Beyond the Kale

GREEN
VILLAGE
INITIATIVE

OUR MISSION IS
TO CREATE SOCIAL,
ECONOMIC AND
ENVIRONMENTAL
CHANGE THROUGH A
UNIFIED NETWORK
OF URBAN FARMS
COMMUNITY
GARDENS AND
SCHOOL GARDENS.

Beyond the Kale

URBAN AGRICULTURE AND SOCIAL
JUSTICE ACTIVISM IN NEW YORK CITY

**KRISTIN REYNOLDS
AND NEVIN COHEN**

THE UNIVERSITY OF GEORGIA PRESS
Athens

Set in 10/12.5 Minion Pro Regular by Kaelin Chappell Broaddus
Printed and bound by Thomson-Shore, Inc.
The paper in this book meets the guidelines for permanence and
durability of the Committee on Production Guidelines for
Book Longevity of the Council on Library Resources.

Most University of Georgia Press titles are
available from popular e-book vendors.

Printed in the United States of America
20 19 18 17 16 P 5 4 3 2 1

Library of Congress Cataloging-in-Publication Data

Names: Reynolds, Kristin, author. | Cohen, Nevin, author.
Title: Beyond the kale : urban agriculture and social justice activism in New York City /
     Kristin Reynolds and Nevin Cohen.
Other titles: Urban agriculture and social justice activism in New York City | Geographies of
     justice and social transformation ; 28.
Description: Athens, Georgia : University of Georgia Press, [2016] | Series: Geographies of
     justice and social transformation ; 28
Identifiers: LCCN 2015043957| ISBN 9780820349497 (hardcover : alk. paper) | ISBN
     9780820349503 (pbk. : alk. paper) | ISBN 9780820349480 (ebook)
Subjects: LCSH: Urban agriculture—Social aspects—New York (State—New York.
Classification: LCC S451.N7 R48 2016 | DDC 338.109747/1—dc23
LC record available at http://lccn.loc.gov/2015043957

CONTENTS

ACKNOWLEDGMENTS

Writing can be a solitary activity, even when the work is about social movements and community activism. Yet we did not feel alone while writing this book. We were fortunate to have been part of a diverse network of individuals—farmers and gardeners, political activists, leaders of nonprofit organizations, city agency staff members, program officers of foundations—who make up New York City's urban agriculture system and who have contributed in significant ways to *Beyond the Kale*.

We would like to acknowledge first and foremost the contributions of the urban agriculture activists featured in this book. Their work to advance social justice remains an inspiration, and the knowledge and opinions they shared with us brought to life the arguments we have made. We extend our heartfelt appreciation for the time and insights they have shared with us over the last few years. We have, with their permission and an opportunity to review for accuracy, used their actual names and quotations in the chapters that follow to highlight, in their own voices, their important efforts. Nevertheless, the analysis is our own, and some of the ideas we have expressed may differ from those of the individuals we interviewed. We also take full responsibility for any errors or omissions in the text.

Our colleagues Navina Khanna, Maya Joseph, and Monica White read early drafts of the manuscript, offering constructive criticism and valuable suggestions. Their feedback enabled us to clarify and focus the text and ensure that we were conveying ideas about race, gender, and class accurately and respectfully. We are truly grateful for their time and assistance. Karen Berman copyedited every single word of the manuscript, making it a much clearer and more accurate and readable document. We are grateful for her editorial talents and attention to detail. We are also thankful for the helpful comments of three anonymous reviewers, as well as Mick Gusinde-Duffy, Nik Heynen, and other members of the University of Georgia Press editorial board and staff.

We were fortunate to have had the support of several talented student research assistants who worked on nitty-gritty aspects of this project. Steven McCutcheon Rubio and Pauline Zaldonis transcribed interviews, searched for journal articles, compiled data, proofread drafts, and performed many other critical research tasks. Brett Silvers and Siu Him (Jimmy) Tang helped design the Beyond the Kale website. In particular, Katherine Nehring was an indispensable assistant over several years. In addition to transcribing interviews and helping with other research tasks, she coordinated activists' feedback on quoted material and helped organize public events—sometimes with very short turn-around time as we worked toward important milestones.

We also acknowledge and thank our dear colleagues Peleg Kremer and Rob Stephenson for their contributions to the book. Peleg created the map of projects discussed in the book, and Rob photographed the featured farms, gardens, and activists. Their work adds important visual elements to the narrative.

Our research, the Beyond the Kale website, and related activities were supported in part by small grants from the Merck Family Fund, the Lucius and Eva Eastman Fund, and The New School. We also received much support from the Environmental Studies Program at The New School, where we were faculty members while researching and writing this book. Alan McGowan, who chaired the program during our research, and Brandon Fischer, Environmental Studies program manager, were especially supportive.

Finally, we thank our families and the many friends who offered encouragement throughout the writing process. Their shared enthusiasm for this work made the research and writing much more rewarding.

Beyond the Kale the book is a beginning, not an end—what we hope is a small contribution to a long-term project to dismantle oppression and advance social justice. We look forward to continuing to work together with the urban agriculture activists described here, additional activists engaged in similar work, and those inspired by the efforts detailed in the following pages.

Kristin Reynolds
Nevin Cohen

PREFACE

The seeds of this book were planted in 2010, when we were part of an interdisciplinary research team that spent two years studying the urban agriculture system in New York City. Our work was part of a project called Five Borough Farm, overseen by the nonprofit Design Trust for Public Space, which sought to develop policy recommendations and evaluation tools to strengthen urban agriculture throughout the city. With other members of the team, we conducted interviews with farmers, gardeners, and staff from nonprofit organizations, foundations, and government agencies in New York, and we reviewed city agency and organizational records to complement what we learned through the interviews. The photographer Rob Stephenson, whose photos appear in this book, captured the vibrancy of New York City's urban agriculture system, and the project's graphic designer depicted important aspects of the system through a series of infographics. A number of the study participants and other individuals familiar with policy making and evaluation served as advisers to strengthen the final recommendations and report.

Through formal research and informal discussions, we gathered information about the overlapping issues related to food, public health, environmental degradation, education, and community-scale economics that farmers and gardeners seek to address through their work. We also learned that while many farmers and gardeners and their supporters were interested in the social justice aspects of urban agriculture—such as providing youth development opportunities and increasing food access in lower-income communities—several had observed race- and class-based disparities among farming and gardening groups. These interviewees spoke about imbalances in funding, access to resources, and connections to key decision makers that gave particular advantage to white middle-class farmers and gardeners. They pointed out that these disparities hindered programs led by people of color, as well as the overall success of urban agriculture in New York City. Both people of color and white people made these observations.

As avid urban agriculture observers (and, at times, practitioners), the two of us were disconcerted by the seeming paradox of an urban agriculture system that was inequitable at the same time that a dominant narrative about city farming and gardening highlighted its social justice benefits. Yet from the perspective of much broader movements for racial and economic justice, gender equity, and LGBTQ rights, these disquieting findings made sense: patterns of disparity among urban agriculture groups were another indication of structural forms of oppression that so often produce unequal balances of power and privilege. In-depth discussions about the roots of food and environmental injustices had been largely absent from the urban agriculture narrative, and we felt compelled to draw attention to this fact.

Despite the importance of these issues, the Five Borough Farm project's final report, published in 2012, included only a brief, rather general section on race and class disparities in New York's urban agriculture system. As researchers and coauthors of the final report, we reluctantly went along with what was, in our view, a less-than-satisfactory discussion of inequity in urban agriculture to stand in for a more radical, and certainly more honest, analysis.

In our view, these factors resulted in a report that made a weaker contribution to a dialogue about racial justice and socioeconomic equity in the food system than it might have, a result that we felt was unfortunate, not least because the report received a fair amount of media and public attention. We had sought to support farmers' and gardeners' efforts; yet despite some of the positive outcomes of the Five Borough Farm project, we had been party to a well-worn pattern of researchers overlooking social structures that granted us privilege in our personal and professional lives. We, along with a number of farmers and gardeners, felt that the lack of substantive discussion about race and class was a conspicuous gap in the report that needed to be filled.

As we reflected on this situation over several months, we began to take closer notice of the tendency for initiatives led by middle-class white people to receive the bulk of attention in the media and in scholarly accounts of urban agriculture. We knew that this focus discounted the work of the many people of color, including recent immigrants from regions of the Global South, who have been growing food in cities for generations. We began to see the lack of attention to these farmers' and gardeners' work as being tied to structural forms of oppression, particularly in terms of the privileges often conveyed to those who are seen as the face of a movement. We wondered whether some of the observed disparities between urban agriculture groups in New York City had resulted from the overrepresentation of white farmers and gardeners, despite the longstanding presence of farmers and gardeners of color.

In the months between finishing our sections of the Five Borough Farm report in the spring of 2012 and its official release that summer, we grew determined to communicate about these issues independently. We also reflected on our own positions as white, upper-middle-class academics with training in critical social science and public policy, time for in-depth research and writing, and relatively ready access to publishing. Knowing that we could not erase our personal or professional identities even if we had wished to do so, we thought about how we might use these privileges as tools to uncover social justice paradoxes in urban agriculture and to help increase recognition and support for the work and leadership of people of color. We were inspired by an idea we had learned from many activists of color: that white people need to engage in racial justice work in their own communities. Ultimately, we decided to write this book as one contribution to this effort.

The title of the book, *Beyond the Kale*, has multiple meanings. Urban agriculture has been portrayed as a newly emerging activity practiced by young, upper-middle-class hipsters, even though it has always been practiced by low-income and working-class urban residents. Similarly, kale has been "discovered" by foodies and restaurateurs, made trendy as a healthy "superfood" and an ingredient in twenty-dollar cocktails, even though it has long been a staple in the diets of people of limited means throughout the world. In this sense, moving "beyond the kale" means looking beyond the trendy aspects of growing food in the city to see people who have been using urban agriculture to make the food system less oppressive and more socially just.

The title is also a play on the phrase *beyond the pale* (outside the bounds of acceptable behavior), which originated in the Middle Ages to describe the land and people living outside of the portion of Ireland enclosed by a fence and controlled by England (the English Pale). Urban agriculture is about much more than food production and can extend to address problems of social justice and political power. "Beyond the kale" thus suggests the need to see beyond the borders of a garden to understand both the broader significance of urban agriculture and the social and political structures in which it is embedded. The title also reflects activists' efforts to move beyond the conventional rules, institutions, and expectations of existing governance and policy-formulation structures to create a more socially just food system through urban agriculture practice.

Finally, although the saying "beyond the pale" refers to working beyond boundaries and conventions, given the contemporary use of the word *pale* to describe lighter colors, the allusion to this word in the title ironically, though appropriately, suggests that those of us—white people in particular—who are interested in advancing social justice through urban agriculture need to see beyond initiatives dominated by white people. People of color, including those living in the Global North or having emigrated there from regions of the Global South, are among the farmers, gardeners, and activists who see in urban food production a resilience strategy and even a path toward urban systems that are more socially just at their core. This book, written as an activist effort, is part of a project that we hope will contribute to far-reaching recognition of these realities as well as to measures to support urban agriculture as a form of social justice activism led by those most negatively affected by food and environmental inequities, and supported by many more.

Unlike many academic publications that keep the comments of interviewees anonymous, this book uses the real names of the urban agriculture activists we interviewed. Our decision to include their words, with their permission and an opportunity to check quotations for accuracy, was an effort to make them and their work more visible, and to give readers an understanding of the interviewees' perspectives as well as our own. We appreciate the degree to which the people we interviewed shared stories, ideas, and concerns with us, and their willingness to be up front about controversial issues. But we emphasize that the questions we asked, the way we used quotes to illustrate general points, and the manner in which we framed the book's perspective involved decisions about curation, interpretation, and analysis that were ours alone, and may thus differ from the perspectives of those we interviewed.

Beyond the Kale

CHAPTER 1

Seeing Beyond the Kale

In the Bedford-Stuyvesant neighborhood of Brooklyn, Yonnette Fleming of Hattie Carthan Community Garden begins one of her food justice workshops with a tribute to the late Ms. Carthan, a Bed-Stuy neighborhood environmentalist and activist after whom the garden is named. The garden's trees provide a welcome respite from the rising city heat on this late-summer day. As the participants settle in, Fleming calls attention to the many other gardeners and community members who have participated in the garden's evolution since its founding in the late 1970s, recounting its history and its importance in this particular community.

Following personal introductions and a discussion about food accessibility in the neighborhood, "Farmer Yon," as Fleming often refers to herself, helps the participants understand various forms of oppression and the ways these forces shape food and agricultural systems. Discussions cover topics such as how racism, patriarchy, and policies rooted in mainstream economic paradigms lead to limited food access, health disparities, and diminished levels of local control in low-income communities and communities of color—in Bed-Stuy and around the world. Fleming calls on participants to think about how these structures may have affected their own lives and what they might do to confront them. She is accepting of individuals' personal circumstances, yet unrelenting in her drive to help them move beyond the type of thinking that perpetuates power imbalances at the individual and societal levels, and to help them experience how agriculture can be at once about food, environment, and liberation.

In addition to Fleming's food justice training sessions, she and other members of Hattie Carthan Community Garden lead regular events that similarly extend the understanding of gardening beyond an activity focused on food. Summer weekends feature two on-site farmers' markets, one of which is held at the "Herban Farm," a second, smaller site that Fleming and other community members have recently transformed from a vacant lot into a vibrant green space. Seasonal events throughout the year celebrate the heritage of the African

Diaspora and feature dishes that Fleming (who is originally from Guyana but has lived in the neighborhood for many years) and other community members have prepared using eggs and produce from the garden and farm. Fleming also leads regular women-only discussions about health and spiritual wellness, along with women-centric events designed to foster leadership and personal empowerment among participants. Beyond the more obvious themes of these events— food access, urban green space, safe spaces for women—the gatherings also focus on community resilience and, particularly through Fleming's leadership, ways that racial justice and women's empowerment can be cultivated through food production, herbalism, community-based markets, education programs for youth of color, and policy advocacy growing out of urban farms. Fleming speaks regularly about how various forms of oppression play out with respect to food and the environment, and she explains, "I'm interested in understanding how women can become true advocates for flora and fauna and justice in the world."

By calling herself a farmer and helping to maintain Hattie Carthan Community Garden as a public green space, Yonnette Fleming underscores the significance of growing food in the city, particularly in historically low-income neighborhoods like Bed-Stuy, where fresh food can be prohibitively expensive or hard to find. She also reclaims the identity of a farmer, as a person of color and a woman, despite the association of agriculture with exploitation among many people of color and despite the stereotype of US farmers as white and male. By growing food, working to break down oppressive social and political systems, and celebrating connections between people and the land, Fleming exemplifies the potential power of longtime neighborhood residents to create change in their own communities.

Advocates of urban agriculture often see city farming as a way to advance social justice, and while this presumption is fraught with paradoxes, particularly with respect to race, class, gender, sexual preference, and community control, activists like Yonnette Fleming demonstrate how farm and garden programs can create food and environmental systems that are more just at their core. In such systems, fresh, healthy, culturally acceptable food is accessible, and environmental and public health risks and benefits are equitably distributed among all communities. In addition, people of color and working-class people are meaningfully involved in food and environmental decision making—and are recognized for their leadership—and governance structures reflect members' articulated social justice values (e.g., see Bullard 1993; Cole and Foster 2001; Mohai, Pellow, and Roberts 2009; Pellow 2000; Schlosberg 2004).

Beyond the Kale examines these aspects of urban agriculture in New York City, as well as the work of people of color and women activists to attain specific social justice goals. It is not a book about the overarching benefits of urban agriculture; many others have covered this topic. Rather, it is about how urban agriculture groups led by people of color and women should, can, and do reflect more socially just systems, and about the processes through which these goals can be achieved.

Urban Agriculture and Social Justice

Urban agriculture, the act of growing crops and raising livestock in cities and their peripheries, is common worldwide but has expanded greatly in the Global North within the past two decades. In the United States, backyard and community gardens have been joined by aquaponic systems (which integrate fish and vegetable production) and rooftop farms, which have redefined growing spaces and helped maximize urban food production, often in unlikely places. As they have for decades, neighborhood residents have organized to clean up vacant lots, but gardeners have also practiced phytoremediation—cultivating plants to remove soil toxicity—and local youth have learned about ecological systems, healthy eating, and leadership skills from working at urban farms. The scope of urban agriculture continues to grow.

Urban agriculture has also become popular among a wider range of city residents, expanding from longtime neighborhood gardeners and people growing food primarily to meet their dietary needs to include so-called locavores intent on eating food grown close to their homes, entrepreneurs capitalizing on consumer interest in supporting smaller-scale farms, and postcollege "hipsters" steeped in do-it-yourself culture. Networks of backyard farms, along with farmers' markets and low-cost community-supported agriculture (CSA) models selling food grown within the city, have expanded opportunities for residents to benefit from urban agriculture, even if they do not garden or farm themselves; similarly, value-added products from salsas to pickles made with urban-grown produce have spawned professional training programs, small-business incubators, and community-based economic development projects linked to urban gardens and farms. Media coverage of these activities has helped fuel their popularity, though at times such coverage has favored initiatives led by young, middle-class white people over those led by people of color who have been growing food for decades—like many of the gardeners at Hattie Carthan, including Farmer Yon.

As urban agriculture has expanded, so too has recognition that farming and gardening projects produce multiple benefits, and many studies have documented these benefits in cities throughout the United States and the world (e.g., Draper and Freedman 2010; Blair 2009; Golden 2013; Bellows, Brown, and Smit 2003; Brown and Carter 2002; K. H. Brown et al. 2002; Kaufman and Bailkey 2000; Smit, Ratta, and Nasr 1996).

Joining those who support urban agriculture for more ideological reasons, landscape architects, designers, and urban planners have examined physical aspects of urban agriculture, exploring both the possibilities of creating inter-connected, productive spaces within city landscapes (Viljoen, Bohn, and Howe 2005) and a number of architectural, design, and planning innovations to integrate farms and gardens into the cityscape (Gorgolewski, Komisar, and Nasr 2011). In a similar vein, government reports and policy papers on urban agriculture have highlighted its potential to foster self-help (through self-provisioning of healthy food, for example) and to encourage community development—though they have just as often defined it narrowly in terms of neighborhood beautification, greening, and increased property values, sidestepping concerns about gentrification and control of public space. Research and policy papers have added to the growing understanding of urban agriculture as a beneficial part of the city, though not always with full consideration of the broader social and political contexts within which farms and gardens are situated.

Many discussions of the benefits of urban agriculture have focused on the ability of farms and gardens to provide fresh, affordable, and culturally appropriate food in low-income communities lacking conventional food retailers. However, some have also recognized urban agriculture as a way to increase green spaces in neighborhoods with few parks, to foster relationships among neighbors of different ethnicities and ages, to improve neighborhood safety by bringing people and activities to neglected spaces, and to help cultivate leadership and job-related skills among youth and adults (Draper and Freedman 2010; Blair 2009; Golden 2013; Bellows et al. 2000; Brown and Carter 2002; K. H. Brown et al. 2002; Kaufman and Bailkey 2000; Smit, Ratta, and Nasr 1996). Studies have found that farmers' markets and microenterprises associated with farm and garden sites are ways for participants to contribute to community economic development and supplement individual and household incomes (e.g., Feenstra, McGrew, and Campbell 1999). Observers have also highlighted the racial and ethnic diversity of urban farmers and gardeners in the United States, suggesting that urban agriculture is a way to bring people from different cultures together (e.g., Hynes 1996; von Hassell 2002).

These and other positive effects that farms and gardens can have on public health, community development, and the environment underscore the fact that urban agriculture reaches far beyond gardens as places for food production or neighborhood beautification. This conventional understanding has led to a broadening of networks, policy initiatives, and funding to support it: Farm and garden enthusiasts have engaged in informal collaborations to exchange information and share supplies. Municipal officials have crafted supportive policy statements, created governmental advisory bodies, and taken actions such as amending zoning ordinances to recognize farms and gardens as legal uses of urban space. City governments have adopted policies granting permission to keep small-scale livestock and have amended building codes to allow for rooftop greenhouses, and both municipal and state governments have created tax incentives for commercial urban farming. Private foundations have expanded or created new funding sources for urban agriculture and related activities, and nonprofit organizations and some university-based extension services have stepped up technical assistance and education (see Cohen, Reynolds, and Sang-hvi 2012; Surls et al. 2015; Reynolds 2011).

As the benefits of urban agriculture have become more broadly recognized, public consciousness about food access and public health disparities has also deepened, leading to policy initiatives and public discussions about the inter-section of socioeconomic status, food, and health. For instance, First Lady Mi-chelle Obama's "Let's Move" campaign was created in 2010 to encourage healthy eating and active lifestyles in response to the finding that nearly 40 percent of the children in African American and Hispanic communities were overweight or obese, a higher percentage than for other racial and ethnic groups (Let's Move 2014). Government agencies and food policy councils throughout the United States have increasingly recognized the connections between access to healthy food and diet-related health issues. At a broader scale, debates about major cuts to the Supplemental Nutrition Assistance Program (SNAP, formerly the Food Stamp Program) in the 2014 Farm Bill elevated public awareness about the links between food access and poverty. This growing awareness of food system ineq-uities has joined decades-old analyses of environmental injustice experienced by low-income communities and communities of color, which gave rise to the environmental justice movement in the late 1980s and early 1990s.[1] Though long recognized by the people and communities who bear the brunt of their negative effects, food and environmental inequities are increasingly part of public and political debates.

Heightened awareness of food system and environmental inequities, along with the growing recognition of urban agriculture's multiple benefits, has led some supporters to see it as a solution to an array of urban problems. When the benefits of urban agriculture are tied to broader issues like urban sustainability, public health, and economic development, for example, increasing the number of farms and gardens can seem like a win-win opportunity for individuals, com-munities, policy makers, and cities writ large. The dominant narrative, which sees farming and gardening as part of building more socially just and sustain-able cities because they provide food and green space, create jobs, and build community, often obscures the underlying social and political structures—such as racism, classism, patriarchy, and heteronormativity—that give rise to the very inequities that supporters hope to address.

Understanding agriculture as a multifunctional and beneficial use of urban space has often glossed over the historical and contemporary processes that have led to food system and environmental inequities. Residential redlining, government disinvestment, and property abandonment, especially beginning in the mid-twentieth century, have concentrated poverty within many neighborhoods of color, discouraged food retailers from locating in low-income communities, and left vacant lots in low-income neighborhoods throughout the United States. Visions of urban agriculture as a way for communities to manage the effects of economic inequities have been fostered by neoliberal political ideology in the US government, which emphasizes community self-help and market-based solutions to societal problems along with a withdrawal of government services and support for basic human needs. Unavoidably situated within this wider context, urban agriculture can be a release valve for pressures on local and national governments to address deeper societal injustices like racialized poverty, educational disparities, and political disenfranchisement that are at the core of many urban problems (e.g., see McClintock 2013; Weissman 2015a, 2015b). These paradoxes give pause to a common assertion that urban farming and gardening build systems that are socially just.

Supporters have often framed urban agriculture in an overly positive light in an effort to bolster its legitimacy in the eyes of potential critics. In doing so, however, they have paid scant attention to the structures that create inequities or to any possibility of deleterious, if unintended, social or political effects. Recently, however, scholars and activists have begun to question the presumption that farms and gardens have only positive or liberatory functions. Pudup (2008), for example, has proposed that community gardens (which she identifies as "organized garden projects") have been used to cultivate "citizen-subjects" who may act either in step with or in opposition to the neoliberal state. Others have asked whether urban agriculture picks up where the state leaves off in terms of ensuring social welfare, allowing neoliberalism and market-based solutions to flourish (Heynen, Kurtz, and Trauger 2012; Weissman 2015a, 2015b; Tornaghi 2014). Still others have argued that for urban agriculture to lead to structural change, it must simultaneously be "radical" in approach and engage with the mainstream capitalist market system (McClintock 2013). Scholars and activists have also observed what many would consider unjust race and class dynamics in urban agriculture systems (Cadji 2013; Cohen, Reynolds, and Sanghvi 2012; McClintock 2013; Metcalf and Widener 2011; Crouch 2012; Markham 2014; Meenar and Hoover 2012) and have argued that urban agriculture can mask deeper structural inequities (Colasanti, Hamm, and Litjens 2012; Cohen and Reynolds 2014; Yakini 2013; DeLind 2015).

Thus, beneath the surface of public enthusiasm for urban agriculture lie some fundamentally different understandings of the origins of inequity and social injustice, along with some ideas about how these issues should be addressed. While we generally agree with the recent analyses of urban agriculture in the context of neoliberal political and economic systems, we believe that dwelling on the neoliberal *question* is not needed in the interest of supporting the work of grassroots groups to address food, environmental, and economic inequity. Rather, examining the structural roots of inequity and contributing to an action-oriented dialogue about how urban agriculture can be (and is being) used to create socially just urban systems are the main goals of this book.

Race, Class, and Urban Agriculture

In addition to debates about whether farming and gardening help solve urban social justice problems in a broader sense, the representation of these activities in public forums presents an inaccurate impression of who is involved in urban agriculture today and how the representation of urban agriculture might connect to advancing racial and economic equity—the goals of many social justice advocates. Urban farming and gardening have long been survival strategies for low-income city residents, many of them people of color, including those with roots in the Global South (e.g., see Hayden-Smith 2014; L. Lawson 2005; Smit, Ratta, and Nasr 1996). However, in the United States, books, magazines, and social media often paint a picture of young white people as the most innovative farmers and gardeners in the post–World War II era, despite the many people of color who have been growing food in their neighborhoods and hometowns for decades and even generations.

For example, as described in chapter 2, urban agriculture has evolved over the course of New York City's history, sometimes practiced as a subsistence strategy among residents living in poverty, and at other times used to spur community revitalization and development. Since the 1960s and 1970s, community gardening in particular has been concentrated in low-income communities and communities of color (Eizenberg 2013, 2008), and community members such as Hattie Carthan in Bed-Stuy have often led in developing gardens on these sites (see the NYCCGC website). Yet community gardening in the New York of the 1960s and 1970s has often been depicted as a process of "urban homesteading" in which gardeners, usually young, middle-class whites, were modern-day "pioneers." At best, this narrative ignores the fact that the neighborhoods in which these "pioneers" and "homesteaders" were creating gardens were well-established communities, often communities of color. Worse, it reproduces colonialist mentalities in which imported white culture should be used to "tame" indigenous peoples.

More recently, mainstream media reports have focused on white-led initiatives as drivers of the contemporary urban agriculture movement. News articles have identified a number of mostly young white farmers in New York City as the "new class of growers" (see Stein 2010), for instance, and have described some of Detroit's white urban farmers as twenty-first-century "pioneers" moving to the economically devastated city to "fight blight" by establishing new urban farms (see "Detroit Foodies" 2013; Midgett 2014). Media pieces on high-tech projects such as rooftop farms and other entrepreneurial urban agriculture initiatives that seek to capitalize on the fashion of growing farm-to-table cuisine have also tended to focus on young, middle-class white people. These and similar pieces have presented urban agriculture as an innovative way to reclaim vacant land, start new businesses, or challenge the industrial food system, yet with scant attention to the race and class dimensions of the movement or of the problems that farming and gardening purportedly solve. Often absent from this narrative is the fact that people of color in New York, Detroit, and many other cities have long gardened and farmed to address the effects of inequity in their own communities.

Recent attention to entrepreneurial urban agriculture projects led by young, middle-class whites may stem in part from the notion popularized by theorist Richard Florida (2002) that members of the so-called creative class—formally educated, young, affluent, and preponderantly white urbanites—are the economic engines of cities. Municipal governments, planners, and real estate developers adhering to this concept have sought to attract members of this creative class to economically depressed neighborhoods as a way to increase property values and tax revenues and strengthen cities' overall economies. While Florida's thesis has been widely critiqued (e.g., Peck 2005; Markusen 2006), the notion that innovation and creativity drives economic development remains, and the idea that the "creative class" consists primarily of white people acts to obscure existing and equally important innovations forged by people of color (see Yakini 2013).

Thus, while not explicitly stating that urban farming and gardening are white, middle-class activities, the portrayal of young white faces in news articles and online forums has suggested white dominance of, and helped reinforce white privilege in, urban agriculture systems (Reynolds 2014; Meenar and Hoover 2012). Media coverage is, after all, a cultural and political resource that can contribute to the maintenance of power among dominant groups (Entman 2007; Ryan, Carragee, and Meinhofer 2001). Coupled with the overall tendency for white people and white culture to dominate US society, the representation of middle-class, white-led urban agriculture in cities with racially diverse groups of farmers and gardeners has added insult to injury by suggesting that urban agriculture, in and of itself, addresses inequities linked to race and class, while reinforcing these very inequities.

In addition to the dynamic of public representation of urban agriculture and its potential effect on social equity, establishing new farms and gardens in low-income communities can stimulate or exacerbate gentrification (the process by which increasing property values and new investments *directly* displace residents and businesses, or *indirectly* lead to displacement as real estate prices and taxes on rising property values become prohibitively expensive for existing residents). Gentrification, too, presents a paradox with respect to urban agriculture and social justice (e.g., see Cadji 2013; McClintock, 2013; Crouch 2012; Markham 2014). For instance, urban farms and gardens can contribute to "ecological gentrification" (Dooling 2009; Quastel 2009), a process through which environmental improvements such as cleaning up toxic sites or converting abandoned lots to green space leads to increased property values and displacement of longtime, often low-income residents. When relatively higher-income, economically privileged people move into historically low-income neighborhoods to establish gardens on vacant lots—or occupy gardens that have already been established and perhaps abandoned—there can be similar effects, increasing property values near the gardens, making the neighborhood unaffordable for longtime residents (Voicu and Been 2008).

In some New York City neighborhoods, like the Lower East Side and Harlem, the establishment of green spaces managed by local residents, together with public policies to encourage the development of luxury and middle-class housing, has facilitated gentrification, leading to displacement of lower-income residents over a number of decades. There are signs of this process taking hold in other New York City communities, such as Bed-Stuy and East New York (Lawhead 2014). For these reasons, farm and garden projects led by (often white) neighborhood newcomers, though typically well intentioned and at times sanctioned or funded by local governments, are not always welcomed by longtime residents (often people of color) because they may lead to displacement. Such projects may be viewed as examples of "outsiders" taking control of community space (Eizenberg 2012a; DeLind 2015; see also appendix 4 for select New York City population characteristics).

These race and class dynamics of urban agriculture illustrate the point that farming and gardening in the city do not necessarily create more socially just systems and can in fact perpetuate inequities that many supporters hope to address. To be sure, many urban farmers and gardeners hope to reduce inequities—even race- and class-based disparities—by growing and distributing food or creating jobs in low-income neighborhoods. This is valuable work. The problem with the trends described above is not that whites, or people with financial means, or new community residents are growing food in cities—or even that their projects may raise property values in a neighborhood. What *is* problematic is that the uncritical embrace of urban agriculture as a solution to a variety of urban inequities, without attention to the racial and class dynamics that underlie them, allows unjust structures to remain unchecked.

The focus that the media, policy makers, funders, and others place on high-tech and other trendy urban agriculture initiatives influences both the kinds of programs and policies designed to support urban agriculture, and, often, the demographic of farmers and gardeners who receive the resources to implement such programs. At the broadest scale, the tendency to support the tactical practice of farming or gardening as way to advance social justice—regardless of who leads and who benefits, or what impact a given project has on specific social justice goals—can mean that already well resourced groups receive a disproportionate amount of support. This unequal distribution of support can perpetuate status quo social, economic, and political dynamics. Ultimately, attention to certain types of farms and gardens limits the success of the urban agriculture system overall by exacerbating disparities among groups and limiting the capacity of organizations that are less well known or less resourced to develop, expand, and sustain their programs.

Seeing Urban Agriculture through the Lens of Structural Oppression

One way to understand urban agriculture's role in advancing (or hindering) progress toward more socially just systems is to examine it through frameworks that illuminate the intersecting forms of oppression that exist at multiple levels of contemporary society. Critical race theory, along with theories of intersectionality and social oppression, help us do just this.

Critical race theory (CRT) explains that racial inequities grow from patterns of implicit racial bias—which exist within whole institutions and extend throughout society—not simply from individuals' explicitly racist beliefs or isolated instances of racial discrimination. Specifically:

- **Internalized racism** exists within individuals, as private beliefs and biases manifest as feelings of inferiority among people of color or as feelings of entitlement among white people.
- **Interpersonal racism** occurs between people as they act on their internal beliefs and biases, often surfacing as racial discrimination or racial violence.
- **Institutionalized racism** is the effect of specific institutional policies and practices (such as school district policies that result in the concentration of children of color in lower-quality schools) that routinely produce inequitable outcomes for groups of individuals, privileging whites and placing people of color at a disadvantage.
- **Structural racism** is the cumulative system of racial bias that extends across society and perpetuates disadvantage among communities of color. Examples of structural racism include unchallenged media portrayals of people of color as criminals, which pervade the public consciousness, and perpetrating discriminatory treatment grounded in an association of all people of color with criminal behavior (Apollon et al. 2014; see also Bonilla-Silva 1997; Conley 1999; Omi and Winant 1994). Often stemming from collective, subconscious beliefs, and often unintentional, structural racism is at the root of many social and political inequities, from police killings of unarmed black men to food retailers avoiding communities of color under the false assumption that people of color do not value, and will therefore not purchase, fresh and healthy food.

Within structurally racist societies, white privilege is understood as whites' historical and contemporary advantages in access to quality education, jobs, livable wages, home ownership, and multigenerational wealth (Bonilla-Silva 1997; The Aspen Institute 2014; Keleher and Sen 2012; Omi and Winant 1994; McIntosh 1990; Taylor 2009). Critical race theory, as elaborated in the United States, thus helps explain the pervasiveness of racial inequity in US society despite progress beginning with the emancipation of enslaved Africans in 1863, extending through the civil rights era and into the twenty-first century, including the election of an African American president.

Of course, questions of social justice and equity clearly extend beyond race and racism. The concept of intersectionality recognizes that individuals have overlapping identities and loyalties, including race, class, gender, sexual preference, spiritual beliefs, and region of origin (Delgado and Stefancic 2012), and that these "shape structural, political, and representational aspects" of the social world (Crenshaw 1991). Further, structural analyses of injustice and its opposite—social justice—also engage with concepts and conditions of oppression. Political scientist and feminist theorist Iris Marion Young identified oppression as having five forms, *exploitation*, *marginalization*, *powerlessness*, *cultural imperialism*, and *violence*, comprising a "system of constraints," though not necessarily resulting from intention on the part of an identifiable oppressor (Young 2009). The resulting lack of power—or "absence of choice" (see hooks 2000, 4–7)—experienced by "oppressed" groups extends beyond the US experience and is thus relevant in considering questions of social justice in the global food system, such as how international trade policies affect Mexican farmers' decisions to emigrate to the United States for low-wage jobs in commercial agriculture or the restaurant industry.

Together, CRT and theories on intersectionality and oppression help us understand that issues such as the lack of income that prevents some households from accessing fresh and healthful food are not merely a function of individual failures to secure employment or manage personal finances, but rather a function of social cues, professional connections, and, often, the intersection of multiple levels of oppression that span generations, as well as political and geographic boundaries. These theories also help us see that individuals' abilities to influence policies affecting their communities stem from the degree of access that their social and professional networks have to policy makers and official policy-making processes, and that discrimination based on gender or sexual preference, for example, is perpetuated by dominant cultural norms that privilege men and those who embody a set of narrowly defined roles and identities. In short, social power and relative privilege are derived not from one sphere, but from the intersection of identities, relationships, and lived experiences that exist in any social or political venue (Crenshaw 1991). Recognizing these dynamics is key both to understanding the sources of inequity among urban agriculture groups and to supporting initiatives to dismantle oppression and advance social justice.

Urban Agriculture as Social Justice Activism

Though farming and gardening are fundamental components of urban agriculture, the physical spaces in which farms and gardens are situated are only *part* of a given city's urban agriculture system. Such systems are composed of interconnected networks of farmers and gardeners, government agencies, supportive organizations, foundations, and investors, as well as the natural environment and the policies and programs that affect the city's food and environmental systems. New York City has one of the most extensive urban agriculture systems in the United States, with approximately nine hundred food-producing gardens and farms ranging from tiny community plots tended by neighbors to commercial rooftop greenhouses producing hydroponic produce for grocers and restaurants (Altman et al. 2014; Cohen, Reynolds, and Sanghvi 2012). As in other cities, this system also includes a wide range of actors beyond gardeners and farmers who support or have some purview over food production. These individuals include nonprofit organization staff who advocate, provide technical assistance, and run farms and gardens; policy makers and government agency officials who provide resources and write laws to make it easier (or more difficult) to farm; staff of private philanthropies who fund agricultural projects; and supporters in many other sectors. (See appendix 2 for a more detailed discussion of New York City's urban agriculture system and appendix 3 for descriptions of groups detailed in this book.)

While some urban farmers, gardeners, and supporters see food production as urban agriculture's primary purpose, for others it is also about creating social or environmental change—a form of activism intended to improve conditions in specific communities and at broader scales. For many gardeners and farmers, urban agriculture is a form of political expression, social activism, or environmental politics. For example, community gardens are for some activists "spaces of contestation" against neoliberal policies and the privatization of urban space (Eizenberg 2012b), and for others they are places where humans redraw connections with the natural environment that have been lost through the processes of capitalist restructuring and urbanization (McClintock 2010). Urban gardens are sites for "everyday resistance" to environmental injustice (Milbourne 2011) and places to enact urban environmentalism (Certomà 2011, 7). For some "urban agriculture activists," as we refer to them throughout the book, urban farms are places to resist food insecurity brought about by the domination of capitalism, and spaces where black and Latino/a community members can reclaim cultural roots, practice self-determination with regard to food and agriculture, or respond to the latent crises of discrimination and government abandonment in "poor and disinvested" [sic] neighborhoods (White 2011a, 2011b; Bonacich and Alimahomed-Wilson 2011; Bradley and Galt 2013; Kato, Passidomo, and Harvey 2013; Broad 2013; Mares and Peña 2010; Myers and Sbicca 2015). Examples of urban agriculture activism can be found throughout the United States, from the San Francisco Bay Area to Detroit, from New Orleans to New York.

As is common among social and political activists, many urban agriculture activists adopt different political positions on different issues and form strategic alliances as political opportunity arises in order to be as effective as possible in achieving their goals (see Hajer 2003; Taylor 2000; Wekerle 2004). Some draw from social movements and intellectual traditions in a framing process that environmental justice scholar Dorceta Taylor (2000, 511) suggests helps activists express social and political grievances and convey the philosophies of their work to potential supporters. This may include describing their farming or gardening using conceptual frameworks such as environmental justice, food justice,[2] or food sovereignty[3] that are recognized within these respective movements and by an increasing number of policy makers, funders, and other potential supporters. Activists also use both long-standing and newer community-organizing strategies, from word-of-mouth networking to running social media campaigns, to build participation in and strengthen the effectiveness of specific initiatives.

Not all urban farmers and gardeners envision their agrarian efforts as a means to social or political change, of course; however, as discussed in chapter 2, activist goals have been at the heart of an increasing number of initiatives in New York and other US cities since the late 1960s. Yet even among decidedly activist-oriented urban agriculture initiatives, not all are focused on social justice as a main objective. Despite the many farmers and gardeners who run programs such as garden education or low-cost farmers' markets (which do have important social goals), relatively few activists engage in efforts to dismantle the oppressive systems—including structural racism, xenophobia, classism, sexism, patriarchy, heterosexism, and the five forms of oppression noted above—that continue to shape food and environmental systems. Fewer still may take into account their own positionalities—racial and ethnic identities, immigration status, class position, gender, and sexual preference—and how these intersecting aspects of identity affect the overall success of their programs. Moreover, because "social justice" can take on different meanings, activists can use this concept to describe their work without clearly articulating what it means in practice.

Urban agriculture activism can also take many different forms. Activists may or may not be focused on social justice issues, and they may or may not clearly articulate what they mean by "social justice" work. Additionally, although some urban agriculture activists use strategic framing to communicate about the significance of their initiatives, others refrain from describing their work as activism *per se*. While individuals like Yonnette Fleming explicitly connect their urban agriculture work to broader social justice concepts like dismantling structural racism and patriarchy, others feel that their efforts to respond through farming and gardening to the day-to-day effects of racialized poverty or government neglect speak for themselves. "Everyday" actions—raising chickens, keeping bees, gardening in abandoned lots—can thus be forms of social and political activism, ecological citizenship, and participation in policy making (Certomà 2011; Travaline and Hunold 2010; Nairn and Vitiello 2009) when they lead to community changes, even if they do not appear at a surface level to be connected to activist goals (e.g., see Bang 2010; Marsh 2011, 76; Kato, Passidomo, and Harvey 2013). The efforts of farmers like Abu Talib (described in chapter 2), whose leadership at Taqwa Community Farm has helped fellow neighborhood residents manage the long-term effects of government disinvestment in the South Bronx, can be considered a form of social justice activism, even when community leaders do not identify their work as such.

Whether urban farmers and gardeners explicitly connect their initiatives to broader social justice frames or work to manage the effects of inequity in their own geographic and cultural communities, the distinction between these and the wider universe of urban agriculture projects lies in their drive to grapple with multiple forms of social and political oppression. Urban agriculture as social justice activism, as we consider it throughout this book, involves dismantling oppression at its core. And while it is important to avoid characterizing individuals' actions in ways that do not reflect their own beliefs, it is also important to understand the significance of different urban agriculture programs, and distinctions between them, insofar as they address specific social justice concerns. Failure to distinguish between programs that are actively working to address the structural roots of food and environmental inequities and those that are less focused on these deeper aspects of justice can limit the support from nonprofit, philanthropic, or government sectors, ultimately limiting possibilities for urban agriculture to help advance far-reaching sociopolitical change. Understanding how urban agriculture activists put their anti-oppression and social justice theories into practice is therefore key for those hoping to engage in or support this work.

Whether people explicitly align their work with broader ideas about social justice, like Yonnette Fleming, or engage in change making through everyday actions that address the effects of inequity, like Abu Talib, these activists embody two important aspects of urban agriculture that are often left out of the dominant narrative. First, although farms and gardens can provide many tangible benefits to individuals and communities, such as access to healthy food and green space, urban agriculture activists can do much more by working to dismantle multiple forms of oppression that play out in food and environmental systems. Second, despite a dominant narrative that has focused on projects led by young, middle-class white people, many urban agriculture programs are led by people of color and first-generation immigrants from the Global South, activists who have long-standing roots in the geographic and cultural communities in which they work. These are key, though frequently overlooked, aspects of the urban agriculture story that *Beyond the Kale* aims to tell.

This Book as an Action Research Project

Beyond the Kale adds to a growing body of critical urban agriculture scholarship and activist analysis by examining farm and garden programs focused on advancing social justice in New York City. But in addition to deepening understandings of the intersections between urban agriculture and social justice activism, the book is part of a broader action research project that we hope contributes to creating more socially just food and environmental systems.

Inspired by the work of feminist economic geographers who use the combined pen name J. K. Gibson-Graham, we see the potential for scholarship to help make improvements in everyday reality. Gibson-Graham proposed that "thinking and writing," which they identified as some of the more tangible products of work performed by scholars, should be viewed as interventions, or processes that shift the understanding of reality and lead to individual and societal change (Gibson-Graham 2008). They also suggested that theory (another potential product of scholarly work) should be used to "help see openings and provide [spaces] of freedom and possibility" in addition to its more conventional role of explaining phenomena (Gibson-Graham 2008). Scholarly work should be used not to "explain why," they argued, but to "explore how," with an interest in "learning, rather than judging" (Gibson-Graham 2008). In contrast to the conventional notion of value-neutral expertise, their stance was that academics can approach inquiry with an interest in participating in social change. They argued, in fact, that scholars have the responsibility to disinvest from stand-alone practices of "critique and mastery" and to undertake instead a more complex praxis of "thinking that [energizes] and support[s]" alternative realities (Gibson-Graham 2006, 6).

While Gibson-Graham's ideas have been influential within critical social sciences, to be satisfied with simply thinking and writing about "alternative realities" would be to fall into the same trap as many alternative food initiatives, such as farmers' markets or farm-to-school programs, which have been critiqued for developing innovative but somewhat limited strategies for change that allow inequitable power relationships to remain unchecked (e.g., see Allen 2008; Allen and Guthman 2006). Indeed, Gibson-Graham's work has itself been critiqued for not going far enough in its analysis of power structures, for not paying attention to the influence of global and national systems over the local, and for not sufficiently recognizing the influence that policy and political processes have over social life (Glassman 2003; Kelly 2005; Laurie 2005; V. Lawson 2005). For scholarly work to contribute to liberation, it must go farther than Gibson-Graham's important conceptualization of scholarship as social action and engage with the multiple and evolving contexts in which oppression is created and reproduced.

With these ideas in mind, we have approached *Beyond the Kale* not as "experts" on the topic of urban agriculture, but as knowledgeable participants in a movement to advance social and environmental justice through urban agriculture work. Our intent in researching and writing this book has been to learn from community-based leaders and to practice shifting the power dynamics between academic researchers and those based outside of academic settings. We have drawn inspiration from a number of scholars whose activist-oriented work has engaged with political aspects of dismantling oppression. Specifically, we have taken to heart lessons learned from author and social activist bell hooks, who identifies "theory as liberatory practice" but emphasizes that "[t]heory is not inherently . . . liberatory, or revolutionary [and] fulfills this function only when we ask that it do so and direct our theorizing to this end" (hooks 1994, 59–75). The suggestions of political scientist and sociologist Francis Fox Piven (2010) have compelled us to do more than simply observe, reflect on, and write about injustice—rather, to engage with community-based activists more as colleagues than as participants in "our" study.

By envisioning ourselves as participants in movements for social justice, we have sought to explore how the process of research and writing about urban agriculture can step beyond explanation and observation into the role of uncovering and co-creating possibilities with activists who are working outside of academic spaces. As noted in chapter 7, our discussions with urban agriculture activists have shaped our perspective on scholar-activism. They have also helped us reflect on how we understand and communicate about scholarship and research. Additionally, we have at times found ourselves in the uncomfortable position of needing to balance the requirements of our academic professions, such as producing particular types of scholarly analysis, with the responsibility to be accountable to our community-based colleagues. The process of engaging in this type of action research has taught us much about the intersections of scholarship and urban agriculture activism and has solidified our commitment to this work.

Overview of the Book

Beyond the Kale examines urban agriculture in critical yet constructive ways, attempting to "energize" efforts to achieve food system, environmental, economic, and social justice writ large. It argues that efforts to address injustice through urban agriculture must attend to social and political structures, such as structural racism and the roots of political disenfranchisement, in addition to providing food, education, employment opportunities, and environmental amenities. Throughout the book we provide examples of urban agriculture activists who work to address multiple forms of social and political oppression in their communities and beyond.

Uncovering urban agriculture activists' deeper analyses and contributing to an action-oriented dialogue about dismantling oppression through urban agriculture are two main goals of this book. Additionally, in an effort to fill in significant gaps in the dominant urban agriculture narrative, the book seeks to lift up the work of people of color who are using urban agriculture to improve conditions within and beyond their own communities. Following Mares and Peña (2011), who argue for the recognition of food practices of marginalized groups as autonomous from those shaped by dominant discourse and paradigms, *Beyond the Kale* specifically and intentionally highlights community-based initiatives, grounded in deep understanding of oppression, that have often been overshadowed by trendy projects. The urban agriculture activists described in this book are primarily, though not exclusively, people of color who run farm and garden programs in New York City. Many of the activists that we spoke with describe their programs as a part of their work to dismantle forms of oppression. Most, even those who do not describe their urban agriculture work as "activist" initiatives, are responding to the effects of structural forms of oppression such as racialized poverty and government abandonment in the communities in which they are deeply embedded. For the purposes of the analysis presented in this book, we consider these individuals to be urban agriculture activists.

Beyond the Kale is based primarily on in-depth interviews conducted in 2013–2014 with farmers, gardeners, and organizational leaders in New York City whose urban agriculture work focuses on eliminating both the causes and effects of inequity and oppression. We prioritized the work of people of color and individuals working in communities in which they are deeply embedded. In addition to interviews, in 2014 we convened a focus group with interviewees and a public forum on collaborations between community-based activists and academic faculty, students, and staff. Our own participation in New York City food systems activism, advocacy, policy making, and planning processes has also informed the analysis presented throughout this book. (See appendix 1 for a more detailed description of research methods.)

The chapters that follow illustrate the prevalence, importance, strategies, and potential impacts of urban agriculture and agriculture-related projects that see "beyond the kale," focusing on achieving food systems and urban environments that are fundamentally more equitable and just. By highlighting individuals and groups that have been trying to dismantle the structural roots of inequity through their work, we hope to make their strategies and practices more recognizable as possibilities that can be replicated, adapted, and potentially scaled up by other farmers and gardeners, policy makers, and diverse supporters. We also explore how urban agriculture activists frame and articulate their work. In doing so, we attempt to explain how these practices relate to broadly recognized movements, and to highlight how some urban agriculture groups are already enacting supporters' ideals. The book also identifies challenges activists encounter that are related to power dynamics, including race-, class-, and gender-based disparities within the urban agriculture system, as well as policies and practices of government agencies, philanthropic organizations, and nonprofit organizations that favor some groups and projects over others—particularly over those that more directly challenge the status quo.

We view our analysis not as truth seeking but as productive inquiry. Using precedents set by the activists and organizations highlighted in this book, along with their visions for future work, we offer ideas that may be used by other farmers and gardeners, funders, organizations, researchers, and policy makers to strengthen urban agriculture's potential to contribute to social justice in food and environmental systems. Though focused on contemporary programs, the book also illustrates how urban agriculture is part of a longer history of community-based social justice activism in order to present a more comprehensive narrative than that put forth by mainstream media coverage and much of the urban agriculture literature to date. While the book focuses on New York City, the lessons drawn from the cases presented here are applicable to urban agriculture and social justice initiatives in many other cities, and in the final chapter, we profile three activist groups in cities beyond New York.

This chapter has provided an overview of urban agriculture, social justice, and activism. Chapter 2 discusses New York City's urban agriculture system, illustrating the history and evolution of food production in the city. Opening with a story from Taqwa Community Farm in the South Bronx, the chapter focuses on several galvanizing historical moments over the last forty years that have led to the diverse and networked farming and gardening system that exists today.

Chapter 3 describes the efforts of farms and gardens to address forms of oppression through the ways in which they grow and distribute food, steward green spaces, educate people from the community, and foster economic development. The chapter begins with a vignette describing Brooklyn Rescue Mission, a social service organization run by clergy and community members in Central Brooklyn that uses its farm-based activities to foster community self-determination.

In chapter 4, we discuss attempts to challenge oppressive structures by enacting social justice theories through distinct organizational structures, representative leadership, and popular education. The chapter opens with La Finca del Sur, a farm in the South Bronx led by women of color and their allies, which has a nonhierarchical structure that leaders view as in line with their social justice theories.

Chapter 5 examines urban agriculture groups' efforts to influence policy priorities and redesign governance structures through formal policy making, strategic collaborations, grassroots advocacy, and "everyday" actions. The networking of Friends of Brook Park and the New York City Community Garden Coalition are highlighted to show how urban agriculture activists ally with other social justice–oriented groups. We also describe other efforts to advance policies that support urban agriculture.

In chapter 6, we turn to the uneven power dynamics that urban agriculture groups have experienced in their work to advance social justice. Rather than reiterate well-documented challenges of insufficient funding, materials, land tenure, and time, this chapter focuses on power imbalances within the city's urban agriculture system as an underlying challenge not often discussed in the literature or the movement. We connect concepts in this chapter to those elaborated by urban agriculture activists including Karen Washington, longtime urban farmer in the Bronx.

Chapter 7 delves more deeply into the intersections of scholarship and activism and discusses research processes and frameworks that can advance the work of social justice–oriented urban agriculture groups. Drawing from farmer and gardener insights and our own analysis, it addresses the role of researchers in this kind of work, as well as collaboration strategies for researchers and practitioners. Opening with a vignette about the public forum we convened to discuss these issues, the chapter also takes the concept of a "scholar" to task.

The final chapter summarizes our findings and connects the themes in preceding chapters to urban agriculture activism elsewhere in the United States, providing examples of initiatives in Detroit, Michigan; Goldsboro, North Carolina; Santa Fe, New Mexico; and El Paso, Texas. It illustrates that urban agriculture as social justice activism, led by people of color and women, extends far beyond New York City.

Our hope is that *Beyond the Kale* and its approach to research and scholarship contributes to both scholarly dialogue and broader efforts to realize social justice in food and environmental systems. At the same time, we have remained conscious of our own social locations and professional status as white academic researchers as we have sought to highlight the experiences and leadership of people of color and working-class people whose efforts have too often been obscured in the dominant urban agriculture narrative. Although the analysis presented in this volume is our own, we rely heavily on the words of these community-based activists to convey meanings throughout the book.

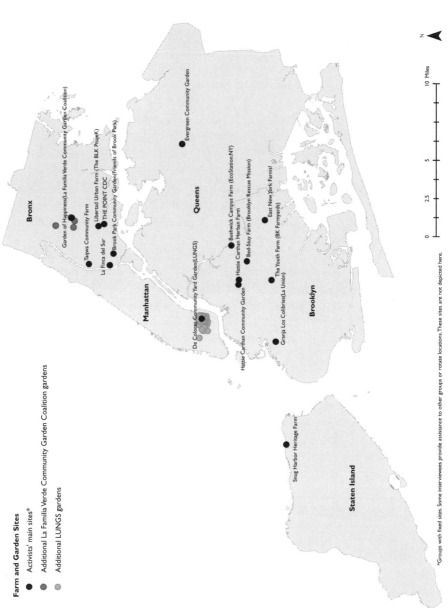

Bronx

Garden of Happiness(La Familia Verde Community Garden Coalition)

Taqwa Community Farm

Libertad Urban Farm (The BLK ProjeK)

La Finca del Sur

THE POINT CDC

Brook Park Community Garden(Friends of Brook Park)

Manhattan

De Colores Community Yard Garden(LUNGS)

Queens

Evergreen Community Garden

Bushwick Campus Farm (EcoStationNY)

Bed-Stuy Farm (Brooklyn Rescue Mission)

Hattie Carthan Herban Mission

East New York Farms!

Hattie Carthan Community Garden

The Youth Farm (BK Farmyards)

Granja Los Colibries(La Unión)

Brooklyn

Staten Island

Snug Harbor Heritage Farm

N

0   2.5   5   10 Miles

*Groups with fixed sites. Some interviewees provide assistance to other groups or rotate locations. These sites are not depicted here.

Locations of farms and gardens included in study. Map prepared by Peleg Kremer.

CHAPTER 2

New York City's Urban Agriculture System

Just a short walk from Yankee Stadium, in the Highbridge neighborhood of the South Bronx, Abu Talib tends a nearly half-acre oasis of vegetables, cherry trees, space for a flock of chickens, and a play area for neighborhood children. In 1992 Talib, together with his son and other community residents, cleaned what was then a trash-strewn lot and turned it into Taqwa Community Farm. Vacant parcels like the one that became Taqwa were the consequence of public policies ranging from urban renewal to scaled-back city services that disrupted social networks, destroyed housing, and contributed to environmental, economic, and public health ills in the South Bronx and other low-income communities of color. Taqwa was created as the neighborhood was rebounding from decades of neglect. Despite New York City's economic growth in the early 1990s, the problems of alcohol abuse, drug trafficking, and gang violence persisted in the streets surrounding the farm. Motivated by a desire to improve conditions in his community, Talib organized a group of volunteers and met with officials from the New York City Department of Parks and Recreation to get permission to garden the site. He and the other neighborhood volunteers turned it into what has since become one of the city's best-known community gardens.

Today, Talib manages Taqwa with his fellow gardeners.[1] During the growing season they gather at the farm to grow food, socialize, and provide a place for neighborhood youth to spend time outdoors with adult mentors. Other neighborhood residents shop at a farmers' market held at the site. Like many gardens and farms that operate on city land, Taqwa has regular open hours for non-gardeners, and it also hosts workshops and classes conducted by the New York Botanical Garden's Bronx Green-Up program and a not-for-profit training program called Farm School NYC. The farm is truly a community space, and it illustrates the power of neighbors to join together, take ownership in revitalizing abandoned lots, and steward them to meet neighborhood needs.

Although Taqwa stands out as an exemplary project, it is grounded in a long history of urban food production and community-based activism in New York.

As noted in chapter 1, New York's farms and gardens are as diverse as the city it-self, ranging from small patches of green space to larger, even commercial-scale, operations, and urban agriculture programs are led by people with varied inter-ests and occupations—hobbyists, activists, farmers, entrepreneurs, chefs, stu-dents—who are part of different racial, ethnic, and socioeconomic groups.

As is true in many diverse systems, individuals and organizations involved in urban agriculture in New York City experience different levels of privilege that in turn affect the extent to which their farms and gardens are successful or help achieve social justice goals. Urban agriculture in New York is rooted in the broad social, political, and historical contexts of the city itself; yet it is also a system composed of different individuals, organizations, and agencies, as well as networks, policies, material resources, and physical spaces (see appendix 2 and appendix 5 for descriptions of this system).

As discussed in chapter 1, some urban agriculture activists explicitly connect their farming and gardening efforts to broad social change objectives. Others, like Talib, see their everyday activities of growing food, mentoring neighbor-hood youth, and maintaining community spaces as a way to address day-to-day symptoms of structural oppression in communities that have long suffered po-litical and economic disenfranchisement and government neglect, even if they do not describe their work as activism per se. To these de facto activists, the significance of their farm and garden programs lies not only in the activities in which they engage and the leadership they exemplify but also in their deep and long-standing relationships with the places and cultural communities in which they work. People like Talib have long histories in New York City's urban agri-culture system, even if their work is overshadowed by higher-profile initiatives. This chapter reviews the overall system, including the pivotal moments that ex-plain the shape of the city's contemporary urban-agriculture-based activism.

The Roots of New York's Urban Agriculture

Urban agriculture is often portrayed as the latest fad, but food has always been produced in cities. In New York, farming and gardening have been import-ant sources of sustenance for low-income residents since the city's founding. Though early forms of urban agriculture in New York City were pragmatic, ad-dressing the need for nearby and relatively low-cost food prior to modern trans-portation, processing, and preservation technologies, city food production has also been promoted during specific historical moments for social and political reasons. Farms and gardens have been thought of as a means to inculcate patrio-tism in wartime, as a way to augment classroom education, and as a remedy for what Progressive Era reformers believed were the ills of urbanization. Agricul-ture in the city has also long been intertwined with class differences, the politics of urban economic inequality, and the use of public space; since the 1960s and

1970s, some participants have engaged in it as a response to urban policies that have exacerbated racial and class disparities.

EARLY FORMS OF URBAN AGRICULTURE IN NEW YORK

Until the early nineteenth century, many New York City residents kept livestock and home gardens for subsistence, but by the midcentury commercial food production became common within the city. Commercial dairies were established during this time because the lack of refrigeration and efficient transportation made it impossible to be far from customers, and some neighborhoods, like the area in Manhattan that is now known as Chelsea, came to have sizable dairy herds (Egan 2005). Other livestock, notably hogs, were kept to manage urban food wastes and for their meat (Blecha and Leitner 2014; McNeur 2011; Tremante 2000). Many of these commercial businesses were owned by recent immigrants seeking financial stability (Tremante 2000). Animals raised for commercial purposes were often crowded into lots close to breweries, rendering plants, and manure lots located in industrial neighborhoods inhabited by low-income city dwellers (Tremante 2000). Although they provided food for the city's growing population, these commercial livestock yards often posed a nuisance to surrounding neighborhoods; indeed, they were among the earliest examples of class-based urban environmental and health disparities related to food.

Public health consciousness took hold in the mid-nineteenth century, and city officials, along with some city residents, became increasingly concerned about the risks of consuming products derived from livestock kept in unsanitary conditions, not to mention the nuisance and health risks of the effluent and carcasses created by these businesses. These concerns set the stage for class-based battles over the legality of urban animal husbandry. As technology allowed for long-distance transportation of perishable products, and in the wake of professional public health campaigns against so-called swill milk (milk produced by cows raised in cities to which some proprietors added whitening substances to improve the appearance), wealthier residents began to buy dairy products from farms located outside of the city, which were deemed more sanitary and of higher quality. Some urban dairies continued production, at times adulterating their products to drive costs down and attract lower-income customers, but in the late nineteenth century, the establishment of a Dairy Commission led to sanitary standards that, with the advent of refrigeration and rail transport, pushed dairies out of the city altogether (Tremante 2000).

Hog production in New York City also differentiated social classes in the nineteenth century. Only the poorest residents in lower-income neighborhoods kept pigs for subsistence and waste disposal, and the efforts of wealthier residents and government officials to eliminate the animals from the city were met with staunch resistance (McNeur 2011; Blecha and Leitner 2014). After a number of cholera outbreaks during the 1830s and 1840s, however, the combination of new municipal regulations, greater enforcement of public health standards, and an expanded inspection and police force resulted in the elimination of hogs from the city by 1859, and of virtually all livestock from public spaces soon thereafter (McNeur 2011).

Vegetable gardens and farm plots persisted throughout the nineteenth and early twentieth centuries even as the city's population grew, in large measure because they were more environmentally benign than livestock. Beginning in the 1890s, New York City's municipal government, like those of other large US cities, supported public gardening programs as a way to address food insecurity among poor residents and prevent civil unrest during economic crises (L. Lawson 2005, 2004). New York replicated a well-known Detroit effort, the Pingree Potato Patch program (named after that city's mayor), which allocated land for subsistence food production to provide relief from poverty during the worldwide economic depression of 1873–1879 (L. Lawson 2004). As economic conditions improved in New York and elsewhere in the United States, these gardening programs generally gave way to development of the land they occupied. Growing one's own food was seen as an emergency measure to stave off hunger and avert protests in times of economic crisis, rather than a means of long-term sustenance for individuals and families living in or at the brink of poverty. Policy makers and planners viewed industrial, commercial, and residential development as better and more profitable use of the land than food production, and the economic activities resulting from development as more appropriate for city dwellers than farming.

PROGRESSIVE-ERA, WARTIME, AND DEPRESSION-ERA GARDENS

During the Progressive Era, a period of social activism and political reform in the late nineteenth and early twentieth centuries, political leaders supported garden projects as an antidote to industrialization and rapid urbanization (Hayden-Smith 2006, 4–5). Gardens and farms were seen as a means to teach agricultural and life skills to a growing urban populace alienated from its rural roots, and to engender cultural reform and "shape cultural values" (Hayden-Smith 2006; L. Lawson 2005). In 1917, the educational philosopher John Dewey advocated expanding the number of school gardens to inculcate "constructive patriotism" in children as well as to supplement food production (Dewey 1917).

During World War I, the US War Department funded initiatives such as the US School Garden Army, the Liberty Garden program, and the Women's Land Army to create new urban gardens, engage schoolchildren in gardening, and train young women to work on farms in place of male farmers sent to war (Hayden-Smith 2014). For the government, the purpose was to augment the output of rural farms, compensate for food sent to troops abroad, free up wartime shipping capacity by reducing food transport, and build support for the war effort by engaging civilians in what was promoted as a patriotic activity (Hayden-Smith 2014, 2006; Hynes 1996; L. Lawson 2005). The programs substantially boosted urban agricultural production. For example, in 1918 Liberty Gardens provided an estimated $520 million worth of food nationally (Hynes 1996, xi). At the municipal level, local organizations in New York City promoted the federal programs by sponsoring demonstration gardens in prominent places like Bryant Park and Union Square in Manhattan and by providing technical assistance to gardeners (L. Lawson 2005). Through the government-funded Women's Land Army of America, women were recruited to work on farms near cities. Barnard College, a private women's liberal arts college in Upper Manhattan, organized a women's agricultural camp in the then-rural suburb of Bedford, New York, to teach 142 "farmerettes" the skills needed to work in area farms (Lai 2009).

After World War I, many of the garden program sites were developed for real estate and other nonagricultural uses, though during the 1920s and 1930s some city planning departments incorporated gardens into their land-use plans (Hayden-Smith 2006). During the Great Depression, the federal Works Progress Administration sponsored relief gardens for food production in urban areas, but these programs were also abandoned after the federal government adopted the Food Stamp Program for farm surplus in 1937 (ibid.). Livestock were still present in urban areas in limited numbers until the 1930s, though they were used more for aesthetic purposes and landscaping than for human sustenance. Indeed, sheep were kept on lawns at the White House during the Wilson Administration, and in New York City's Central Park, until 1934 (Blecha 2007, 14–15).

After the United States entered World War II, four different federal agencies launched a second national garden initiative. As during the First World War's Liberty Garden campaign, the Victory Garden campaign of World War II promoted gardening in rural, suburban, and urban areas as a duty of civilians to participate in the war effort. Wartime propaganda encouraged Americans to grow their own food to enable the government to divert commercial agricultural products to the troops and Allies abroad (*Victory Gardens* 1999; L. Lawson 2005, 170–181; Hayden-Smith 2014). In part because many urban residents were already growing their own food, often in response to scarcity in the Great Depression, World War II–era Victory Gardeners were able to produce an estimated 44 percent of the nation's vegetables during this period (Hayden-Smith 2006, xii; Hynes 1996). Many families also raised chickens and livestock along with vegetables, though animal husbandry was not a part of the national Victory Garden campaign (Blecha 2007; Bellows et al. 2000).

By 1943 New York City had an estimated four hundred thousand Victory Gardens, and an additional fifty thousand were added in the 1944 growing season—an unprecedented increase in urban food production (Jenkins 1944,

1943). Mayor Fiorello LaGuardia's administration supported the effort, yet not with significant financial resources, as the city was struggling to recover from the Great Depression. Moreover, the city was ambivalent about the feasibility of maintaining sizable spaces for food production in densely built areas. A report on Victory Gardens in New York City published by Cornell University, the state's land-grant college, cautioned that "in the closely built areas, particularly in Manhattan, Victory Gardens are out of the question. . . . The [smaller] home garden is by far the most satisfactory" (New York State College of Agriculture 1943).

POSTWAR URBAN AGRICULTURE

Urban agriculture waned during the 1950s. Government wartime gardening programs ceased, the US economy grew, and the food distribution and retail system industrialized and centralized. Supermarkets replaced smaller grocers as the predominant source of food for urban (and suburban) residents. As public policies like federal funds for interstate highways and federally insured mortgages for veterans supported the growth of racially segregated suburbs, aesthetic preferences among the white, middle-class suburbanites who populated these communities turned toward manicured lawns instead of vegetable patches (Hynes 1996, xiii–xiv; L. Lawson 2005, 205–7). Some of the wartime Victory Gardens remained as urban community gardens, and public housing authorities in larger cities like New York actively promoted gardening for beautification and to engage residents in sponsored social activities (Hynes 1996, xxiii–xiv; L. Lawson 2005, 205–7). Urban livestock husbandry also continued in this period, especially among immigrants who carried on the cultural practices and dietary customs of their home countries, which often emphasized freshly raised meat (Bellows et al. 2000; Blecha 2007, 14–15). Still, city gardening and farming were far less prominent than they had been in previous decades.

The Re-emergence of Urban Agriculture in New York City

Urban gardening re-emerged in the 1960s and 1970s, this time as a grassroots effort, in contrast to the government-led programs that had been designed to meet the pragmatic and political needs of wartime mobilization and the Depression (L. Lawson 2005). One of the most visible manifestations of urban agriculture in this period was the proliferation of neighbor-led projects to create community gardens on vacant lots.

The resurgence of urban gardening was a response to broad economic, political, and social changes in New York and other large cities. In the postwar period, most suburban developments were racially and socioeconomically segregated through neighborhood covenants, deed restrictions, and bank redlining—the practice of not lending money in communities of color, areas bankers identified as financial risks, indicated by red boundaries drawn on lenders' maps.

As middle-class white families moved from cities to suburbs, so did retailing, resulting in reduced tax revenues for municipalities. An increasingly interconnected global economy also meant that firms were more easily able to relocate to locations with lower-cost labor, inexpensive land, and newer infrastructure. These developments led to an exodus of industry from older cities, along with stable manufacturing jobs and associated tax revenues. Often, the only infrastructure that remained consisted of obsolescent and contaminated industrial sites. Remaining residents were left to fend for themselves in accessing necessities from medical care and fire protection to healthy food.

These changes accelerated the flight of middle-class whites, causing population declines in inner cities. Beginning in 1949, federal funds became available for cities to condemn and clear low-income neighborhoods (designated by city planners as slums) to entice new development, a process known as urban renewal. These urban renewal projects often targeted communities of color, uprooting large numbers of black and Latino/a residents, and in the process increasing racial segregation within cities, breaking up the social networks in these neighborhoods, and disrupting intact low-income communities. Federal housing funds also financed the construction of public housing, which in New York City took the form of high-rise towers. These projects concentrated low-income people of color in buildings that were often physically isolated and class-segregated, further disrupting communities and social networks.

In New York City, these economic, demographic, and policy changes reduced the city's tax base while increasing the need for public services, putting the city on the brink of bankruptcy by 1975 and shutting it out of the capital markets (Fuchs 2010). To stave off bankruptcy and regain access to capital, the state created the New York State Financial Control Board, which had the power to require the city to cut its budget. The board reduced the discretionary portion of the city's operating budget, slashing services funded by municipal tax revenue, such as garbage collection, firefighting and policing, schools, hospitals, and libraries. Over the course of the 1970s, some one in five city jobs were lost due to attrition or mandated layoffs. The police department was reduced from 31,000 employees in 1972 to 22,000 in 1980 (Newfield and Du Brul 1981, 7). Despite increases in political power among people of color during this period, from a successful campaign for community control of public schools to a strong mayoral run by Puerto Rican political leader Herman Badillo, these cutbacks still fell disproportionately on low-income communities of color from the South Bronx to Central Brooklyn.

More insidiously, the budget cuts were part of a strategy of "planned shrinkage," in which services were reduced in neighborhoods with declining populations, ostensibly to improve efficiency by concentrating remaining resources in neighborhoods with stable populations and income to support them, but also to accelerate the depopulation of low-income communities that were labeled "pathological" by political leaders like Daniel Patrick Moynihan. Paradoxically, the reduced services in the communities designated for planned shrinkage led to initial population losses that were considered evidence of community decline, justifying further service cuts.

Reductions in municipal functions like policing and sanitation had pernicious effects, but the city's decision to close and consolidate fire companies in low-income neighborhoods was particularly damaging. Relying on modeling by the Rand Corporation that was subsequently discredited, in the 1970s the city closed or consolidated dozens of fire companies and reduced the Fire Department's workforce, mostly in low-income communities of color in the Bronx and Brooklyn, even though these were often densely populated, with older yet more intensively used housing that was therefore at greater risk of fires and fire damage. Closures of fire companies continued throughout the 1970s, even as the numbers of building fires grew to a peak of 56,000 in 1976. Fires forced mass movements of low-income residents within and between neighborhoods, directly and indirectly displacing an estimated 600,000 black and Latino/a residents (Wallace and Wallace 1998, 18). The fires destroyed large numbers of housing units, prompted landlords of nearby buildings to neglect and abandon their properties, and accelerated the movement of middle-income residents to other neighborhoods and out of New York City. The psychological, social, and physical disruptions caused by these upheavals led to declining public health, reduced public safety, and shorter life expectancy (ibid., 17–19). Many of the city's gardens and farms are on the vacant lots created by this period of malignant government and property-owner neglect of low-income communities of color.

In the wake of the city's fiscal crisis, municipal leaders in the 1980s adopted neoliberal growth strategies that relied increasingly on business subsidies and fiscal austerity to stimulate economic activity (Fainstein and Fainstein 1989). Then-mayor Ed Koch, mirroring a political philosophy espoused by the Reagan administration, played a significant part in lowering expectations of the city government's responsibility for solving urban problems, emphasizing the need for public-private partnerships and private-sector leadership to produce needed affordable housing and to stimulate economic development, responsibilities that in the past had been assumed to a much larger degree by city government with federal funds. Though motivated by different political views, the shift to neoliberal municipal policies was consistent with demands for greater citizen engagement and self-help at the neighborhood scale, supporting the growth of activities like vacant lot cleanups and community gardening. But it also had negative effects on low-income communities of color that depended to a large extent on public services because residents lacked the personal wealth to supplement diminished city functions like education, health care, parks, libraries, and sanitation with private services.

Economic and demographic changes during the 1980s also played a role in the growth of community gardening activity. Cities began to grow economically, particularly those like New York that were centers of finance connected to the global economy. Population losses began to reverse, and cities attracted young, white, affluent residents who were able to compete in the postindustrial economy, even as large numbers of low-income residents remained disconnected from the rapidly growing financial and real estate sectors.

Moreover, as private investment began to return to some low-income neighborhoods close to the central business district, like Manhattan's Lower East Side, many of the black and Latino/a residents who had borne the brunt of city disinvestment in the 1970s but were not protected by tenancy in public housing were displaced. The city and the private sector supported this process of gentrification by promoting a vision of low-income communities as the "urban frontier," encouraging young, middle-class, white people to act as urban "pioneers" and "homesteaders" by populating these communities building by building, block by block (N. Smith 1996). As noted in chapter 1, these so-called pioneers often used the cleanup of rubble-strewn lots and the creation of gardens as a way to beautify, and take control of, the neighborhoods in which they were "settling," though perhaps disregarding the fact that their "homesteading" drove up real estate values and intensified efforts to displace longtime residents, many of them low-income people of color who were already gardening. In gentrifying communities, however, people of color and new residents did often work together to create gardens, focusing on the immediate benefits of lot cleanups and safer green spaces and not the secondary effects of these gardens on real estate values and how a real estate boom induced by neighborhood greening might make the gardens vulnerable to development pressures. Many of the gardens were created on city properties taken from private owners who stopped paying their taxes on properties that lost much of their value due to municipal disinvestment. In areas of the city not yet subject to gentrification, such as Harlem, the South Bronx, and Central Brooklyn, residents were focused on reclaiming sites lost to urban renewal, abandonment, and fires, creating safe and healthy spaces and growing food to improve their neighborhoods.

URBAN AGRICULTURE AND THE GRASSROOTS

Community gardening, the most prevalent form of urban agriculture in 1960s and 1970s New York, was thus a response to interconnected economic and political trends, although gardeners were motivated by other factors as well. For residents unwilling or unable to leave their neighborhoods, creating something positive by turning a rubble-strewn lot into a garden was often a survival strategy. For neighborhood newcomers, whether conscious of their role as gentrifiers or unaware of the consequences of their actions, turning vacant spaces into gardens was a process of "taming" that urban frontier (N. Smith 1996). For some activists involved in civil rights, feminist, and mainstream environmental movements, urban gardens were both spaces for community organizing and opportunities to solve problems like crime, environmental injustice, and the need for more educational opportunities for youth (Hynes and Howe 2004; Stephens et al. 1996). In contrast to gardening programs led by progressive reformers in the late nineteenth and early twentieth centuries, or those sponsored by federal government programs during wartime and the Depression, urban agriculture in this period grew out of grassroots organizing (L. Lawson 2005).

Many discussions of urban agriculture activism of this era point to the theatrics of white activist Liz Christy and her self-proclaimed band of "green guerillas [sic]" composed of Christy and other young, middle-class artists living on the Lower East Side (known as Loisaida by Latino/a residents). In an effort to reclaim the many abandoned lots in the community, Christy organized neighborhood residents to toss seed "green-aids" (a mixture of mud and flower seeds) over fences separating lots from the street, plant flowers in median strips, and transform a heavily trafficked corner into a community garden. The organization she helped form, Green Guerillas, emphasized neighborhood residents' "self-help" over reliance on city services to clean up abandoned and rubble-strewn city lots (Hynes and Howe 2004, xiii; L. Lawson 2005, 205–8).

Christy's goals were to improve conditions for the existing residents, to emphasize the value of urban greening, and to support community control of land. However, these intentions and her success in creating gardens notwithstanding, the long-term results were decidedly mixed. The gardens contributed to increased property values on the Lower East Side and to the neighborhood's gentrification, while also serving as spaces of resistance to development. Green Guerillas exists to this day; it emphasizes a grassroots-organizing and community-driven model of change.

Less frequently included in written accounts, yet arguably more important in terms of the extent of New York City community gardening, are the many black and Latino/a gardeners in Upper Manhattan, the Bronx, and Brooklyn who were also early leaders during this era (New York City Community Garden Coalition n.d.). Low-income neighborhood residents, including many black and Latino/a gardeners, also took managing the effects of government abandonment and private disinvestment into their own hands. They, too, organized neighbors to clean and plant rubble-strewn lots that were abandoned by landlords and taken over by the city for unpaid taxes. They turned these lots into green spaces and community centers, often with vegetable plots, botanical landscaping, and, in some gardens, *casitas* (traditional Puerto Rican wooden structures used as meeting places within gardens) for community activities. Churches, community organizations, and associations of neighbors often supported these activists.

The sweat equity of neighborhood residents often filled in for diminished municipal services like sanitation and policing. From this perspective, the gardens can justifiably be understood as supporting government devolution and neoliberal policies. Yet the spaces also served as community gathering places for grassroots organizing and political activism (L. Lawson 2005). Though written historical accounts to date do not pinpoint one individual as a spearhead of these initiatives led by people of color, their efforts to convert vacant spaces into gardens and farms, in addition to the work of white-led groups like Green Guerillas, set the stage for the unfolding of urban-agriculture-based activism throughout the city.

GOVERNMENT SUPPORT AND DEVELOPMENT CONFLICTS

New York City's urban agriculture in the late 1960s and early 1970s was enabled by urban policies, even if municipal agencies didn't set out to create a large network of gardens. By the late 1970s, however, City Hall stepped into the field of urban agriculture, recognizing that gardeners were cleaning up vacant parcels and restoring order to communities at virtually no cost to the city. In 1978 the Koch administration allocated federal Community Development Block Grant funds to create Operation Green Thumb (today the New York City Parks and Recreation Department's program called GreenThumb), which provided technical support to gardeners and helped them manage city-owned garden sites.

The Green Thumb program supported hundreds of urban agriculture projects throughout the city's low-income communities, as required by the funding. In contrast to the wartime and Depression-era programs, the goal of the Green Thumb program was not to simply encourage production. New York City's decision to launch Operation Green Thumb was based largely on the desire to engage city residents as stewards of vacant city-owned land until development opportunities arose. Another consideration was the potential for gardens to spur investment by making the surrounding neighborhoods attractive to higher-income individuals and real estate developers. In the words of the parks commissioner under both the Koch and Giuliani mayoral administrations, the program was "where you could park land for interim use. . . . You don't want a rubble-strewn area, so you park it in Green Thumb and let it be used as a garden. But the key word is 'interim'" (Raver 1997). The increasing popularity of community gardens and the availability of federal community development dollars to fund Operation Green Thumb eased the political decision to support this interim use.

Additional government programs that supported urban agriculture in New York during this time included the Garden and Greening program of the New York City Housing Authority (NYCHA) and local cooperative extension programs (typically funded by the US Department of Agriculture [USDA], county governments, and state land-grant universities). NYCHA's Garden and Greening program evolved from a 1963 citywide resident garden competition (New York City Housing Authority 2014a). Initially a flower garden contest, it expanded to include a vegetable gardening competition and eventually a full-fledged program that today also includes tree plantings and environmental education (New York City Housing Authority 2014b). This program was motivated by the desire to provide what NYCHA viewed as wholesome activities for residents of low-income public housing facilities and to put to productive use some of the vast, yet frequently barren, landscapes of the city's high-rise "tower in the park" housing projects. Cornell University Cooperative Extension's Master Gardener Program (part of a national system of similar programs initiated in the early 1970s, which still operate throughout the United States) trained volunteers to provide advice on home gardening (Stephens et al. 1996; Reynolds 2011), and the USDA-sponsored Urban Garden Program, which existed from 1976 through 1994, employed cooperative extension agents to teach about gardening, small-livestock husbandry, and nutrition in twenty-six cities, including New York (ibid.). These programs were designed to help low-income city residents access fresh food at a low cost.

By 1980, real estate development had begun to pick up in Manhattan (and to a lesser extent in other boroughs), and displacement of lower-income residents was occurring in neighborhoods adjacent to the city's central business districts (Sites 1997, 545). City agencies and private developers sought to capitalize on increasing demand for housing, and the city adopted policies to create more units. During the previous decade, property abandonment and disinvestment had made the gardens, and the sweat equity of gardeners, appealing to city officials. However, as the economy rebounded, many of these sites were viewed as valuable development parcels, and the gardeners as obstacles. This shift was particularly true in neighborhoods like the Lower East Side, where a decade of gentrification had made market-rate housing construction financially feasible and the garden sites more lucrative to developers. In 1986, the city's destruction of the Garden of Eden, a revered community garden in this neighborhood, contributed to the 1988 riot in neighboring Tompkins Square Park, which was largely a reaction against city policies supporting gentrification, and foreshadowed what would become a much larger conflict over garden displacement in the 1990s (Zukin 2011).

While the gardens of the East Village and Lower East Side were targeted for development, the gardens in low-income communities of color in Brooklyn, Queens, and the Bronx faced less pressure from real estate development but were not invulnerable. These neighborhoods had ample vacant public land and faced far less private-development interest than communities in Manhattan; as a result, community gardens continued to be created on city-owned lots there throughout the 1980s. Yet seeds of conflict were being sown. In 1986, the Koch administration announced a $5 billion housing plan to build or rehabilitate 250,000 apartments in ten years in communities that had suffered from property neglect and abandonment in all five boroughs. Production of affordable housing in low-income neighborhoods accelerated as the administration formed partnerships with nonprofit housing development organizations to construct new units. The city began transferring the control of some gardens from the Parks Department to the Department of Housing Preservation and Development (HPD) so the latter could assemble easy-to-develop sites for larger-scale housing projects (ibid.).

The conflict between housing production and community gardens continued through the 1990s as the local and national economies grew. Land values in some communities with gardens continued to increase, and news of plans to convert particular sites into housing caused all community gardeners to worry about their tenure on city-owned parcels (Howe 1994). Under Mayor Rudolph Giuliani, the city stopped approving new GreenThumb gardens in 1994 and attempted to sell off all of its vacant land, including parcels occupied by gardens, in 1996 (Elder 2005, 777). A critical moment for New York's urban agriculture system came in 1998 when the city stopped renewing existing GreenThumb licenses and initiated the process of auctioning 114 garden sites (Englander 2001). Mayor Giuliani framed the issue in terms of needing the land to build new housing, emphasizing that constructing new apartments to open up units for lower-income residents was more important than gardens, that housing (and not food production) was a basic right for city residents, and that property owners of newly constructed market-rate housing would stabilize "impoverished" neighborhoods and help existing residents of all income levels. Activists in the community gardening, environmental justice, parks and open space, and affordable housing movements countered by arguing that "the public the Giuliani administration was interested in cultivating was that of the white middle class, real estate and development interests, and potential donors," pointing out that there were many other parcels of vacant land available for housing, and suggesting that the administration feared the garden sites as places for the mobilization of people opposed to its policies (Staeheli, Mitchell, and Gibson 2002, 200).

The ensuing struggle involved legal challenges by the gardeners and public protests (C. Smith and Kurtz 2003; Elder 2005). Lawsuits were filed based on claims that the proposed sale violated state and city environmental review laws and that they disproportionately harmed people of color, in violation of the Civil Rights Act of 1964 (Elder 2005). The courts dismissed these claims, holding that the city had the right to balance the benefits of housing development, community facilities, and construction jobs against the loss of open space (ibid., 783). Despite these legal losses, however, advocates for the gardens were able to convince then–New York State attorney general (and gubernatorial candidate) Eliot Spitzer to file a lawsuit against the city, largely based on the original claim of city officials' failure to follow environmental review laws. The suit resulted in a temporary restraining order barring the sale, opening up an opportunity for singer-actress Bette Midler's nonprofit New York Restoration Project (NYRP) to buy fifty-one gardens and for the national nonprofit Trust for Public Land (TPL) to buy an additional sixty-three parcels, most in communities of color and gardened by people of color.

In the wake of the Spitzer lawsuit, the purchases by NYRP and TPL, and the emergence of a newly energized and organized activist urban agriculture community that extended beyond community gardeners to environmental justice and other activist groups, the Giuliani administration agreed to NYRP's and TPL's purchases and eventually relented on the sale of many other gardens. Giuliani's successor, Mayor Michael Bloomberg, settled the attorney general's lawsuit shortly after taking office in 2002, maintaining most of the remaining gardens by transferring their control back to the Parks Department or to other nonprofit groups (Eizenberg 2013). As a result of this battle, most existing garden sites were spared from development, though community garden preservation and land tenure remain contentious issues between gardeners and New York City government to this day (Cohen, Reynolds, and Sanghvi 2012; Moynihan 2013). Gardens on city property do not have permanent or even long-term tenure, which many gardeners feel is important for maintaining community green spaces in their neighborhood, in addition to justifying the gardeners' significant investment of time and energy in maintaining the sites. As this book is going to press, the Housing Preservation and Development Department has solicited private developers for new residential buildings to be located on HPD-controlled vacant land, including active community gardens.

GARDEN ACTIVISTS

Overall, the period that began in the late 1990s galvanized a strand of activist-oriented urban agriculture in New York that characterizes an important part of this system today. The experience of fighting to save community gardens strengthened advocacy groups that support urban agriculture, like the New York City Community Garden Coalition, a grassroots group formed in 1996 (largely to address the threats to community gardens discussed above). These events had helped frame gardens as an integral part of the city's landscape. Also, some residents saw gardening as a way to claim a "right to the city" (Eizenberg 2012b, after Mitchell 2003), even as New York's prodevelopment municipal government continued to regard urban agriculture as merely an interim use of city-owned parcels. The development of some garden sites and continued threats to community gardens overall highlighted their vulnerability.

One lasting outcome of this battle was the creation of a group of community gardens with permanent land tenure and management staff, namely those operated by NYRP, various land trusts, and larger nonprofit organizations. These privately held gardens are recognized as productive spaces providing instrumental value to the city. They have helped establish food production as a legitimate urban land use. However, for those GreenThumb gardens on city land (mostly in communities of color) and thus not protected with permanent tenure, it has become ever more apparent both that the act of gardening in New York City is politically charged, and that the stakes of *not* engaging in political activism can be high for the gardens, the gardeners, and the residents of neighborhoods in which gardens are situated.

By 2010, as urban agriculture gained popularity throughout the country and concerns about diet-related public health disparities became politically salient, the city adopted new rules granting licenses for gardens in the city's Green-Thumb program to operate on city property. The rules include provisions for automatic renewal provided that gardens comply with the license terms and conditions, with a mandatory public review if the city wishes to evict gardeners and develop a site (City Record 2010). Despite these required procedures, the city is still able to develop garden sites for housing or any other public purpose.

New York City's Contemporary Urban Agriculture System

Urban agriculture in New York City today builds on the farming and gardening movements of previous eras but with growing spaces, practices, and motivations that make use of new technologies and take advantage of a moment in which concerns about the food system and addressing social inequities are both popular and politically salient. In addition to long-standing community gardens, small-livestock husbandry (notably chicken keeping) has become more common, and beekeeping has been legalized. Food production intended to address urban food insecurity has also returned, as has commercial farming. "Guerrilla" gardening has become more sophisticated, with the use of geographic information systems technology to map vacant lots and publicize property ownership data to help would-be gardeners identify and gain access to possible sites.

Conflicts over the use of vacant space for food production versus development remain intense, especially as the number of vacant city-owned parcels has declined and real estate values have risen. Yet the Bloomberg administration, which drew to a close in 2013, for the most part spared community gardens and other urban agriculture sites even as it rezoned many neighborhoods to increase development density. Moreover, the notion that farming and development are incompatible has begun to change as city housing agencies and private developers have found ways to integrate urban agriculture spaces into the city's infrastructure, including on rooftops of new affordable housing projects and older commercial buildings, in upscale restaurants and supermarkets, and on temporarily stalled development sites.

Yet as noted above, conflicts remain as the administration of Mayor Bill de Blasio, who was elected in 2013 on a platform of addressing inequality throughout the city, seeks to build or preserve 200,000 units of affordable housing. In fact, there is no formally adopted city policy to preserve existing gardens and farms on public land or to expand urban agriculture. Strategy documents issued by elected officials (e.g., New York City Council 2010; Office of Manhattan Borough President 2009, 2010, 2015) and iterations of the city's sustainability strategy (City of New York 2007, 2015) discuss the value of urban agriculture and describe plans to create new gardens and farms. However, short of issuing long-term licenses for gardens and farms, mapping the sites as parkland (which cannot be developed without state approval), or turning the sites over to land trusts or nonprofits, these remain merely intentions of the administration.

Historically, New York City's position on urban agriculture as a way to use public space has shifted in response to the social, political, and economic climate of the moment, and there is no guarantee that current support will continue. In the absence of firmer commitments to urban agriculture, activism remains a key focus for some farmers and gardeners, but it extends beyond preserving gardens themselves. Activists such as Abu Talib and Yonnette Fleming continue to use farm and garden spaces as venues to address both neighborhood-level concerns and much broader social and political issues.

Disparities in New York City's Urban Agriculture System

Urban farmers and gardeners in New York City must confront many of the same challenges faced by their counterparts in other US cities. As discussed in more detail in chapter 6, in addition to garden tenure, these challenges include accessing clean soil, compost, seeds, and tools; finding sufficient funding to support food production and related programs; working with city policies affecting farming and gardening; and identifying enough people to manage a variety of activities and program tasks. And yet within New York's urban agriculture system, individuals and organizations often experience these challenges differently according to their own race, gender, and class, as well the demographics of the communities in which they work (e.g., see Cohen, Reynolds, and Sanghvi 2012; Reynolds 2014). For example, accessing clean soil and compost for raised beds is important in many urban environments, since urban soils tend to be low in nutrients and high in contaminants (McClintock 2012; Duchemin, Wegmuller, and Legault 2008). However, contaminated soil is particularly common in areas with mixed industrial and residential land, and these areas often are communities of color and/or neighborhoods with predominantly low-income residents (e.g., see Sze 2007). As a result, these farm and garden organizations must take additional precautions (often requiring financial and material resources and technical help) merely to ensure the safety of the food they produce (see Vigil n.d.). Soil quality is just one example of how general challenges to urban agriculture may be different from community to community, often with disproportionate burdens placed on farmers and gardeners situated in historically low-income communities and communities of color in New York.

Disparities also exist between urban agriculture groups themselves. Interviewees in the Five Borough Farm project (discussed in the preface and Appendix 1) characterized the city's urban agriculture system as two distinct communities, one with significantly more financial resources, stronger relationships with influential groups, and/or a white leadership that created or took advantage of opportunities to expand their operations. As one (white) farmer noted:

> There are two very unique and distinct aspects of this urban farm movement going on. . . . One is very middle class and white, and one is not. One is of color and very low income. And they are . . . very separate. Unless they are brought together, I don't know that the success of either is going to continue. The needs [of each group] are completely different.

When asked for examples of the different needs, this farmer suggested that lower-income gardeners in communities of color often lack financial resources and carry out their work without being paid, while white middle-class urban farmers are more concerned about whether they can make a living farming—covering basic expenses is less of a problem. Other interviewees in that study claimed that organizations led by people of color faced greater difficulty securing resources, in part because they were less connected with political leaders and groups with financial resources (e.g., foundations and private donors). The interviewees based their opinions about these disparities on their own experiences in trying to obtain funds and other resources for their projects, as well as their observations of resources available to urban farms and gardens led by middle-class whites (Cohen and Reynolds 2015). But these opinions also suggest that white privilege and intersectional forms of oppression, as discussed in chapter 1, may be one source of the disparities among urban agriculture groups. One (African American) farmer cautioned that disparities made New York's urban agriculture system unsustainable, stating:

> I'm afraid right now that the way [urban agriculture is] looking is white-led. And people of color are being pushed to the side. I don't want crumbs. . . . And . . . if this movement is [going to be] sustainable, it has to be equal. Because right now I'm starting to see a trend whereby the people with the most power, the most voices, are getting the money and the people who can't speak as well are [not].

While New York's urban agriculture system is a network of diverse people, organizations, policies, materials, and physical spaces like farms and gardens, disparities between groups, particularly disparities based on race and class, keep this system from being as successful as possible. As discussed in chapter 6, recognizing these as significant challenges that are rooted in uneven dynamics of power and privilege is key to urban agriculture as social justice activism. As one farmer proclaimed, urban agriculture "can empower people to have political . . . and economic power," though only if the disparities in power are reduced or eliminated.

Roots of Urban Agriculture Activism

As this chapter has illustrated, New York City has a long and diverse history of urban agriculture that has been about politics and social justice as much as it has been about food production. Gardening and livestock husbandry performed by poor city residents and commercial operators in the nineteenth century gave way to Progressive reform-oriented garden projects at the turn of the twentieth century and subsequent government-sponsored programs that were prominent throughout the United States during the two world wars and the Depression. After a hiatus in the mid-twentieth century, urban agriculture re-emerged in New York City in the form of grassroots "guerrilla" and community gardening beginning in the 1960s and 1970s. The roots of contemporary urban agriculture activism in the city can be most directly traced to this era, when community gardening was a means to rebuild neighborhoods that had borne the brunt of public and private disinvestment. Despite a frequent association of this movement with white, middle-class activists, people of color throughout the city were also leaders in this period of urban agriculture.

As the economy grew in the 1980s and 1990s, community gardeners and urban agriculture organizations had to defend their rights to the spaces they occupied and reaffirm the value of the gardens to city officials who viewed them largely as a temporary use for sites that were slated for development. This galvanized a strand of urban agriculture activism focused primarily on preserving and maintaining gardens situated on city-owned land. The Giuliani administration's largely unsuccessful attempt in 1999 to sell a large number of city-owned garden sites required gardeners and farmers to become more politically active and to ally with sympathetic political officials, nonprofits, and philanthropic organizations.

The 1999 crisis produced several outcomes that have stabilized urban agriculture while also creating tensions in this system: the gardens preserved through the New York Restoration Project and the Trust for Public Land became permanent (privately held) green open spaces, establishing the viability and value of working urban landscapes; and a strand of activist-oriented urban gardening took hold through the organizing efforts of the New York City Community Garden Coalition. However, the process of protecting the gardens also made what had been a transgressive use of public space part of the status quo. Most of the gardens remaining on city land were spared development and were given additional protections from eviction—though not permanent tenure—alleviating some but not all of the tensions between gardeners and City Hall.

Contemporary New York City urban agriculture comprises an increasingly diverse network that builds on historical legacies but makes use of innovations like aquaponics and rooftop farming and engages with current social and political concerns. A small number of larger community and commercial farms have also joined long-standing community gardens, while relatively new technologies have been used to publicize key information about existing and potential farm and garden spaces. City agencies, including those responsible for low-income housing and environmental protection, have invested in integrating urban agriculture into housing facilities. They have also subsidized urban farms and gardens as stormwater management infrastructure and have established policies to help commercial urban farms and greenhouses, thereby advancing the notion of urban agriculture as a source of entrepreneurship, job creation, and tax revenue for the city. The embrace of urban agriculture at the city level has mirrored the growing popularity of the practice at the national and global scale. Yet race- and class-based disparities among urban farmers and gardeners detract from the sustainability of individual projects and the system overall.

Since 1999, urban agriculture activism has continued to gather momentum and has also diversified. Today, gardeners and farmers still advocate for policies affecting their day-to-day and long-term agricultural practices, most notably garden tenure and legalization of specific activities like beekeeping. However, some urban agriculture activists also focus on broader social, environmental, and economic justice concerns. An overlapping group of New York City activists, many of them people of color and women with long-standing roots in their communities, use urban agriculture as one strategy to address tangible inequities such as community food insecurity and lack of green space, as well as much deeper historical social problems including structural and intersectional forms of oppression.

As discussed in chapter 1, some of these activists frame their work in terms of specific concepts or in line with various activist and intellectual traditions. Others, like Abu Talib, simply speak of their farming and gardening efforts as a proactive way to address the ongoing effects of concentrated poverty in their communities. While their labors bring important benefits that reach far beyond providing food in their communities, these activists' work is often overlooked in mainstream accounts of urban agriculture, reproducing cycles in which public recognition and social capital reinforce disparities between comparatively privileged (often white) groups and those with fewer economic and political resources.

Simply documenting what is wrong with this system does not go far enough in shifting the narrative toward one that supports the leadership of people of color and women whose work is focused on dismantling oppression. Highlighting existing leadership among activists of color (and like-minded white activists) and the various ways in which they use farm and garden programs to advance social justice is a key element of this project, to which we turn next.

CHAPTER 3

Growing More than Just Food

Robert and DeVanie Jackson of the Brooklyn Rescue Mission Urban Harvest Center grow produce and raise chickens at Bed-Stuy Farm, a project of the center, which they cofounded with other Bedford-Stuyvesant community members in 2002. The nonprofit organization is a faith-based Christian ministry, but it serves community members regardless of their religious or spiritual beliefs and practices. The mission provides food, clean clothing, and other support services to low-income and homeless individuals in this Central Brooklyn neighborhood. The Jacksons see service through feeding people as a central part of the Christian mission, and they act on this belief through numerous community activities that they lead.

Brooklyn Rescue Mission began providing food to the community through an emergency food pantry but in 2005 expanded its programs to include a garden, a greenhouse, fruit trees, chickens, and an aquaponics system to raise fish. The organization also runs a CSA program and two farmers' markets, through which it distributes produce from its own farm and two farms in upstate New York. The markets regularly feature healthy-cooking demonstrations to help neighborhood residents, many of whom have diet-related health concerns, integrate healthful foods into their meals. Local entrepreneurs sell value-added products like jam and baked goods at the markets; the Jacksons see this as a way to promote economic development. Brooklyn Rescue Mission also runs a youth internship and employment program, as well as a senior citizens' program that provides food and various social activities for neighborhood participants. These are just a few of the ways the Jacksons put their faith into practice.

On the surface, Brooklyn Rescue Mission appears to be like many other contemporary urban agriculture groups in New York and elsewhere that grow food, manage on-site farmers' markets, run educational programs, and offer an oasis from the built-up urban environment in hopes of improving city life. Yet the mission's food and agriculture activities are grounded not only in Christian social justice values but also in a structural analysis of the persistent racialized economic inequities affecting residents in this historically low-income neighborhood. The Jacksons see the food system disparities that affect African American communities as a consequence of systemic economic disenfranchisement. Robert Jackson's analysis is that "food is based on economics and politics." He asks, "How are you going to have control over access to your food if you don't have . . . economic power?" Jackson contextualizes these comments in historical patterns, noting, "When was the last time you went to a meat shop and saw an African American own it? These are things that have to be adjusted." Both Robert and DeVanie Jackson speak about urban agriculture as "the starting point for a self-reliance movement" and suggest a related belief in self-determination as an important element of socially just systems—a belief shared by black food and environmental activists (e.g., see White 2011a).

The Jacksons' analysis of power in the food system has developed through up-close awareness of structural racism and the ways that it plays out in people's everyday lives through multigenerational poverty and lack of economic opportunity. Food production is a central activity at Brooklyn Rescue Mission and is one thing that distinguishes it from other social service organizations. Equally central to this work is the recognition that food system disparities grow out of historically inequitable power relationships that, in turn, convey social and economic advantage to some over others.

While the day-to-day activities at Bed-Stuy Farm resemble those at other farms and gardens, the Jacksons use urban agriculture to cultivate a different sociopolitical and economic reality in which people of color have more control over the food systems in their own communities, and in which low-income communities have more economic power. This chapter examines how urban agriculture activists like the Jacksons put their social justice beliefs into practice, using urban food production and the diverse activities that surround it to foster resistance to oppression and to support community self-determination and resilience.

Growing Food as Resistance

Producing one's own food in the city can be a strategy for personal and political resistance to many aspects of the conventional food system, from the monopolistic effects of corporate consolidation in US agriculture to the social and environmental ramifications of industrialized farming, such as soil degradation and the economic challenges faced by small family farms. As the stories from Hattie Carthan Community Garden (chapter 1), Taqwa Community Farm (chapter 2), and Brooklyn Rescue Mission suggest, for members of socially marginalized groups, it can also represent self-determination and political agency—the ability to effect political change in one's community—especially in the face of "racial and economic apartheid" (White 2011a). Also, it can be a resilience strategy in the context of social, economic, or ecological crises (Kato, Passidomo, and Harvey 2013). Urban agriculture can be a form of resistance not only to specific exploitative practices that have shaped the U.S. agricultural system—for example, enslavement, forced removal from ancestral lands, and enactment of abusive agricultural labor laws—but also to the persistent, structural forms of oppression discussed in chapter 1. Resistance can take the form of everyday acts of food production practiced *despite* the social and legal systems that keep many people of color and low-income people at a disadvantage within dominant society. It can take the form of dialogue about the connections between individual food system inequities and broader social patterns, such as the idea that disparate food access is a result of disinvestment in and government abandonment of low-income communities and communities of color. It can involve demonstrating how activities such as urban farming and political advocacy can help dismantle oppression by fostering economic and political empowerment and community resilience.

Observers and practitioners of urban agriculture have noted that many African Americans today associate food production with oppression because of the legacy of slavery, and later sharecropping, in the Jim Crow–era agrarian South (Kaufman and Bailkey 2000; Meenar and Hoover 2012; White 2011b; Yakini 2013). This deeply ingrained social memory has kept some individuals from participating in urban farming, a reality that some agriculture activists have recently begun to counteract through farming, teaching, and raising awareness about black farmers and other farmers of color throughout the United States (see Yakini 2013; Penniman 2015; Bowens 2015; Farms to Grow n.d.).

Moreover, African Americans' experiences with agriculture are also those of resistance to oppression (White 2011b; Yakini 2013). As sociologist Monica White argues, food production has long been an act of resistance, as well as a "sign of the possible," with potential for reshaping material realities and countering internalized oppression among African American farmers (White 2013, 2011b). These analyses have helped reframe the understanding of farming within some black communities, a shift with implications for a new view of agriculture in urban environments.

Analyses of resistance through urban agriculture put forth by White and others detail the experiences of African American communities, but their observations can be extended to many racial, ethnic, and cultural groups. For example, urban farms and gardens can help members of indigenous communities and immigrants from many regions of the Global South to resist the cultural oppression they may face as a result of living in a new setting that is not supportive of their own traditions. Importantly, urban agriculture can also help participants refute the image of people of color as victims with no agency to affect their own realities. Thus, rather than functioning as a defensive act, urban farming and gardening can help (and has helped) members of many communities of color and immigrant communities in the United States cultivate social resilience. These are important, yet often overlooked, ways in which urban agriculture can help build community power from within.

RESISTING CULTURAL OPPRESSION

Granja Los Colibries, a farm in Sunset Park, Brooklyn, provides one example of how urban agriculture groups resist oppression by keeping alive community knowledge about agricultural heritage and traditional food practices. The farm is a project of La Unión, a six-hundred-member organization consisting primarily of immigrants from the Mixteca region of Mexico, which focuses on advancing social, economic, and cultural rights within the local community and in the members' home countries. The organization specifically addresses equity in education, youth development, and food justice and also advocates for immigration policy reform. These are issues that affect daily life for La Unión's members, many of whom have low incomes, speak limited English, and have family members residing in Mexico who hope to immigrate to the United States.

Granja Los Colibries grew out of a collaboration between youth participants in La Unión's Youth Action Changes Things (Y-ACT) program and some of the organization's adult members, many of whom have experience growing food on rural farms or in their backyards in Mexico. In 2010, Y-ACT conducted a community food assessment, documenting the lack of fresh produce available in the neighborhood. The assessment fueled a growing interest within the organization in turning a lot between two neighborhood apartment buildings into a community garden. Over the course of that year, members cleaned the space and transformed the lot into a very small farm managed by Los Granjeros, La Unión's farm and garden committee. Members of Los Granjeros cooperatively oversee the cultivation of vegetables and herbs and keep a small flock of hens, using and adapting traditional practices for the small space and urban environment. They also share their agricultural knowledge with other members, including the youth participants who have not had prior experience with food production.

Through Granja Los Colibries, the farmers engage in autotopography, a practice through which people use agriculture and landscape management to create a familiar space in new surroundings (see Mares and Peña 2011, 2010). Farming and gardening in this sense are important not only because they help the farmers themselves maintain a part of their agricultural heritage (in addition to supplementing fresh food available to their families) but also because they help participants resist the loss of culture-specific knowledge that often follows immigration to a new cultural setting. As La Unión's executive director Leticia Alanis explained, "Because most of the people who participate in the garden grew up ... working the soil, ... for them, the garden is like an oasis. ... People feel a lot of pride and also connect with their roots ... and then we all are connected as a new generation to that experience of taking care of living things." The farm provides food, but perhaps even more importantly, it helps participants within this mostly immigrant community resist cultural oppression as they forge new livelihoods in the United States.

La Unión is not the only group in New York City using urban agriculture to resist cultural oppression. Farms and gardens throughout the city, from Evergreen Community Garden in Queens to sites throughout the Bronx, provide such opportunities for participants. At Taqwa Community Farm in the Bronx, Abu Talib, himself a garden elder with agricultural roots, recounted having helped plant two cherry trees in the early years of this garden as a way to access fruit that he had been accustomed to eating as a child growing up in the South. Years later, he explained, he continues to invite children from the neighborhood surrounding Taqwa to pick and eat cherries from the trees, sharing small parts of his own farming knowledge with the children, as he does in other ways with some of the garden's adult members. Talib does not speak of his gardening work in terms of cultural resistance per se, but his stories convey the fact that agriculture in the city is a way that he has retained, and helps share, a piece of his own heritage as an African American growing up—and growing food—in the rural South.

RESISTING THE IMAGE OF VICTIMIZATION

In addition to helping participants resist cultural oppression, urban agriculture activists use their programs to demonstrate that farming need not be connected only to exploitation or victimization among people of color (White 2011a, 2011b), and that even those who have experienced political injustice can be actively involved in changing policies that adversely affect them and their families. Having analyzed archival data, Monica White demonstrates that although some African Americans today associate agriculture with enslavement, they do not have a historically negative relationship with the land, or with agriculture, but rather have a negative relationship with oppression through agricultural enslavement and subsequent laws and social codes that kept (and still keep) black farmers at a disadvantage. White drove home this particularly important point in a keynote address to the 2013 Black Farmers and Urban Gardeners conference in Brooklyn. Through stories ranging from the Transatlantic Slave Trade—such as African women's practice of carrying seeds braided into their hair and planting them on arrival in the Americas—to present-day urban farming in Detroit, she emphasized the many ways that Africans and African Americans have exemplified resilience through agriculture.

Similar narratives of resistance to victimization through food production are present in New York City. At Hattie Carthan Community Garden, for instance, farm activities are envisioned as a way for "youths and elders [to] share the rich tradition of agriculture" (Hattie Carthan Community Market 2013) and a means to help rewrite agricultural history in participants' minds. As discussed in chapter 1, events at this garden often pay homage to community elders and African ancestors who have experienced, and in many cases sought to eliminate, structures of racism and patriarchy. Through conversations that take place during less formal gardening and farming, elders and garden leaders also teach members of the community, particularly younger people who may not be aware of the diverse experiences of their ancestors, about the legacy of agriculture and social justice activism in their communities. Yonnette Fleming underscored the relevance of these activities in her community's context: "We're [working for justice] through the empowerment and the development of people who have been excluded in matters of the environment, and have been relegated to slave labor in the history," she explained, "so it means that every time we show up, it's a move for justice."

At La Unión in Sunset Park, the garden site also provides a venue for discussing interrelated social and political issues that affect its members directly. Alanis explained, "Usually when we have activities at our garden, we have . . . a guided reflection on [broader food system] topics, whether this is how we eat, how we could eat better, or . . . [the conditions of] the people who work to produce the food." Discussions may center on community food security and whether a community has access to healthy, affordable, and culturally acceptable foods, or they may explore issues like the food justice aspects of subsidized school lunch programs (in which many of La Unión's member families participate).

Gardeners may also talk about the status of farm workers, a topic intertwined with the organization's focus on immigration policy reform and an issue that is particularly relevant to the mostly Mexican members of La Unión. A 2008 analysis found that 40 percent of all hired farm workers in the United States are foreign born, with 37.3 percent originating from Mexico. Of Mexican immigrant farm workers, 90 percent are not US citizens (Kandel 2008). Discussing these facts within the context of the garden helps members connect political issues affecting their own lives with the act of growing food as resistance, and it helps build the integrity of the organization's focus on food and politics.

By coupling the act of food production with discussions about broader food systems and social justice issues, programs at La Unión and Hattie Carthan help participants address the need for improved access to fresh and healthy foods (albeit on a very small scale in the case of Granja Los Colibries) and contextualize some of their day-to-day experiences in surrounding local, international, and political systems. For La Unión, this practice also enables the organization to draw connections between urban agriculture and its advocacy efforts for policy and educational reform. In demonstrating multiple ways in which urban agriculture represents and is connected to empowerment and community agency, these organizations help resist persistent and erroneous images of people of color and recent immigrants from the Global South as passive victims of economic and political disenfranchisement. The fact that these discussions take place in the garden is important because it connects abstract concepts, like agricultural policy, to tangible activities and everyday realities.

Fostering Self-Determination through Markets and Entrepreneurism

Although it is easy to focus on the food production aspects of urban agriculture, farms and gardens are staging grounds for diverse marketing activities through which activists aim to address their social justice goals. These activities include on-site farmers' markets and CSA programs through which farmers and gardeners sell their products (often at low or sliding-scale prices). The market programs like the one at Brooklyn Rescue Mission (described at the beginning of this chapter) often aim to help low-income community members more easily access fresh, healthy, culturally appropriate food, and at the same time they contribute to community economic development by providing a few jobs. They also help foster microenterprises through which individuals can supplement their incomes by selling farm-based products like homemade jam or botanical-based beauty products while gaining entrepreneurial skills.

As with food production, these value-added marketing activities are common among urban agriculture organizations. As noted in chapter 1, on one hand such activities can be read as "self-help" strategies in line with the neoliberal view that the capitalist market should (and can) solve social problems (see McClintock 2013; Agyeman and McEntee 2014; Weissman 2015a, 2015b). Yet these activities can also be understood as efforts to foster self-determination in light of economic realities and historical economic disenfranchisement as Robert Jackson describes them. Activists we spoke with use urban-farm-based market activities not to *solve* the problems caused by economic inequity or government devolution (as chapter 5 discusses, many such activists also advocate for policy advocacy changes to address these issues) but rather as a way to help community members assert agency in managing the effects of long-term disenfranchisement from the city's mainstream economy. Their on-site markets are a way to build their communities' economic power, even if they represent only a small percentage of the food and body-care product sales in their community.

As an example, Deborah Greig, agriculture director at East New York Farms! in Brooklyn's East New York neighborhood, explained that running a farmers' market is one way in which the project works toward its mission of addressing food justice by supporting local sustainable agriculture and community-led economic development. "We involve [members of the community] pretty significantly," she explained. "We try to work with local vendors and local gardeners to grow food for our market. So, [we're] growing food [and increasing] access in the neighborhood [and also] creating some income around that." East New York Farms! (ENYF!) is a project of the United Community Centers (UCC), a community-based organization founded in 1954 that provides various services and support to community residents. The farm project began growing and selling food in partnership with local residents in 1998 through a farmers' market that at first had just two vendors, both selling food grown in the city. Two years later, in 2000, the establishment of the UCC Youth Farm as a part of the ENYF! project, along with distribution of USDA Farmers' Market Nutrition Program coupons in East New York starting the same year, made the market products more affordable for nutrition program participants (Daftary-Steel and Gervais 2014), and these changes helped ENYF! expand.

Greig, who is white, explained that initially ENYF!, due to its small size and modest revenues, was not able to pay the community members who worked at the market. However, after increasing the number of vendors both from within the local community and from farms in upstate New York, it has been able to employ neighborhood residents to run some of the market activities and has thereby contributed to their incomes. These contributions are important in East New York, which has a significantly lower median household income and higher rate of unemployment than the city overall (see appendix 4). Although the number of jobs created through the market has been relatively small, by involving community members in all stages of market production—from growing food to selling it—ENYF! creates opportunities for participants to take ownership in efforts to improve their community's economy and provides work experience that may help prepare them for other jobs.

Beyond East New York, other urban agriculture activist groups have facilitated the creation of microenterprises that use products from the farm or garden. In these cases, entrepreneurialism is envisioned as a way to help individuals gain experience owning and operating a business, and supplement their incomes in the process. Such was the experience of one farmer at La Finca del Sur (see chapter 4) who makes and sells beauty products from lavender grown on the farm. Nancy Ortiz-Surun, one of the farm's founders, explained that this farmer-entrepreneur is the sole provider for her special-needs child and herself, and that as she has gained experience as a small business owner, she has expanded her market and "her horizons." Similarly, Yonnette Fleming at Hattie Carthan Community Garden and Herban Farm (see chapter 1) discussed supporting women-run microenterprises as a way to foster "alternative economies for populations that are disenfranchised by [mainstream] occupational systems." With help from other farm and garden volunteers, Fleming has organized seasonal on-farm artisan markets where women entrepreneurs sell hand-crafted products such as fruit preserves, jewelry, and herb-infused soaps. Fleming explained that beyond providing an occasional venue for the women to sell their products, the market is designed to help female artisans "move into entrepreneurship thinking" in order to learn new methods "to acquire money for life."

These market and entrepreneurial activities provide not only financial benefits but empowering experiences that reach beyond the conventional job training and part-time paid work that urban agriculture organizations commonly provide. Several activists noted that on-farm markets had also helped invalidate disempowering stereotypes about their communities, setting the stage for similar initiatives. For example, there is a common misperception that the dearth of food retailers in low-income neighborhoods results from insufficient demand for fresh produce due to individual preferences or lack of knowledge about healthy eating (e.g., Alkon 2012; Guthman 2008b) rather than private-sector and political choices about where to build supermarket chains, or policies that favor large grocery firms over small grocers, cooperatives, direct marketing outlets (like farmers' markets), and other forms of independently owned food businesses. Deborah Greig explained that the longevity and growth of the ENYF! market demonstrates that there is, in fact, demand for healthy, fresh food among low-income community members. Karen Washington, a Bronx-based farmer and activist who is among the founders of a garden coalition called La Familia Verde, echoed this sentiment, pointing to the success of one of the markets that she and community members also founded: "[Our] farmers' market . . . came out of the fact that we were told low-income neighborhoods can't *afford* organic food, fresh food, that it's too *dangerous* for farmers to come, and it's too *far*. This will be our tenth year having the La Familia Verde farmers market [in the Bronx]. It's a testament to the work that the community has done to bring in fresh produce, and the connection the community has made with the urban farmers and the rural farmers, [all] working together to bring fresh produce to *my* neighborhood."

The markets and microenterprises described here are situated in low-income parts of New York City and are run by individuals and organizations with long-standing roots in the communities in which they work. The activists use their farm and garden programs to address the effects of economic disenfranchisement and economic inequality, which are critical concerns in the lives of many members of their communities. Ray Figueroa, director of social-ecological community development projects at Friends of Brook Park (a community-based environmental organization in the South Bronx that also operates an urban agriculture program), explained: "If you come up in the 'hood and say, 'Yo, what's the main issue in the community?' folks'll say, 'Man, not enough jobs, man. You got jobs?'"

These activists do not propose to eliminate unemployment through farmers' markets and farm-based microenterprises. They do not envision markets as the primary solution to economic inequality or limited food access. Nor do they aim to create a *completely* local, self-reliant economy or remove themselves entirely from the mainstream market economy. Rather, they hope to reframe community members' thinking about economic livelihood and to reach beyond teaching job skills to foster independently owned and community-based businesses as a means to economic empowerment. By connecting food and flower production to community-driven entrepreneurship, these organizations begin to demonstrate how urban agriculture can help community members determine for themselves the types of food available to them, the ways in which these foods are marketed, and who receives the economic benefit from growing and distributing food.

Urban Agriculture Education as Social Justice Activism

Education and youth development are also common activities for urban farm and garden projects, nationally, but relatively few of these programs would be considered "activist," and even fewer explicitly address social justice issues. In New York City, as in other cities, school garden programs teach a wide range of topics including nutrition and healthy eating, environmental awareness and appreciation, self-esteem, and life skills, and they may also include lessons that satisfy state or federal standards for science education (Blair 2009; Grow to Learn NYC 2014). A growing number of farms and gardens on high school and college campuses teach about food and urban farming and also teach skills such as teamwork and project management (Parr and Trexler 2011). Beyond school gardens and farms, educational programs help adults and young adults learn about horticulture, farm management, business management, and broadly relevant job and communication skills (Hynes 1996; Pinderhughes 2003; Feenstra, McGrew, and Campbell 1999). Yet few programs are organized around deeper social change objectives.

In contrast to these common types of education programs, the urban agriculture activists described throughout this book engage quite deliberately in what bell hooks (1994) describes as teaching as a form of activism. Through formal and informal educational programs, they use their gardens and farms, and the activities within them, to teach about the nature of political, economic, and social structures that produce oppression. Although these activist farmers and gardeners do teach about ecology, nutrition, culture, and life skills, these subjects are often approached through the lens of social justice. Organizations like La Unión and Hattie Carthan Community Garden infuse discussions about injustice in food systems into garden activities and events, and they offer participants opportunities to see how agriculture can be used to resist oppressive forces and cultivate community resilience. Some activists also develop and use formal curricula and experiential-learning activities to help participants understand complex social constructs such as structural racism and the intersections between race and class. Today's urban farm and garden educators also have diverse goals, and several New York City urban agriculture activists we spoke with have designed and operate formal educational programs to help students understand the connections between agriculture, food, and justice while they learn practical farming or gardening skills.

One example of such a program can be found at BK Farmyards, a farming collective that runs the Youth Farm (a project of Green Guerillas) at the High School for Public Service in the Crown Heights neighborhood of Brooklyn. The group's on-farm educational programs for high school students and apprentices include formal discussions about racial and economic justice, and these topics are also included in a health and environment course that BK Farmyards members, most of whom are white women, co-teach with the high school's faculty. Often, informal discussions on the farm emphasize racial justice, and BK Farmyards has hosted outside groups to provide racial justice and anti-oppression training programs for youth and adult staff in order to strengthen this emphasis in its activist work.

Bushwick Campus Farm, also situated on the grounds of a public high school in Brooklyn, provides another example of an urban agriculture education program focused on social justice, and, more specifically, on educating about and dismantling the multiple forms of oppression discussed in chapter 1. The farm and its educational programs were managed by Maggie Cheney, director of farms and education at the nonprofit organization EcoStation:NY at the time of this study. Cheney, who is white and a queer-identified farmer, explained that in the summer job-training program, "We're training about racial disparities, [and] we're also training about homophobia—isms of all types—[and how they're] connected. . . . I'll ask 'How many people in here have someone they know who is obese? How many people have a family member who's diabetic? Raise your hand.' Then I say, 'Well, why are they?' And then I say, 'Do you think this is the same problem here in Bushwick as it might be in the [wealthy] Upper East Side or Upper West Side? Is this is the same problem that all people have regardless of race, class, gender, ethnicity, if you're a recent immigrant or not?' And then [we] discuss that."

Discussing racial and economic inequities in the context of farm activities helps participants begin to understand complex social and political dynamics that affect many aspects of life. Such programs often provide in-depth education about society (through critical pedagogy) to which lower-income youth participants, in particular, may not have access. As Greig observed, the youth in the ENYF! program "just don't get [this type of education] in the schools that they go to." These programs also help participants understand food system inequities in ways that emphasize the structural and intersectional forms of oppression, rather than seeing inequities as the results of individual circumstances—a skill that many youths and adults in the United States have not developed. For instance, Yonnette Fleming's food justice courses examine how patriarchy and racism play out in the food system. They also include discussions about how certain policy-making processes perpetuate disenfranchisement from decision making related to public health issues that affect participants and their community. The course helps demystify the concept of food justice for community members who, Fleming has noted, often find this term overly abstract. She has also observed that the youth with whom she works often understand these concepts more quickly or more thoroughly than the adult participants. Fleming believes that such programs are important for shifting long-term public understanding of social justice.

In addition to examining broader sociopolitical dynamics (like structural racism and its effects on food security and public health), farm and garden programs like these provide students with the language to talk about racism and oppression in other situations, such as in their classrooms, at work, and in everyday interactions. The impact of these lessons may also reach beyond the individual participants. Specifically, communicating about structural forms of racism is a tactic that racial justice advocates argue can help shift public discourse from mainstream narratives about individual acts, such as racial bias, to much broader societal and historical patterns (Apollon et al. 2014). Helping people focus on structural forms of oppression rather than on interpersonal or isolated circumstances can reduce white people's resistance to recognizing racism and thus can lead to more productive antiracist work. Similarly, expanding consciousness about how structural oppression surfaces within the food system—and helping participants develop the vocabulary to communicate about these structures—is a strategy that activists use in the hope of advancing social justice beyond the garden gates.

Teaching as activism is taken to a larger scale by Farm School NYC, one of the more extensive adult urban agriculture education programs in New York and nationally. Launched in 2010, the two-year adult training program began as a project of the nonprofit Just Food, which runs a number of community programs designed to address racial and economic justice issues in the food system. The school was designed and is guided by representatives of numerous organizations and agencies throughout the city, including many of the activists discussed in this book. Social justice is as core to the school's curriculum as growing food is, as demonstrated by the school's mission to "train New York City residents in urban agriculture in order to build self-reliant communities and inspire positive local action around food access and social, economic, and racial justice issues." Students take courses in urban agriculture growing techniques, business planning and marketing, community organizing and leadership, food-based education, and community food arts (canning, pickling, and fermenting, along with state food safety standards). Jane Hodge, Farm School's director until 2014, explained that social justice topics are incorporated into all courses to help the program achieve its mission. For example, in the school's "Growing Soil" class, students and instructors discuss land ownership, the connection between land and identity, and how these relate to issues of race and class. Farm School NYC follows Just Food's emphasis on popular education, meaning that teachers are practitioners in their respective fields and students are encouraged to teach the concepts and skills they've learned to fellow community members outside the school.

Other organizations also use urban agriculture education to provide experience in community organizing and popular education as a part of advancing social justice, even when they don't describe it as such. Green Guerillas today runs a "Youth Tillers" program, through which it employs high school students in paid internships that involve building and supporting community gardens and organizing events to educate other youths (Green Guerillas 2014). Executive director Steve Frillman emphasized that Green Guerillas doesn't explicitly seek to address predefined notions of social justice, but rather aims to help community gardeners realize their gardens' goals. The Youth Tillers learn about this approach to grassroots community organizing when they participate in Green Guerillas meetings with participating gardeners. Frillman, who is white, explained, "[We] connect with community gardeners, sit down with them in their gardens or in a community center in an evening and say, 'What are your goals, what do you need, how can we help you get there?'"

The principle that Green Guerillas embodies is to build projects around community needs rather than impose its own priorities on gardeners and the places that they cultivate. Indeed, all of the programs described in this book approach urban agriculture education from a perspective that sees community members as potential agents of social change. The formal educational programs are designed to help students understand the structural roots of food system injustice, along with their historical and contemporary contexts, and activists also use the farms and gardens for more informal teaching about these dynamics. Further, as suggested by the examples above, many of the activists with whom we spoke insist that advancing social justice in the food system involves not merely educating people *about* urban agriculture or health, or even *about* disparities, but also facilitating the development of participants' critical-thinking and problem-solving skills, beginning with the knowledge they already possess from lived experience.

Stephen Ritz, a Bronx teacher and founder of a school-based urban agriculture program called Green Bronx Machine, explained: "You don't need a PhD . . . to figure out what kids get off at [this subway] stop and who stays on the train to get off at the Bronx High School of Science.[1] My kids know all too well the reality of their community. What they *don't* understand is how they're being marketed to, and what they *don't* understand is what healthy, fresh food is. So, when they learn to grow it, they learn to eat it, and they learn to sell it, that's a game-changer." Sharon de la Cruz, a program coordinator at The Point Community Development Corporation in the Hunts Point neighborhood of the South Bronx during the time of our study, further illustrated this notion, explaining, "The reality is, most people in Hunts Point have an average household income of fifteen thousand. . . . [How do you really teach folks to eat healthy] when eating healthy is quite expensive?" The Point is a youth and community development organization that has run urban garden and nutrition education programs with an emphasis on whole systems and community assets. Empowering people, de la Cruz noted, "is about really starting from the basics. And 'empowering' doesn't mean that I am teaching them things that they don't know. It's more just, 'OK, in your current situation—which is of being [from] a low-income neighborhood—how can you improve your [dietary] choices?'" She emphasized the importance of acknowledging individuals' personal situations and showing respect for the decisions they make based on their economic realities: "[It's] not making folks feel ashamed about their context . . . but meeting people where they are."

Thus, these activists use their education programs to build participants' abilities to improve the everyday reality of individuals and communities. In addition to providing education about important aspects of the food system, such as how food grows or the elements of a healthy diet, teaching is, for these individuals, a form of activism aimed at helping program participants understand the social structures that produce inequities and develop the skills to make deeper individual and community change. In doing so, they both refute and disprove racist and classist stereotypes of low-income communities and communities of color as deficient in social and human capital. This work becomes another "sign of the possible" that those who are most directly affected by food system injustice can be leaders in realizing a more equitable food system.

Urban Farms and Gardens as Safe Spaces

Farms and gardens can serve as natural oases in the built environment that dominates many urban neighborhoods, and they can be places for participants to cultivate cross-cultural and intergenerational friendships. They can also provide physical and metaphorical safety for members of socially marginalized communities. In her analyses of urban farming in Detroit, Monica White draws from the work of sociologist Patricia Hill Collins to suggest that urban farms can provide safe spaces to "foster the conditions for black women's independent self-definitions" (2000; cited in White 2011b). This idea can be extended to encompass farms as safe spaces for women of many backgrounds, queer youth and adults, young black men, and other individuals who experience marginalization from dominant social settings based on their identity or social location.

La Finca del Sur provides one example. One of the main goals of this South

Bronx organization is to provide a safe place for women farmers and gardeners to grow food, herbs, and flowers and to participate in activities that are often otherwise dominated by men. In addition to agricultural production, activities at the farm include all-women's spoken-word events and women's healing workshops. La Finca has also hired participants in another local organization called Nontraditional Employment for Women—which supports women's economic independence by training and placing them in careers in the construction, utilities, and maintenance trades—to build a small greenhouse at the farm. These activities, and the organizational structure of La Finca del Sur itself, have been designed in a way that one of the group's cofounders, Annie Moss, described as "more relevant" to the values of the women who created and run the farm.

Other urban farms act as safe spaces for queer-identified farmers who, as Maggie Cheney at Bushwick Campus Farm observed, "may not feel comfortable in rural areas" that don't have strong LGBTQ communities. Cheney explained that she works with a citywide organization called Make the Road New York, which has organized Gay-Straight Alliances (GSAs) throughout the city. At the time of our study she coordinated a GSA chapter at the high school where the farm is located. She recounted several ways that youth in the program reacted to it: "[They'll say,] 'Oh, let's have a rainbow-colored garden box' and 'Why don't we do our GSA outside, and farm?' and 'What if we go to this conference and do a cooking demo, and be gay and cooking farm food?' They're coming up with all these ideas, that I'm just kind of there, because that's who I am—these are my worlds."

Due to Cheney's leadership, Bushwick Campus Farm and some of the activities it houses have functioned as "queer autonomous spaces," which geographer Gavin Brown has suggested serve as venues for participants to "question the social relations that normally restrict the free expression of their sexuality" (G. Brown 2007; see also Sbicca 2012a). Cheney has also used farm activities to challenge heteronormativity and to help all of the students she works with, regardless of their sexual orientation, to reconsider traditional gender roles. Cheney explained that farming is "another tool to [teach] about gender equality . . . and an amazing way to really cross gender lines" and that "agriculture is a perfect example of something that demonstrates all different types of gender roles—construction, cooking, sowing seeds, digging in the dirt. You see all these things that you could pinpoint, and say, 'Oh, that's stereotypically male, and that's stereotypically female.' And then you're given this beautiful opportunity to discuss that, and to try to have students understand that they don't have to be in either of those boxes if they don't want to be."

At a larger scale, urban agriculture may also provide a metaphorical autonomous space for queer-identified farmers. Bee Ayer, co–farm manager and market manager at BK Farmyards during the time of our study, noted that being a queer farmer can be difficult and alienating in many rural areas. She explained that in her experience there is often a larger queer farming community in urban centers and that "there is a lot of camaraderie between all the people who identify as queer and work in the urban ag movement in New York City. . . . [A] lot of us do know each other and talk with each other and share with each other and get together more socially." Similarly, Cheney mentioned that some of the youth participants in the Bushwick Campus Farm program have led food justice workshops available to the broader New York City LGBTQ community. For the youth leaders, the workshops are an opportunity not only for them to "empower themselves" but also for workshop participants to understand why people in the LGBTQ community, specifically, want to learn about these issues. "Both groups [are] teaching each other—straight-identified, gay, black, Latino, white. We were all brought together around food."

In the South Bronx, Friends of Brook Park (FBP) provides safe space for youth involved in the criminal justice system through its Youth Farm Initiative, an alternatives-to-incarceration program. The city's Department of Probation refers teenagers to the program, where they engage in farm work complemented by mentoring. Ray Figueroa at FBP explained, "We sit, and we talk . . . we have group meetings, and then we complement that with actual physical engagement in the youth farm. It all helps to . . . reconnect these young people in a way that's looked upon by the courts as very productive." Figueroa, who directs FBP's youth programs, pointed out that the on-farm meetings help make "concrete community connection[s] to provide [young people] an opportunity whereby they can be engaged in growing, cultivating, harvesting food, and in the process, growing, cultivating a sense of efficacy." In fact, FBP emphasizes community connections through all of its youth programs, which specifically draw inspiration from radical human rights groups led by people of color working in the South Bronx in the 1960s and 1970s. Figueroa explained that their educational programs "go into something of the historical struggles, and the historical campaigns that have been carried out in the community through a street organization known as the Young Lords Party and the Black Panther Party. Both were very active here in the South Bronx [and] food was very key to their organizing efforts. . . . [Both groups] used to do food distribution . . . [and there] would be a critical community conversation around what is going on in the community. . . . So we do the same [at our meetings] . . . we talk about the history of struggle for social justice."

Nationally, two-fifths of incarcerated juveniles are African American and one-fifth are Hispanic,[2] despite their lower overall representation in the US population (Mendel 2011). In New York City, nearly 60 percent of youth in residential correctional facilities in 2007 were African American, and 24 percent were Latino (New York [State] Task Force on Transforming Juvenile Justice 2009). By providing a venue for productive activities and mentoring, and by teaching youth of color about the legacy of social justice activism in the South Bronx,

FBP's Youth Farm Initiative helps participants see ways to interact with their surroundings that may help keep them out of the so-called school-to-prison pipeline.[3] It also provides a safe space for black and Latino/a youth who may have experienced various forms of marginalization from mainstream society based on their race. And by teaching about the historical precedents of contemporary food and social justice activism, FBP helps youth see (and see themselves as) assets in their community. These programs, along with those at La Finca del Sur and Bushwick Campus Farm, are perhaps different kinds of "oases," but they are no less important than the lush green spaces that the term often conjures in the imagination.

Growing Environmental Justice

In addition to the social and educational aspects of urban agriculture activism discussed above, farming and gardening in the city can serve to advance environmental justice, especially when the farms or gardens are situated in communities that are disproportionately burdened by environmental degradation and when they are led, or result in leadership by, individuals affected by environmental racism and other forms of environmental injustice. Participation in farming and gardening can also foster ecological citizenship, helping city residents become aware of and active in policy- and decision-making processes affecting the environment (Travaline and Hunold 2010) and ideally leading to policies that are environmentally beneficial or at least environmentally benign. Additionally, the vegetation in farms and gardens can help reduce urban heat island effects (Gómez-Baggethun et al. 2013), support environmental remediation, and, as green infrastructure sites, possibly help reduce combined sewer overflow (Cohen and Ackerman 2011; Cohen and Wijsman 2014).

These environmental amenities are commonly cited as benefits of urban agriculture, but they are particularly important in communities like the South Bronx in which policies have led to a preponderance of vacant lots, insufficient public open spaces, a high concentration of industrial facilities and truck traffic contributing to high asthma rates, and elevated surface and air temperatures from the urban heat island effect that pose acute health risks. The environmental benefits of urban agriculture become environmental *justice* benefits in low-income communities, often low-income communities of color, that experience a disproportionate burden of environmental pollution and degradation and tend to have less political and economic clout (see chapter 1). Urban agriculture can serve as a strategy to help advance environmental justice by mitigating the inequitable distribution of environmental degradation and limited access to environmental benefits.

As noted in preceding chapters, many activists in New York City, including many people of color, have cleaned up abandoned lots as a necessary first step to building farms and gardens, and many such projects could be considered environmental justice activism, predating the movement per se (cf. Taylor 2011). Although some sites were transformed in the 1960s and 1970s, others have been turned into gardens relatively recently after years of neglect, or years of being what one gardener in Bed-Stuy described as "a place where [people] dumped things."

Beyond removing trash and transforming what some residents have considered eyesores into more pleasant spaces, some urban agriculture activists have used their farms and gardens to contribute to environmental remediation or to address urban environmental issues that are broader in scope. For instance, sections of La Finca del Sur that are located on an Environmental Protection Agency–designated brownfield served as a test site for a phytoremediation study that involved planting sunflowers and observing the plants' removal of toxic compounds from the soil. The findings from the study, which also included other test sites, were included in a publicly available guide to phytoremediation (see "Brownfields to Greenfields" 2011).

In a separate project, Friends of Brook Park received a grant from the New York State Energy Research and Development Authority to plant trees as part of an initiative to mitigate heat island effects in the South Bronx, helping achieve a long-term goal to reduce air temperatures citywide. Ray Figueroa underscored the environmental justice aspects of this work: "There's a lot of industrial activity [in the South Bronx]: manufacturing, there's the FedEx [shipping facility], there's [a] waste transfer station right on the waterfront. All of that contributes to the environmental health issues [in this community]." He emphasized that for Friends of Brook Park, the initiative was not just about planting trees but also about environmental justice, pointing out that it was important to appreciate the potential significance of the project in "a community that's struggling."

To understand urban agriculture as a form of environmental justice activism is not new, of course. As noted in chapter 2, activists in communities disproportionately affected by environmental degradation have long used gardens to improve conditions in their neighborhoods. Yet urban agriculture is more commonly framed as a general environmental amenity. Seeing contemporary urban agriculture as a strategy to advance environmental justice is quite different from seeing it as simply a way to beautify or even "green" a neighborhood. Because environmental justice intersects with issues of social equity and public health, and because, as a movement, it emphasizes leadership by people who bear the brunt of environmental degradation, understanding the environmental justice dimensions of farm and garden programs in low-income communities of color is key to understanding their social justice significance. An environmental justice framework is also important in terms of farmers' and gardeners' ability to garner political and financial support for their initiatives. As they do with the food production side of urban agriculture, the activists described throughout this book regularly draw connections between the immediate environmental benefits of their work and the sociopolitical structures that make it necessary. Urban greening is one benefit of city farming and gardening, but environmental justice is often an equally important aspect of these activists' work.

Beyond Food and Sustainability

The activities described in this chapter are, at a basic level, about food production and food access, community economic development, jobs and education, cultural memory, open space, and other environmental amenities. But they are also about far more than that. Food production and direct environmental improvement are what make the work of the urban agriculture activists described here distinct from other forms of social service work or environmental activism. Meanwhile, as discussed in chapter 1, their on-the-ground analysis of the roots of inequity is what differentiates them from those urban farmers and gardeners whose programs are not particularly focused on social or environmental justice or on dismantling oppression. The activist groups highlighted in this chapter use urban agriculture activities to confront injustices that have historical, structural, and political roots.

Farmers and gardeners at La Unión and Hattie Carthan Community Garden in Brooklyn and Taqwa Community Farm in the Bronx help members of their communities resist cultural domination by maintaining and passing on culturally specific knowledge about food and agriculture. They also refute the image of their communities as passive victims of an unjust system by helping participants understand food system injustice in the context of broader sociopolitical systems. Activists at Brooklyn Rescue Mission, La Finca del Sur, and East New York Farms! foster self-determination in the communities in which they live and work by operating farmers' markets and providing venues through which individuals can develop microenterprises that contribute to their income. The hope is that these enterprises can also help strengthen their communities' economies. Leaders of BK Farmyards, Bushwick Campus Farm, Friends of Brook Park, Hattie Carthan Community Garden, and Farm School NYC run educational programs to give participants opportunities to develop both the analytical skills to understand root causes of food system inequities and the community organizing and communication skills to help dismantle them. Beyond their focus on food and agriculture, many of these activists also advance environmental justice at the neighborhood and citywide level by cleaning trash-strewn lots, planting trees, and helping participants understand the social justice aspects of environmental improvement and leadership through the lens of environmental justice.

In understanding these common urban agriculture activities as strategies to cultivate resistance and empowerment, or as "the starting point for a self-reliance movement," as Robert and DeVanie Jackson claim, it is still important to recall that urban agriculture is not a panacea. Farming and gardening will neither "feed the city" nor eliminate racism, patriarchy, or any other manifestation of social or political oppression. Rather than a cure-all for inequity (or an anticapitalist project), urban agriculture is for these activists a tool that can help individuals and organizations create more socially just systems within their communities. By combining tangible activities such as farming, gardening, selling food and plant-based products, and cooking with dialogue about structural dimensions of social justice, and by helping build participants' communication and entrepreneurial skills, these activists are growing power in their communities. Some activists also enact their ideas about less oppressive systems through the structure of their organizations, as described in the following chapter.

CHAPTER 4

Embodying Socially Just Systems

La Finca del Sur is a two-and-a-half-acre community farm and garden in the South Bronx led by Latina and black women and their allies. Founded in 2009 in collaboration with another local nonprofit organization called More Gardens!, the farm is part of the women's strategy to build healthy neighborhoods in an area of New York City that has experienced some of the most negative effects of government abandonment, disinvestment, and environmental racism. At street level, the farm site appears to be a less-than-ideal place to build an outdoor community space, as it is bordered by a local thoroughfare, an interstate highway exchange, and an elevated rail line that carries daily commuters between Manhattan and nearby cities in New York and Connecticut. Viewed from above, however, its colorful flowers and vibrant community garden plots flourish in stark contrast to their industrial surroundings. For La Finca's founders, the farm is exactly where it needs to be.

Like many of the activists described in this book, La Finca's leaders aim to increase food access, advance environmental justice, and contribute to community empowerment through activities such as growing food and providing a community meeting place. They also focus on the many positive assets in the South Bronx and their own connections with people and cultures throughout the world. The founders chose the name (which translates to "Farm of the South") to reflect both the Latino/a heritage of many of its members and their collective roots in regions of the southern United States and the Global South. Harvest festivals, educational tours, and other seasonal events emphasize the rich ethnic and cultural connections among residents in the wider South Bronx community, the majority of whom are black and/or Latino/a. The relationships among food, agriculture, people, and place—and their connection to social justice—are at the heart of La Finca's programs.

Alongside its focus on community, the nonprofit organization that also bears the farm's name is intently focused on fostering women's empowerment, particularly among Latina and African American women. On-farm activities such as women's open-mic nights, women's herbal healing workshops, and after-school programs for middle school girls (run in collaboration with a local low-income housing development) provide opportunities for participants to perform, teach, and learn in a venue that is supportive and safe. The organization has supported women-run enterprises, such as the lavender business and the organization Nontraditional Employment for Women discussed in chapter 3, and it extends its focus to encompass women farmers of color worldwide. Cofounder, farmer/ director, and creative educator Nancy Ortiz-Surun notes, "Women do much of the world's farming but only get a tiny fraction of the recognition, and a tiny fraction of the direct economic return." La Finca was thus created in part to shift understandings about the roles of women as farmers both within and beyond the South Bronx, and to carry out the founders' ideas about socially just systems in which women lead and are recognized for their leadership.

La Finca del Sur uses agriculture and on-farm programs to accomplish its mission, but the group's work is deeper than these visible activities. The founders designed the structure of the organization itself to align with the values they place on representative leadership and cultivating collective power among women of color. Though officially a nonprofit organization, La Finca's leaders describe the organization as an urban farmer cooperative. The five-member advisory board is composed primarily of women who self-identify as Latina and/ or black (though white women were among the founders and have also been on the board), and the board's bylaws make it a de facto nonhierarchical leadership body. Members take on roles that fit their individual strengths and that evolve to meet the organization's changing needs. The board members, along with a core group of member-farmers who help guide the farm's trajectory, make their decisions collaboratively. By positioning themselves as leaders of a cooperatively managed nonprofit organization, the women of La Finca challenge white-dominant, patriarchal social structures and top-down organizational design. One of the cofounders, Annie Moss, who is white, explains that La Finca's governance structure is better aligned with the cooperative's vision of a less oppressive world than more conventional organizational models in the United States.

Many activist groups like La Finca del Sur attempt to align their organizational structure with leaders' and members' ideals, grounding their governance practices in specific conceptual frameworks and theories of change (e.g., see Taylor 2000). In addition to using farm and garden activities to challenge oppression within *existing* social structures (as discussed in chapter 3), many groups strive to put in place an organizational structure that is a model for the social system they want to see. Yet the ideas behind the innovative board structures, leadership development processes, decision-making procedures, and informal practices often remain behind-the-scenes, overshadowed by the more visible day-to-day activities.

It is common to recognize the actions that often define a social justice movement or an activist effort but to miss the "intense thinking that [takes] place regarding the project of creating a more democratic society" (Heynen and Rhodes 2012, 394). Yet understanding these motivations offers important lessons for contemporary activist initiatives that aspire to achieve deeper social and political transformation through their actions. With respect to urban agriculture and social justice, seeing only farming, gardening, and educational *activities*, without recognizing the leaders' underlying theories about how organizational processes align with their visions of more liberatory systems, limits the extent to which other activists might understand and incorporate deeper lessons from successful initiatives into their own. Raising up the praxis of activist organizations, or what Wakefield (2007) describes as the process of "giving life to ideas about the way the world is—and could be—by acting on one's (theoretically informed) convictions in daily life," can help identify "openings of freedom and possibility" (Gibson-Graham 2006) for various actors in an urban agriculture system.

Thus, uncovering the distinction between activities (such as food production or on-farm education) and the ways that activists attempt to model their social justice ideals within their organizations can help others envision themselves participating in more socially just realities that may otherwise seem marginal or nonexistent (e.g., see Gibson-Graham 2006). It may also offer perspectives for supporters (such as those in philanthropic organizations and government agencies) to consider when they design programs to enable food systems and social justice work. To these ends, this chapter explores how urban agriculture activists in New York City "give life" to their broader social justice and anti-oppression ideals through the structures and practices of their programs.

Leadership, Beyond Diversity

A fundamental part of some social justice activists' work is ensuring that people who have historically been excluded from political decision making play leadership roles in solving problems affecting their communities. As noted in chapter 1, among the factors that led to the formation of the US environmental justice movement in the 1980s and 1990s was the belief among activists that people who are most negatively affected by environmental racism—racial discrimination with respect to environmental risks and benefits—should be involved in both defining what is meant by "environment" in the movement and developing solutions to environmental problems (Gottlieb 2005; Pellow 2000; Taylor 2011, 2000; Sze 2007; Cole and Foster 2001). A similar emphasis on self-determination undergirds some strands of contemporary food justice activism in the United States and is among the key principles of the global food sovereignty movement, which some activists are adapting to the US context (e.g., see Block et al. 2012; Newtown Florist Club Writing Collective 2013; Mares and Peña 2011; "Declaration of Nyéléni" 2007; Patel 2009; Redmond 2013; Kurtz 2015; Alkon and Mares 2012; Alkon et al. 2013).

Yet although low-income communities and communities of color remain disproportionately burdened by environmental pollution, degradation, and diet-related public health disparities in the United States, middle- and upper-middle-class whites continue to outnumber people of color in the leadership of mainstream environmental and alternative food organizations.[1] A recent study of two hundred mainstream environmental organizations, foundations, and government agencies found that only 12 percent of the organizations studied had people of color in leadership positions—despite the fact that together Hispanics, blacks, Asians, Native Americans, and Pacific Islanders represented 38 percent of the total US population in 2010 (Taylor 2014, 43). Though there has been no similarly extensive study of mainstream alternative *food* organizations, scholars and activists have observed that the leadership of and values articulated by the mainstream food movement is also exceedingly white (see Guthman 2008b; Yakini 2013; Slocum 2006).

To be sure, many mainstream food and environmental organizations recognize that they must address racial and ethnic diversity within their organizational structures to remain relevant in a nation in which, according to a government study, minority groups are predicted to constitute 57 percent of the US population by 2060. To address racial homogeneity within their organizations, some mainstream environmental groups have broadened their applicant pools for staff positions, increased outreach in racial and ethnic minority communities, and consulted with people of color who are environmental professionals (Taylor 2014, 68). Mainstream alternative food and agriculture organizations have given their (often volunteer) outreach and diversity committees the charge of encouraging more people of color to participate in their meetings and events, and many groups have consciously featured people of color in their newsletters.[2]

These and similar initiatives have had some success in increasing staff and membership diversity within organizations (e.g., see Taylor 2014) and have therefore been important in making mainstream groups more representative of the overall US population. However, diversity measures per se do not address power imbalances within alternative food and environmental organizations, or in mainstream food and environmental movements writ large (see Slocum 2006; Bradley and Herrera 2015; Mares and Peña 2011; Reynolds 2014; Taylor 2014). *Leadership* is different from *diversity*, and without explicitly addressing the demographics of organizational leadership and how this relates to power and privilege, efforts to merely add diversity actually risk perpetuating white, middle-class dominance as the status quo.

For certain scholars and activists, white dominance in the mainstream alternative food movement is antithetical to the ideals that some organizations espouse. For example, food justice is often characterized as addressing the political *and social* structures that underlie inequities in the food system (e.g., see Mares and Peña 2011). And although the *concept* of food justice has gained traction within many food organizations, the structure of those organizations has not always reflected the demographics of a given community but instead has replicated patterns of white-dominant society (Bradley and Herrera 2015). Emphasizing this point, Karen Washington, a veteran urban agriculture leader and among the cofounders of La Finca del Sur, insisted:

> When we're talking about social justice, then let's look at the institutions that are controlling the social justice movement. . . . A lot of food organizations are run and managed by whites. . . . When we're talking about food justice, and we [people of color] are the dynamic, [we need to look at] who has the power; who is in positions of power. And the majority of [those] people are whites. . . . The people that have the power are white, and the people that are impacted are people of color. . . . You're talking about food and social justice, but there's not a black or Latino person, or a woman on your board of directors [or] . . . heading your organization?

This comment underscores the incongruence between idea and action that pervades some food organizations when it comes to social justice, and offers an example of how diversity measures that do not result in leadership and power among people of color can perpetuate existing white-dominated systems.

The disconnect between organizational theory and practice extends beyond race. Diversity measures also often overlook the role of class privilege in replicating and sustaining existing organizational structures. Professional connections with those in influential positions and fluency in the communication styles common within typical business environments (i.e., "professional" etiquette) go a long way toward helping individuals attain leadership positions, potentially putting those who do not possess these forms of cultural capital at a disadvantage. For example, unpaid internships help younger people obtain entry-level jobs and gain experience that, over the long term, prepares them to lead organizations, but such internships are more feasible for those financially well-off enough to work for free. Among midcareer and more senior professionals, board membership (one form of organizational leadership) is also often unpaid. In fact, being a board member frequently requires making a direct financial contribution or actively fund-raising, thus limiting board membership to those who have the financial means or connections to donors that enable them to take on financial responsibilities or commit to fund-raising quotas (e.g., see Taylor 2014). These patterns can exclude working-class people from leadership positions, since it is easier for people with social privilege, financial means, and spare time to commit to a time-consuming, unpaid job. As discussed in chapter 1, these forms of privilege are often experienced by middle- and upper-class whites. Racialized wealth disparities thus affect leadership diversity in organizations, insofar as they stratify the pool of potential leaders along lines of race and class.

SEEING LEADERSHIP WHERE IT EXISTS

The study of environmental groups cited above found a tendency among leaders of mainstream environmental organizations to subconsciously believe that people of color lacked the knowledge, qualifications, or skills to lead environmental initiatives, despite ample evidence disproving these beliefs (Taylor 2014, 174). Further, some respondents in that study believed that racial and ethnic minorities were not a core part of the "environmental movement" (ibid.), notwithstanding the existence of the environmental justice movement, which has been driven by people of color since its coalescence at the First National People of Color Environmental Leadership Summit in 1991. Marcs and Peña (2011, 200) have identified a similar blind spot within what they call the "mainstream alternative food movement," arguing that white-led alternative food systems are regarded as "the center by which all other practices [are] judged," despite the long-standing "alterNative" food practices of Native American and indigenous peoples, which were developed and exist autonomously from white-led groups. These observations betray a belief among some members of white-led movements and organizations that mainstream movements are the only legitimate force in food system and environmental advocacy.

The tendency to not recognize knowledge, skills, and existing leadership among people of color has perhaps helped justify the persistence of white leadership within mainstream food and environmental organizations, as well as in their respective movements writ large. If white leaders fail to identify "viable" candidates of color for key positions, status quo leadership structures may seem prudent. Within this paradigm, if sympathetic philanthropies and government agencies see mainstream (again, most often white-led) movements and organizations as the real drivers of food system and environmental activism, support for initiatives led by people of color and working-class people might not seem to be an effective way to achieve change. When taken seriously, this connection (albeit often implicit) between understanding and practice compels mainstream organizations interested in advancing food and environmental justice to "walk the walk" by attending to power imbalances *within* their organizations, agencies, or movements rather than maintaining status quo leadership structures. To this point, Hugh Hogan, executive director of North Star Fund (a private foundation that supports grassroots activism in New York City and has funded urban agriculture efforts), explained that his organization's theory of change is that "the people most directly affected by injustice and oppression need to be in the driver's seat." Hogan, who is white, explained that this approach is important not only because it alters some of the power structures that perpetuate the inequities, but also because community members have up-close knowledge about how particular problems affect their communities and unique perspectives on how they can be solved. "If [community members are not able to] inform the policies or changes that need reforming," he noted, "the best theories are just that."

And yet, as Mares and Peña (2011) underscore, mainstream groups are only part of a broader array of food and environmental movements and practices, and a focus on the practices of white-led groups can itself undermine the project of dismantling oppressive systems. People of color, including indigenous communities and recent immigrants to the United States, are already leading food systems change and engaging in food and agricultural practices that are also the focus of many mainstream alternative food groups. Recognizing skills, experience, and existing leadership among people of color and working-class people is a crucial aspect of creating and supporting food and environmental systems that are more socially just at their core. This approach goes far beyond increasing diversity, or even racially diverse leadership, in white-led groups and is more in line with ideas about self-determination and community-led change.

The urban agriculture activists we spoke with understand these dynamics of organizational and movement leadership firsthand, and many have taken the initiative to address them directly. For example, Black Urban Growers (BUGS), an organization that advocates for the interests of African American and black farmers and gardeners in New York City and beyond, was formed in part to address the dearth of leadership among people of color in mainstream (white-dominated) sustainable agriculture groups. Karen Washington, who cofounded the organization, explained that the importance of its mission is clear because when she attends sustainable agriculture conferences, "I don't see people like me." Washington, who is African American, helped start BUGS as a vehicle for black farmers and gardeners to lead and participate in the exchange of knowledge and networking on food and agriculture topics relevant in their own communities. Since its founding in 2010, BUGS has held several conferences in New York City, Detroit, and Oakland, California. Washington noted that the growing numbers of attendees has demonstrated that the observed "whiteness" of alternative food and agriculture movements is not due to disinterest in agriculture or food system change among people of color. "We had an open house in October [2012]," Washington explained, "and it was standing room only. So, it just goes to show you that . . . food doesn't know color, race, religion. . . . It sort of dispels the notion that people of color, women, they don't want to farm."

Several other activist groups in New York also consciously embody self-determination as a part of their vision for more socially just systems. The cofounders of La Finca del Sur created the organization and farm in order to give women of color more opportunities to collectively lead food system change in their South Bronx community. La Unión, the Sunset Park organization led mainly by first-generation immigrants from Mexico, emphasizes leadership by those who are directly disadvantaged by immigration, education, and agricultural policies (La Unión 2014). Rather than opposing or attempting to change "mainstream alternative" food systems or organizations, these groups provide opportunities for and models of food systems and environmental leadership *by and for* people of color and working-class people. They also demonstrate that while mainstream organizations may receive more public recognition as agents of food and environmental change, they actually exist alongside organizations and initiatives led by people of color.

To be clear, groups like La Unión, BUGS, and La Finca del Sur have not completely separated themselves from mainstream food organizations. As discussed in chapter 5, urban agriculture activists regularly collaborate with diverse mainstream organizations and government agencies to accomplish common objectives. Still, their work remains focused on building power among individuals and groups that have not historically had as much clout in food and environmental decision making in the United States, particularly compared with the members of mainstream food and environmental groups. And while mainstream alternative food organizations may view ideas such as "nurturing collective black leadership" (part of BUGS's mission) or immigrant-driven policy reform (one of La Unión's advocacy goals) as beyond the scope of their missions,[3] objectives focused on representative leadership are among these urban agriculture activists' central concerns.

Modeling "Just" Social Structures

As mentioned above, some activists weave their vision of less-oppressive systems into the fabric of their organizations, modeling different power structures such as nonhierarchical leadership and collaborative decision making. La Finca del Sur stands out as a nonhierarchical organization, and cofounders, including Nancy Ortiz-Surun, Annie Moss, and Karen Washington, regularly and publicly discuss how these structures fit into their vision of socially just systems. But other urban agriculture groups in New York City also engage in this form of social justice praxis.

Farm School NYC, described in chapter 3, provides another example. The idea for this adult education program took root in 2007 as John Ameroso, Cornell University Cooperative Extension's longtime urban agriculture extension agent in New York City, neared retirement. Ameroso had been leading urban agriculture education programs throughout the city since the 1970s, often in collaboration with the nonprofit Just Food and other urban garden technical-assistance programs. He and a number of Just Food's educators are white, but having spent decades supporting urban agriculture throughout the city, they knew that there were many gardeners and farmers of color, including recent immigrants, who could train the next generation of practitioners in a more formal way than what they were already doing informally at their homes or community garden sites. Around the same time, a group of women involved in community food and urban agriculture (including members of Just Food's board and staff and several of the activists described in this book) came together to envision their next steps with food production. They, too, knew firsthand of many individuals who grew, prepared, and preserved foods like fruit jams and salsa, and who could teach others if they received some training in pedagogy. The vision for Farm School NYC was thus collaborative and nonhierarchical from the beginning, and planning involved both white people and people of color.

Farm School NYC thus grew out of a need for more educators (especially as interest in urban farming and gardening had increased over the previous decade) and a desire to facilitate community-led education. But the cofounders also envisioned a school that reflected their values about collaborative and representative leadership. Over a three-year period, a network of individuals and representatives of various organizations worked collaboratively to plan and seek funding for the farm school project (Just Food n.d.). Jane Hodge, the school's first director, explained that during the planning stages, "We had a really great participatory visioning process and all kinds of different voices in the room. We use[d] a [consensus facilitation] method taught to us by the Institute of Cultural Affairs[4] . . . Basically, [the focus was,] 'How do you make decisions? How do you make group visioning happen?'"

The planning group ultimately won a three-year USDA grant to fund a start-up phase, and Farm School NYC launched its first courses in early 2011. The executive board and the Academic Planning and Community Partnership Committees are composed of representatives from various agencies and organizations (including one of the authors of this book), as well as individual community-based farmers and gardeners. The board and committees use collaborative decision-making processes to guide the school's trajectory, helping the school put into practice its mission to "build self-reliant communities and inspire positive local action around food access and social, economic, and racial justice issues" through teaching about urban agriculture (ibid.).

BK Farmyards provides a third example of how activists have attempted to align their organizational practices with their vision of socially just systems. As noted in chapter 3, the group is a farming collective composed mostly of women farmers who run a Youth Farm and an on-site farmers' market at the High School for Public Service, a public school in Crown Heights, Brooklyn. Its members consider social justice a core part of their urban agriculture work, and they see nonhierarchical decision making and leadership as being in line with their ideals. Bee Ayer (co–farm manager and market manager at the time of this study) explained that the group makes collaborative decisions about farm and organizational management: "We don't have [a] director who makes decisions about programs or funding priorities [without the input of the other members]. . . . We come together for strategic planning meetings four times a year, [with additional meetings] throughout the year if we have new ideas . . . or we want to rearrange things, evaluate our programs or how we are working together. . . . The individual . . . in charge of [a given] program . . . handles the specifics."

By modeling collaborative and nonhierarchical processes, these three organizations aim to challenge conventional structures that in effect grant authority to one social group over others. Ayer explained the reasoning behind the structure of BK Farmyards, connecting it to the members' experiences: "All of us have worked for nonprofits before . . . and we've seen . . . how the [organization] itself [can] actually not [be] that sustainable. They overwork their workers; they have a hierarchy that really limits the capacity of the people doing on-the-ground work [to take ownership in the organization]; they don't share decision making with their community; they're often not running programs in a way that will really build the capacity of program [participants] to actually have those types of jobs." Referring to La Finca del Sur, Annie Moss explained, "We've structured our organization . . . to reflect a different kind of leadership and a different kind of organizational structure that we think is more . . . relevant to women and to women of color." She added, "[We're] stepping outside of the system because it's not working for people in this neighborhood."

La Finca del Sur, BK Farmyards, and Farm School NYC also provide various models of how urban agriculture activists can bring the operation of an organization or movement into sync with the ideals behind the programs they run. They may even act as microcosms, giving those within and outside the urban agriculture social justice movement a glimpse of real, not merely potential, alternatives—alternatives that these activists, and perhaps others, may find "more relevant" to their social justice ideals.

Liberatory Education

Chapter 3 discussed activists' use of urban farms and gardens as sites for critical pedagogy and anti-oppression education. Some groups also use specific pedagogical practices to disrupt conventional power dynamics between teachers and students. Here again, Farm School NYC is one of the most far-reaching examples in the city. The school emphasizes popular education and leadership development through approaches that draw heavily from the work of Brazilian educational theorist Paolo Freire. In his classic *Pedagogy of the Oppressed,* Freire wrote about a contradiction in what he called "banking education," in which the teacher is presumed to be the singular source of knowledge in a classroom setting. He argued for seeing educators and learners as "simultaneously teachers *and* students" (Freire 1993, 72, emphasis in original). Farm School NYC attempts to put this philosophy into practice. As Jane Hodge explained, during the first semester of the program, "students learn about participatory education models and . . . [discover] that Farm School is not a top-down approach, but [rather] all of us creating a learning environment together."

Farm School NYC requires its teachers to use participatory and experiential teaching techniques that they learn through the school's "Training of Trainers" (TOT) course. The course was created by Owen Taylor, who was another of Farm School's founders and taught TOT for a number of years. He explained that although the course had originally been developed by the nonprofit Heifer International, he had adapted it by drawing from Freire's work and from examples of civil-rights-era Citizenship Schools and work on experiential learning elaborated by educational theorist David A. Kolb. The goal was to develop a course that would facilitate individualized skill development rather than merely provide students with information. Taylor explained that Farm School NYC teachers are required to take this course with students, and that the process of learning "shoulder-to-shoulder" helps break down the dichotomy between "expert" and learner. He emphasized that the course is not only about *how to teach* but is also a "very transformative group process" in which teachers and students learn and evolve together. He added, "The way that we teach embodies our social justice values."

Challenges of Operating Differently

Urban agriculture groups in New York City thus "give life" to their ideas about social justice through representative leadership that works toward self-determination in food and agricultural systems; through nonhierarchical and collaborative organizational management; and through pedagogical practices that challenge expert/student dichotomies. Organizations like BUGS, La Finca del Sur, and La Unión not only bring racial, ethnic, gender, and class diversity to efforts to change the food system, but they also serve as models for systems in which people of color, women, and recent immigrants have social and political power. Through their organizational practices, groups like La Finca del Sur, BK Farmyards, and Farm School NYC disrupt conventional notions of top-down leadership; and Farm School NYC explicitly steps away from "banking" models of education that have become ever more prevalent in an era of standardized testing and Common Core curricula.

Although the leaders of these groups described their approaches as successful in reflecting their social justice goals, some also noted that not conforming to conventional hierarchical roles was difficult at times. La Finca's leaders faced this challenge in incorporating as a nonprofit organization, a process that requires naming a set of specifically defined officers—usually a board president, a treasurer, and a secretary. Moss recalled, "At first we weren't even thinking about [those roles], but then we started to have the conversation and it was like, 'Why would we even try to put ourselves into that? We don't operate as a hierarchy *at all*.' It was weird to even talk about who would be what . . . even if it is just . . . on paper. . . . [We thought that it would be] so much more meaningful [to] scratch [those words] out and put in something else [for our own use]. So that's what we did, and we basically just came up with titles that reflect the roles that we have, which are all . . . integral and necessary. And not at all . . . hierarchical."

Another challenge that some activists discussed was the complexity of operating in collaboration with large, bureaucratic institutions and foundations that were not accustomed to interacting with youth who questioned social norms that are often taken for granted. Ayer described her own views of how BK Farmyards had to grapple with the Department of Education's institutional culture and policies, explaining, "We have often struggled working with the higher power within these bureaucracies . . . they don't take us seriously because we are mostly young women, they don't take our youths' concerns seriously. . . . I don't think they have any experience, or were ever taught how to communicate with people who are different than them, or [how to] receive feedback from people that they may look down upon."

Ayer, who is white, also described her views of the challenges with having high school students who had learned about structural forms of race- and class-based oppression—through activities BK Farmyards had helped facilitate—uninhibitedly express their feelings of "being used" by funders to "[fulfill] their own ideas of what [funding] will accomplish." She explained, "Our students will sometimes just ask the funders, 'Well, if you actually care about this, why are you holding on to all this money? Why don't you just, you know, distribute [the money] in a more fair way, and then we could actually make decisions for ourselves based on what we think are the best uses?'" She noted that these conversations, which had taken place during a site visit with some of BK Farmyards' funders, provided teachable moments to "talk with students about the structure of our economy and the distribution of wealth." She added, "Our students don't want to be interviewed [by] people from foundations all the time and we have to respect that and sometimes [say no to foundation representatives]. . . . It puts us in this hard place because we are respecting our values, and the students' [values] . . . but . . . we are also sometimes less likely to get funding to do our work."

For Farm School NYC, one of the biggest challenges has been attracting a racially diverse student body, a goal that is closely aligned with the founders' vision of training people of color and low-income city residents to be urban agriculture educators. Student selection is based on the applicants' demonstrated commitment to social justice, connection to a New York City community, articulation of how they will use skills gained through Farm School, and previous gardening or farming experience. The committee applies these criteria and also selects for demographic and geographic diversity. Although the goal is a diverse group of students, Hodge explained that "the vast majority of applicants are people [who] are white, women, born in the '80s, and live in Brooklyn." She attributed this imbalance in applications to mainstream media and online coverage of the school, which she felt had tended to reach this demographic. Less clear is whether the composition of Farm School NYC's leadership and current students deters people of color from applying (Hodge, who is white, was the only full-time paid staff member at the time of this study and was therefore often seen as the face of the program), or whether the required time commitment makes participation difficult for people with lower incomes. Since the time of our interview, Farm School NYC has begun to publicize its programs in different venues in an effort to increase student racial, ethnic, and class diversity. Additionally, when Hodge left her position to pursue full-time farming, Farm School hired an African American woman, Onika Abraham, as the new director, which may make a difference in terms of how the project is perceived among potential students of color as the now-independent organization grows under Abraham's leadership.

Walking the Talk

It is common for outside observers to focus on the visible aspects of urban agriculture programs: produce donated to food pantries; schoolchildren tasting carrots pulled from the soil; people of different races, ethnicities, and ages farming together. But as every gardener knows, what lies beneath the surface—soil structure, nutrients, and rootstock—is critical to the success of the plants above. To the activists described in this chapter, creating socially just organizational structures that embody the kind of society they aspire to are as important to their long-range goal of combating oppression as the more visible farm and garden programs they run. Success, to these activists, involves nurturing leadership among people of color and women, making decisions collaboratively, rejecting hierarchical organizational design, and creating an organizational culture that does not replicate the oppressive leadership styles and structures of traditional nonprofits and businesses.

These activists have taken different approaches, but they all weave their ideas about social justice and anti-oppression into the structure of their organizations and programs. They are subverting conventional organizational structures to empower women of color. They are setting in place the kinds of cooperative, collaborative, and egalitarian decision making that rejects hierarchical control. They are practicing educational methods that blur the line between teacher and student and that incorporate politics and social justice into an agricultural curriculum. Their programs have been successful as agricultural projects, though they have also confronted challenges that stem from operating organizations that resist the status quo.

"Giving life" to social justice ideals is thus a key aspect of the groups high-lighted in this chapter. Indeed, this form of *organizational* praxis is part of what makes their work so compelling—once it is understood. But again, the visible activities in which activists engage often overshadow the theories and analyses that inform their practices. Uncovering ways in which the activists embody their anti-oppression ideals can thus help reveal possibilities for social justice praxis. Following Gibson-Graham's framework, understanding the theories behind the actions can also help legitimize "marginal"—or simply underrecognized—expe-riences as everyday reality, providing finer-grained examples of how urban agri-culture can be used to model, and potentially support, fundamentally different social and political systems.

And yet, as we note in chapter 1, to rest on the idea that simply legitimizing alternative realities within a dominant system will lead to "social justice" would be naive at best. Because their work exists within broader power structures, pol-icy change is also essential to achieving their broader anti-oppression goals. To this end, chapter 5 considers ways in which urban agriculture activists engage in policy advocacy.

Abu Talib, Taqwa Community Farm, South Bronx.
Photo by Rob Stephenson.

Bed-Stuy Farm, Brooklyn Rescue Mission Urban Harvest Center,
Bedford-Stuyvesant, Brooklyn.
Photo by Rob Stephenson.

East New York Farms! project,
United Community Centers,
East New York, Brooklyn.
Photo by Rob Stephenson.

Hattie Carthan Community Garden,
Bedford-Stuyvesant, Brooklyn.
Photo by Rob Stephenson.

La Finca del Sur, South Bronx.
Photo by Rob Stephenson.

Mural at Granja Los Colibries, La Unión,
Sunset Park, Brooklyn.
Photo by Rob Stephenson.

Ray Figueroa, Friends of Brook Park, South Bronx.
Photo by Rob Stephenson.

Snug Harbor Heritage Farm, Staten Island.
Photo by Rob Stephenson.

Stephen Ritz of Green Bronx Machine, South Bronx.
Photo by Rob Stephenson.

Tanya Fields and daughter, The BLK ProjeK, South Bronx.
Photo by Rob Stephenson.

CHAPTER 5

Cultivating Policy

One summer evening, Friends of Brook Park (FBP) hosted a meeting of a local community development corporation called Nos Quedamos. The gathering took place in Brook Park Community Garden, which FBP oversees, and was a strategic move on the part of the two organizations. FBP's Ray Figueroa, Director of Social-Ecological Development, explained that the idea was to bring the two groups together to build a broader network of activists working on related issues in the South Bronx community. FBP focuses on urban ecology and environmental justice; the garden and a related youth farming project are among its core initiatives. Nos Quedamos runs projects to increase financial literacy, clean up brownfields, and build affordable housing in the Melrose community of the South Bronx, also issues of concern to gardeners at Brook Park and about a dozen other community gardens with which Nos Quedamos works. For FBP and Nos Quedamos, gardens are perfect spaces for coalition building, as they are both literally and figuratively common ground where community organizers from housing, environmental justice, and other social justice movements can build political strength in neighborhoods lacking the clout that wealthier communities take for granted. In describing the organizing process, Figueroa explained, "We share our struggles, and coming together is a way to share our strengths as well. So it's old-fashioned boots-on-the-ground, reaching out, visiting with folks, and reciprocating."

Following the Brook Park–Nos Quedamos meeting, the two organizations continue to work together with other city groups to advocate for policies that address fundamental social justice issues: poverty and unemployment, racial and gender discrimination, and environmental racism. FBP has also worked with networks that include a homeless advocacy group and a housing-rights organization to advocate for policies that recognize the inherent connections between food and housing as basic human rights.

Policy advocacy is clearly important to these groups, since municipal, state, and national policies have an immediate effect on urban agriculture, affordable housing, and other social and environmental issues, and frame how these issues are considered in the future. In the case of groups like Friends of Brook Park and other organizations situated in lower-income communities, policy activism is also important because of the history of political disenfranchisement of these communities, which has contributed to many of the issues these groups aim to address through their programs.

FBP's activities also illustrate that policy making happens both within and outside conventional policy structures, through diverse means, and with unique roles for activists. Building on the legacy of community garden activism discussed in chapter 2, Ray Figueroa and other urban agriculture activists in contemporary New York use strategies that reach beyond conventional policy advocacy techniques such as collecting signatures on petitions and speaking at public hearings and community board meetings. Carrying out tactics similar to those of generations of community gardeners that came before them, they employ social-movement and community-organizing methods of coalition building, reframing issues so they are politically salient, and forming strategic, if temporary, partnerships to accomplish common policy objectives (e.g., see Taylor 2000; Wekerle 2004).

These initiatives are examples of "new political spaces," a term used to distinguish a broader shift in governance that has occurred over the last several decades, from conventional "classical-modernist" political institutions (Hajer 2003) like legislatures and administrative agencies to wider networks that include diverse stakeholders outside formal governmental bodies (Innes and Booher 2010; Agrawal and Lemos 2007; Dryzek 2010). These new political spaces do not take the place of conventional government institutions and practices— policies are still devised by various government officials and passed into law by legislative bodies; formal legislative and regulatory mechanisms remain core to policy implementation, and urban agriculture activists participate in these processes. However, policy making in new political spaces involves many more people, interest groups, belief systems, and practices than conventional governmental processes (Innes and Booher 2010; Agrawal and Lemos 2007; Hajer 2003).

The FBP–Nos Quedamos example illustrates how some urban agriculture activists operate in new political spaces, using gardens as places to foster networks and to advocate for policies pertinent not only to garden tenure (the ability of gardeners to maintain use of a site) but to a broader range of issues that connect to their particular concerns. Often these concerns are fundamentally about social justice. Beyond the explicit policy activism that they carry out through common advocacy tactics, within their own organizations they implement social justice practices that go well beyond existing laws or regulations. These practices represent the policies they wish to see, and indeed, some might eventually be put into law. In this sense, they are influencing formal policy as "everyday makers" (e.g., see Bang and Sørensen 1999). Activists' strategies to shape public policy thus go beyond conventional notions of what it means to participate in policy making, and they reflect the more complex, diverse, and nuanced manner in which policy is forged. This chapter examines these additional processes that urban agriculture activists use to create supportive political systems that advance social justice in food and environmental systems.

Network Building

The activities and strategies of different individuals and organizations are often fluid and networked across different interest groups, sectors, and geographic scales. They may include both established routes to policy making and informal extra-governmental activities. For example, official food policy councils created by a municipality might advise on urban agriculture policy, while agency staff and nongovernment stakeholders might informally collaborate on new policies. These informal arrangements can include unofficial networks and ad hoc interagency committees formed by municipal staff, as well as groups brought together by advocacy organizations, philanthropies, academic institutions, and other nongovernmental organizations to address specific issues (Aarsaether, Nyseth, and Bjørnå 2011). Programs organized by nonprofits, "citizen science" projects (in which people without formal training in research methods collect data about topics relevant to their own communities), and many other forms of influence may operate in parallel with conventional legislative or budget-setting processes to inform policy making related to the urban food system. For example, for Yonnette Fleming at Hattie Carthan Community Garden, networking is an essential part of advancing food justice. She noted that it was important to form a working group that can "begin to sit at the table and talk about food justice and take small bites from [large] problems."

Virtually all activists in this book shared Ray Figueroa's desire to build a richer and more diverse network of activist organizations to work more effectively toward common social justice objectives. The focus of the groups involved in these networks varies; some are only tangentially involved in food and agriculture but are connected to urban agriculture through their concerns about issues such as inequity and human rights, and others work on issues more obviously related to urban agriculture such as garden tenure, food access, or nutrition. The New York City Community Garden Coalition, of which Figueroa serves as president, has been particularly active in building advocacy networks of urban agriculture groups throughout the city. In advance of the 2013 mayoral election, for example, the coalition held a forum for candidates that also involved a teach-in led by diverse grassroots social justice organizations, including those focused on affordable housing and rights for homeless people, as well as Loisaida United Community Gardens (LUNGS), a coalition of community gardens in the Lower

East Side that sponsors community events and advocates for the preservation and support of member gardens, including the De Colores Community Yard garden, among whose members we interviewed. Figueroa said that his goal for the forum was to "get these other groups to come—in the spirit of solidarity, but [also] to . . . begin the process of networking and organizing with each other."

In networking with other organizations to build political influence, urban agriculture activists like Figueroa and others described in this book have expanded the issues that their farm and garden programs address. For example, in 2015 several social justice organizations and a network of urban agriculture activists (including Figueroa, representing the New York City Community Garden Coalition; Karen Washington; Onika Abraham of Farm School NYC; Tanya Fields at the BLK ProjeK in the South Bronx; and the Reverends Robert and DeVanie Jackson) circulated an open letter to New York's governor calling for a policy to create food distribution infrastructure to explicitly address the needs of farmers of color and communities of color. The letter urged the state to address structural racism in its decision making; to create programs to support landownership for black farmers; to direct economic development resources to communities of color; to include urban farmers in the state's agriculture census; to finance community-scale food distribution infrastructure, particularly in communities of color; to link community-based black and Latino entrepreneurs to food production infrastructure; and to provide financial support to community-based food organizations led by people of color (Cooper et al. 2015).

Some activists have deliberately created alliances to work on issues *not* germane to farming and gardening but considered important to broader movements for social justice. For example, Leticia Alanis of La Unión explained that "on immigration [advocacy], we work with the New York Immigration Coalition and with other groups. . . . When there is a network it's easier just to plug in. . . . A network of advocacy organizations in terms of immigration allows us to contribute. In education [advocacy], we are part of education task forces. . . . We work with the New York Immigration Coalition . . . [health and education task forces]. . . . And we advocate for the rights of immigrant parents and students in the school system. But then, we have other networks as well, like the Participatory Action Research Center for Education Organizing (PARCEO) and Advocates for Children." Figueroa also described reaching out to networks and coalitions not directly involved in urban agriculture to create solidarity among these organizations: "I've been in meetings with housing [groups], like residents associations, and they're like, 'Community gardens? Trees?' They didn't see the value of what we were talking about in terms of a community garden. But . . . over the last year and a half . . . I've invested a lot of time and energy in going out to a variety of meetings, coalition types of meetings, [like] South Bronx Community Congress, supporting Picture the Homeless, so, one, it's in the spirit of solidarity, and two, to begin to parlay that into 'Hey, let's talk about this.'"

For some activists, the networking process itself has helped their organizations shift or expand the scope of the issues they tackle as they connect with other groups working on a particular issue. For example, Nancy Ortiz-Surun described La Finca del Sur's participation in a campaign to stop the food-delivery retailer Fresh Direct from moving to a site in the South Bronx. There had been considerable community opposition to Fresh Direct's initiative because the city offered the company public subsidies, yet it would take up prime property that many in the community had envisioned as open space. It would also bring a fleet of diesel delivery vehicles to a neighborhood already suffering from high rates of respiratory disease due to a concentration of industry and highways. The opposition campaign was led by Friends of Brook Park and other community groups, yet Ortiz-Surun had felt that La Finca del Sur needed to be involved because the campaign aligned with La Finca's broader focus on social and environmental justice.

When they support issues espoused by other groups, some urban agriculture activists believe that their new allies will in turn support policies to strengthen farming and gardening. Figueroa in particular underscored these types of synergies, such as the idea that the same sweat equity that goes into creating and managing a community garden can be used to engage people in building and maintaining affordable housing. He added: "We have been doing some very strategic, come-up-out-of-our-silo, kind of cross-fertilization of movements, saying, 'Hey, it's all about land and what happens with that land. It's all about city property and the disposition of that property. And because it is . . . public property, how can we really work to maximize the public good?'"

These activists are thus adept at forming coalitions with other activists to address policy concerns that extend beyond farming and gardening to broader issues of social justice. For example, Figueroa's alliance with Picture the Homeless, an organization founded and run by homeless people, involves advocacy for policies to support community control of public land for affordable housing *and* gardens through mechanisms like community land trusts. Urban agriculture activists also address economic justice and community control of urban space through supporting rent regulations to preserve housing affordability and stabilize communities, and they have raised awareness about the potential for gentrification to displace longtime residents of communities of color.

Networking is also a strategy to achieve political support to advance the work of the gardens and farms themselves. As urban agriculture activists seek to build political power to support their projects and strengthen the urban agriculture system, they have enlisted elected officials and agency staff in their efforts. For example, Ortiz-Surun explained that one strategy La Finca del Sur had used was to develop a sympathetic group of local political leaders who would support strengthening the "asset that the community now has in this farm." Annie Moss explained that efforts to convince agencies to provide basic infrastructure for La Finca, including fencing, had helped establish working relationships with agency staff, which she hoped would be beneficial to the organization's efforts in the long run. She noted that the original goal of getting the Parks Department and the Department of Transportation—the two city agencies that control land on which La Finca is situated—to fence the site was to improve safety for women farmers and gardeners. However, success in convincing city agencies to support the farm also became a means of political empowerment. In her words, "If we can develop those contacts with the different agencies and have [the farm] be more established, then we will be more empowered to deal with [other] issues when they come up." Borrowing from community-organizing and social-movement tactics, these urban agriculture activists work to develop diverse networks to accomplish their common interest in advancing social justice in the city. Some of the political work is narrowly focused on the needs of the gardens and some is aimed at benefiting the communities that the garden projects attempt to improve.

In addition to the various interests represented within them, policy advocacy networks also include activists, organizations, and government agencies working at different geographic and political scales. Fleming, whose farm and farm-based entrepreneurial initiatives tend to focus on problems facing the local Bed-Stuy community, pointed out that activists form strategic partnerships with both community-based organizations and larger advocacy groups. Though intently focused on people living in what she often refers to as the "local geography," Fleming acknowledged the value of allying with larger New York City food advocacy organizations, such as Just Food, and even national groups to achieve policy change. She stated: "I don't plan to stand alone. What I'm doing is moving out and creating partners and streams with national organizations, understanding their agendas . . . so that we are able to tweak this system in small ways." Likewise, Figueroa described how the New York City Community Garden Coalition worked with community garden and land-access groups throughout the state to leverage an expansion of the New York State Office of Community Gardens' authority and the establishment of a state Task Force on Community Gardens, both based within the New York State Department of Agriculture and Markets.

Additionally, a number of activists have been involved with initiatives of the US Food Sovereignty Alliance (USFSA), a coalition of organizations working to advance principles of the international food sovereignty movement in the United States. Many of the issues that food sovereignty activists address are inherently political, as they pertain to control over land and the right to self-determination in the food system. Urban agriculture activists have thus been able to link their policy advocacy in New York City—to gain long-term or permanent tenure for gardens and farms and to give local residents more authority over land-use decisions that affect their communities—to related issues at a global scale.

Figueroa, for example, explained that he is part of a USFSA working group on "land grabbing," as some activist groups have come to refer to government and/or private parties' rush to acquire large tracts of agricultural land. "Land grabbing is happening as much here in New York City as it is happening around the country and internationally," he stated. He described how the working group's efforts in New York connect to international food sovereignty activists: "[As a result of our work] with the US Food Sovereignty Alliance, [we are] connected with La Via Campesina [the group that first introduced the concept of food sovereignty in 1996]. So we work with folks from [places like] Venezuela. We haven't been there yet, but we do collaborate and share information about best practices and real struggles." The Food Sovereignty Alliance links the political actions of different food sovereignty groups, from Restaurant Opportunities Centers United's campaign to raise wages for tipped workers to protests by students at the University of California, Berkeley, to stop the sale of the university's farm. Realizing that there are national and international groups fighting for land access and the right to grow food gives context to and legitimizes FBP and the New York City Community Garden Coalition's advocacy of policies like permanent tenure for gardens, veto power by community boards over land-use decisions, and participatory budgeting.

New York City groups are not literally working on the same policy campaigns as national and international organizations, but they are working on common issues, and their efforts are mutually supportive. For example, the Reverend DeVanie Jackson of Brooklyn Rescue Mission has met with Via Campesina members from Indonesia and Nicaragua, finding commonality between her work as a person of color addressing food access issues in Bed-Stuy and farmers' struggles for their rights in the Global South (Schiavoni 2009). Nancy Ortiz-Surun, Leticia Alanis, and Karen Washington all played roles in presenting the annual Food Sovereignty prize to the Korean Women Peasant Association in 2012, highlighting issues faced by women farmers in the Global South that have received increasing attention among policy advocates in the United States and elsewhere. Thus, even if urban agriculture activists have limited time to engage in policy advocacy beyond the municipal level (which is often the case), many try to support broader-scale initiatives through network building not only because it feels empowering, but because they understand that national and international policies affect their own organizations and the social justice issues they aim to address through their work.

Framing the Issues through Discourse

In new political spaces, policy development often involves working to frame, or define, an issue from the point of view of urban agriculture and social justice constituencies. This work can include assembling political resources, ideas, and knowledge to help identify and describe problems in a particular way; propos-

ing policy solutions; and producing program design prototypes to guide decision making (McCann and Ward 2012; Sørensen and Torfing 2005; Ansell and
Gash 2007; Binz-Scharf, Lazer, and Mergel 2011). By shaping discourse, activists
can shift the public's understanding of the causes of policy problems, sometimes
contradicting the focus, emphasis, or perceptions of government officials and
other interest groups. Some activists contextualize their discussion of issues
through existing political frameworks—such as the way some urban agriculture
activists use food sovereignty or environmental justice frameworks—to connect
these issues to or frame them within the context of larger social and political
movements (e.g., see Taylor 2000). Networks of social justice activists can use
these frameworks to identify and draw attention to particular problems that
might otherwise be overlooked, or to describe them in ways that favor certain
policy solutions, such as those that aim to help communities that have been
disadvantaged by previous policies or economic trends. In the process, activists
aim to make the problems that they target, as well as their preferred solutions,
more politically salient.

Individuals and groups choose to work on particular policy issues for a variety of reasons. Some participate in networks whose members have elected to
work to advance specific policies. Others strategically choose to work on certain policy problems when it seems to be the most opportune time to achieve a
desired outcome. But some urban agriculture activists also try to influence the
salience of particular issues by framing them so that they resonate with other
activists and policy officials. Through various forms of communication, activists
highlight, shape, and make politically relevant various urban agriculture policies. They can also elucidate connections between urban agriculture activists
and city agencies beyond the more obvious Parks Department (which runs the
GreenThumb program) and agencies that control disparate garden sites. These
include efforts such as the New York City Community Garden Coalition's meetings with GreenThumb staff to negotiate garden licenses, and the citizen-science
project Farming Concrete's collaborative effort with agencies and gardeners to
measure the quantity of produce grown.

To be sure, much of the discussion that has occurred among farmers, gardeners, and government agency officials in New York City has related to the
gardeners' desire to secure more land, permanent land tenure, and access to basic resources such as compost and soil, water, and technical assistance. Getting
these discussions started has often required cultivating relationships with staff
in agencies such as the Department of Sanitation or the Police Department by
attending community meetings and speaking with district and borough staff.
Such interactions have at times resulted in changes to agency policies or practices at the service-delivery level, such as increasing trash collection at farms
and gardens. But they have also helped demonstrate that agencies that are not
readily recognized as having much to do with urban agriculture (e.g., the De-

partment of Sanitation) actually affect, and can help or hinder, farming and gardening initiatives. Short of yielding a citywide urban agriculture plan that would commit the city to maintaining farms and gardens as a permanent part of its landscape, activists' efforts to reframe the discourse about municipal support for farming and gardening have, in recent years, helped city officials recognize urban agriculture as a cross-cutting theme in working papers on various policies and in the city's sustainability plan (City of New York 2014, 2015).

Activists also engage in policy change through attempts to reframe the discourse about urban agriculture in ways that include broader social justice concerns. For example, the open letter to the governor, discussed above, raised a broader set of issues having to do with structural racism in the food system that had been considered beyond the scope of the food hub task force's work. The task force thus served as a strategic opportunity for activists to bring race into what might otherwise be viewed as an issue of supply-chain logistics. Even if the letter ends up having little effect on the substance of the task force's work (as this book goes to press there has been no decision about this issue), putting structural racism on the table makes it part of the policy discourse so that it is more likely to be included in subsequent policy debates.

Another example of how urban agriculture activists have attempted to shift policy discourse is in their efforts to frame community garden stability as an issue of the rights of city residents to have access to and manage public space (Eizenberg 2012b, 2013). Some activists have critiqued the methods used to evaluate future land use and introduced to their advocacy platforms the notion that gardens play a critical role in urban sustainability and public health, a role that has been overlooked or insufficiently valued by public agencies. In doing so, they have made the case for land-use decisions that are based on community needs and goals instead of narrow economic criteria.

Activists like Figueroa compare community gardens to the old English commons, noting that public spaces can provide "individuals the means by which they can live their lives in dignity, and grow their food, and go forward." He frames the control of land as a way to achieve some degree of food sovereignty and empowerment. To Figueroa, focusing on the future economic value of vacant land and using primarily financial criteria to determine future use favors some uses—and users—over others while masking the power dynamics behind those decisions. Financial criteria also undervalue community food production, which might not be economically efficient but is important to neighborhoods in many other ways. "Basically," Figueroa explained, "it just boils down to getting the city to respect places." He added that "these are not just spaces. They're *places*, in the sense that they have meaning; they've been cultivated. These are community-cultivated places of meaning that really provide an opportunity for the community to build itself."

Some activists have elaborated more radical notions of land control. Tanya

Fields, executive director of the BLK ProjeK, argued that even private prop-erty owners should be compelled to use their property to meet the needs of the community. The BLK ProjeK is an organization in the South Bronx that seeks, through its Libertad Urban Farm and other initiatives, to address food justice and public health issues as they specifically relate to women and youth of color. Fields acknowledged that this concept of landownership and control is a radical one, based on the idea that public policies should give people "more access to land in their community, whether . . . public or private." Yet she has criticized on a "spiritual level" the ability of some private landowners to keep vacant land from being used for gardens simply because it is privately owned: "This idea that you can say, 'Okay, I've got this land and I paid my taxes and I'm going to sit on it for twenty or thirty years waiting for an upswing; in twenty, thirty years I'll give it to my kid who will sit on it for fifteen to twenty years and they'll sell it.' And then the community in which [the land] exists has no place [in decision making]. This is the very basis of injustice. We all live in this community, we are investors in multiple ways, we are stakeholders in multiple ways. And somehow, something that sits here [and] lays fallow around us for decades at a time, we have no say about it because some person living in [nearby] Westchester or Put-nam County owns it?! That's bullshit, right?!"[1]

Fields also echoed belief systems that are common in many indigenous com-munities in the United States and elsewhere around the world, arguing that land is different from other commodities in that its use has an effect on other people, that humans have a biological and ecological connection to the land, and that we cannot be separated from it. She insisted that when vacant lots are converted to other uses, they should bring benefits to the surrounding community, and that community members should have a stake in these types of land-use de-cisions: "I think there [needs to be] a much more public process for people to vet . . . what happens in their community."

Fields's comment illustrates that despite having ideas that may come across as radical, urban agriculture activists are often strategic in their policy discourse, using language that resonates with different audiences, including government officials and others who care about the economic value of urban agriculture. For example, Figueroa explained that while his personal interest in getting per-manent status for community gardens has much to do with the meaning that these places hold for the gardeners, he also uses the language that the city uses in assessing the value of property, such as metrics about productivity and the eco-nomic value of what is produced on site: "We try to be very literate and versed in terms of how the city looks at its lots, and [we] try to make [our] argument from a metrics perspective." Karen Washington (who, in addition to her work with La Familia Verde, La Finca del Sur, and BUGS, has served as president of the New York City Community Garden Coalition) similarly noted the impor-tance of measuring agricultural production because it can translate into dollars and jobs, demonstrating the economic value of urban agriculture. Washington explained that it was important for urban farmers to be counted in the national Census of Agriculture to strengthen the case for federal agriculture funding to support food production in the city. In her view, "If we are counted, we can start getting a piece of [the] pie."[2]

Figueroa discussed the importance of getting community gardeners together to speak as one voice about permanent tenure for the city's gardens: "My agenda is to get more aggressive with the city and to, you know, figure out a way to do the massive community organizing that we need to just tell them, 'Hey, you're violating human rights.' Short of eliminating poverty . . . we need to have things that allow people to live with dignity, and that acknowledge their human worth. . . . This is a real tactical thing that I'm entertaining here in terms of influencing policy, but yeah, they need to permanently preserve gardens; that's what needs to happen."

Many of the urban agriculture activists we spoke with also work to reframe broader food policy discussions (i.e., not just those related to urban agriculture) so that the structural causes of food, health, and environmental inequities, and even deeper systemic issues such as multigenerational and concentrated poverty, are part of the debate. For example, over the past decade there has been significant discussion of the fact that low-income communities face limited access to healthy food in New York City. Increasingly, this social problem has been discussed in terms of "food deserts," an idea that many social justice activists refute because it obscures structural and political causes of food inequities.[3]

Often, the policy response to the dearth of accessible, affordable food in certain neighborhoods has been to encourage supermarkets to open in low-income communities by providing financial incentives and eliminating barriers to supermarket development, such as restrictive zoning. Yet some activists have raised the point that poverty, underemployment, and disparities in both public and private resources are actually at the heart of the problem, and that policy responses need to tackle these injustices to address food access. Figueroa proclaimed, "Food desert? We didn't invent that term. The community didn't invent that term. But it's the analytical paradigm that informs a lot of well-meaning organizations that say, 'Oh man, it's a food desert. Let's teach people how to eat better. Let's have cooking classes.'" Figueroa explained that this characterization results in policy solutions aimed at enhancing services within a community rather than addressing sociopolitical issues causing the dearth of healthy food retail. He added, "Social justice is not about services. It's about how the community can improve itself and really deal with the fundamental issues that got them in this place. We can't 'service' our way out of this issue of food access. . . . Yeah, you can say it's an issue. But it's not the root issue. [The issue is] people that are displaced from being meaningfully engaged as human beings. And that's [because of] poverty and unemployment."

Figueroa and other activists have thus attempted to shift the framing of food inaccessibility from the notion that low-income communities are food "deserts," needing mainly financial incentives for grocers to locate in them and educational programs to teach people different eating habits, to an explanation that recognizes that structural obstacles like poverty are the principal barriers to accessing healthier food.

In fact, Figueroa's main urban agriculture project, the Youth Farm at Brook Park, addresses one root cause of poverty: high rates of incarceration of people of color, which can prevent access to jobs, college, and public housing. Teaching the youth to grow food is not the program's main goal (though they do supply peppers for a locally produced hot sauce); the main goal is to reconnect them to the community and enable them to see themselves as stewards, not criminals.

Similarly, to Sharon de la Cruz at The Point Community Development Corporation during the time of this study, the important context for addressing these problems is the history of the community in question. Referring to her South Bronx neighborhood, Hunts Point, which faced disinvestment and property abandonment in the 1970s and was plagued by the widespread use of crack cocaine in the 1980s and 1990s, de la Cruz pointed out, "You had trash everywhere, you had arson fires everywhere, the crack epidemic was happening. . . . And that took a toll." The core policy questions in de la Cruz's view are how to address the economic problems facing the neighborhood and how to ensure that the large businesses located there (including the Hunts Point Produce Market, which bills itself as the largest wholesale produce market in the world) give back to the community. Activists like de la Cruz, Figueroa, Fields, and Washington have found that framing these issues as social and economic justice concerns is more politically powerful and more closely aligned with community needs than focusing exclusively on increasing the number of healthy food retailers, addressing blight, or even creating more community gardens.

Beyond reframing the discourse about broader social justice issues, many of the urban agriculture activists we spoke with try in other ways to shift how government agencies see their basic services, interpret regulations, and distribute resources. Activists recognize that the policies that urban agriculture groups deal with on a day-to-day basis are often existing agency rules and practices that support or regulate their activities, not proposed legislation or potentially supportive programs pertaining to agriculture in the city. Such reframing might therefore involve convincing an agency to see the connections between an activity like growing food and a group's core mission. Yonnette Fleming, for example, engaged in discussions with the New York City Department of Health and Mental Hygiene about the importance of treating community gardens as a means to improve public health. Fleming was a member of a task force led by the Health Department, and in that capacity she observed that the department hadn't factored community gardens into its research on improving access to healthy food:

"The conversation [in the report] was about stores, supermarkets, and bodegas. So when I read [it] I said, 'Wait a minute, isn't there another part of this? In Central Brooklyn we have sixty-something gardens in a small concentration. How can you *not* factor that in unless you think [growing food] isn't [related to] public health, or you think public health is *you* taking care of *us*?'"

Some of Fleming's efforts to reframe the way the Department of Health understands and therefore approaches urban agriculture have not been as successful as hoped, in that they have not yet resulted in policies that specifically support gardening as "health work," as Fleming refers to it. However, her discussions with agency officials, and the fact that she runs a farmers' market connected to a farm in a low-income community (an activity in which numerous other urban agriculture activists are also engaged), have contributed to a shifting discourse about the potential for farmers' markets and gardens to support healthy eating and the strong demand for farm-fresh produce in low-income neighborhoods. This shift has led to the creation, continuation, and expansion of programs to supplement federal food benefits for low-income customers who wish to shop at farmers' markets. Moreover, despite her critique of the department's approach, Fleming continues to work closely with its staff to try to influence how they consider gardens in their programs. In fact, Hattie Carthan Community Farmers' Market (a project led by Fleming that is separate from the farm) receives funds from the agency to run health and nutrition education programs on market days. The market also accepts Department of Health–administered Health Bucks, a city program that supplements Electronic Benefit Transfer (EBT) purchases at farmers' markets, allowing customers who receive federal benefits to stretch the buying power of their funds. This fluidity illustrates the type of strategic framing and network building in which many urban agriculture activists engage.

As does the broader strategy of creating new political spaces, the process of shaping policy discourse occurs in different venues. Urban agriculture activists we spoke with raise issues of social justice whenever they are engaged in policy discussions about the food system. As a member of an interagency task force on urban agriculture, for example, Figueroa reminded city officials that "you guys are talking about food access and improving people's eating habits, but the elephant in the room is poverty and unemployment! You're always citing the correlating issues going on, but you don't address those issues!" To Figueroa, the policy goal should be to "have food-based economic development that is environmentally sustainable and that . . . does so in a way that promotes equity." Similarly, the Reverends Robert and DeVanie Jackson at Brooklyn Rescue Mission regularly raise issues about social justice and food when meeting with city officials. Robert Jackson explained, "In the dialogues that we have [about policy] we've [been] very vocal . . . on the matter of poverty and food that comes from food banks . . . [and about] why there has to be farmers' markets with farmers and farm associations." For his part, Figueroa admitted that when he brings up these issues, city officials react "like I'm from Mars," yet this has not discouraged him from speaking his mind, as he feels strongly about focusing attention on the root causes of food and environmental disparity.

Policies through Everyday Practices

New political spaces also include what might otherwise be dismissed as the mundane practices, experiences, and actions of everyday life. Everyday practices can shape policies by differing from and conflicting with existing conventions, regulations, or policies (Coleman 2007; Marsh 2011, 76; Wagenaar and Cook 2003). For example, gardening on public land, composting organic matter, teaching cooking skills, and harvesting rainwater stand in stark relief to aspects of the food system that are unjust or unsustainable. These everyday activities demonstrate innovations and help generate potential solutions (Wagenaar and Cook 2003). Once these activities reach a certain scale, policy makers and their constituents may feel the need for a policy response. This form of policy making occurs through the activities of what Bang and Sørensen (1999) describe as "everyday makers," individuals engaged in community-scale projects that affect laws, programs, agency practices, and other policies. Their everyday projects might range from the daily practices of a group of community members to the activities of new businesses that either reinforce or challenge existing policies or normalize activities that might otherwise be considered inappropriate. The everyday nature of this mode of policy making is often not recognized as such by governmental officials or even the "makers" themselves.

Activists also become involved in oppositional activities aimed at shaping policy at various scales, including engaging in "everyday *resistances*" to existing policies (Wekerle 2004; emphasis added). A particular practice, such as keeping bees illegally, may elevate a conflict between beekeepers and the city over whether the practice is appropriate and ought to be legalized, precipitating policy change, as noted below. These are not large-scale actions but rather involve ignoring and bending rules to draw attention to ineffective or unfair policies and highlight the need to change them. Individuals who engage in everyday resistances might not do so with the intention of changing policy, but activists can make otherwise apolitical acts of gardening or farming politically salient by illustrating how common and beneficial they are.

Urban agriculture activists in New York City engage in policy making through their everyday actions as they implement projects and find ways to work around existing rules and regulations. Four examples of this are the following:

- Increasing numbers of beekeepers flouted the law by keeping what the city's Health Department considered a wild animal, leading Just Food and the New York City Beekeepers Association to launch an ultimately successful policy advocacy campaign to legalize beekeeping in New York City in 2010 (Brustein 2009).
- Community-based composting projects and on-farm composting have demonstrated the feasibility of composting organic matter in residential neighborhoods and public interest in source-separating organic waste, leading to City Council legislation requiring studies of the feasibility of waste composting and a pilot compost collection program of the Department of Sanitation.
- Entrepreneurial efforts to grow food on vacant lots, which have expanded the urban agriculture system and demonstrated the demand for land to be used for food production and the viability of community-managed farm and garden sites, have led to policy support for expanding urban agriculture.
- Educators have worked to incorporate urban agriculture and social justice into the core curriculum of public school garden and farm programs, and through this process have helped build support for school-based urban agriculture education.

Not all of these actions specifically address social justice in the way that the activists highlighted in this book discuss it. However, they *are* examples of how the everyday activities of urban agriculture can foster policy change, either by raising awareness among government officials of the prevalence and importance of specific farm and garden activities, or by causing agencies to develop policies that pertain to these activities. The extent to which urban agriculture activists are able to leverage their activities to garner political support for their social justice programs depends in part on the strength of their networks and their ability to frame their issues in ways that make sense to decision makers at a given moment.

Encouraging Participation in Conventional Policy Making

While the term "new political spaces" refers mostly to new governance processes, there is a physical dimension to the concept as well. In the case of urban agriculture, policy making literally takes place in new *physical* spaces, such as gardens and farms—outside City Council chambers, agency conference rooms, and other traditional governmental spaces. As the vignette at the beginning of the chapter illustrates, community farms can be venues in which groups organize social justice campaigns, teach about social justice and politics, and cultivate leadership to develop new policy advocates in their communities. The control of a particular place is thus important not merely as a political issue in and of itself (as community members struggle to gain access, tenure, and longer-term stewardship of land) but also as a space for policy-making activities.

The urban agriculture activists we spoke with use their farm and garden programs as spaces to empower community members to engage in more conventional policy advocacy as individuals. For instance, Deborah Greig noted that East New York Farms! supports community gardening interests through efforts such as attending rallies, writing statements of support for funding requests, or speaking to the press. For local policy issues ENYF! gets involved directly: "We were pretty involved with the legalization of beekeeping, because that directly affected a lot of our gardeners, and us." ENYF! staff encourage community members to become involved in these efforts as much as possible so that community desires are heard and residents are actively engaged in shaping policies that affect their lives. To schoolteacher Stephen Ritz, a critical part of engaging in policy making is getting kids involved with elected officials and encouraging them to register to vote:

> Well, we want kids to vote. We've registered hundreds of voters, and that's really cool. . . . I'm thrilled . . . that the Bronx borough president knows my kids by name, and they know him by name! They know state senator Gustavo Rivera. They know [our] congressman, José Serrano. They recognize these people, and they know these people, and to me, that's important.

For some, participation in various public meetings held by governing bodies not only serves to enable farmers, gardeners, and activists to voice their opinions in an official forum but also is a way to meet and establish connections with community leaders and agency officials. For example, the members of La Finca del Sur participate in meetings of the local community planning boards.[4] Ortiz-Surun noted: "We try to have representatives of the farm attend meetings, which is difficult when you have a largely volunteer staff, many working long days. We do try to have members attend each month; it's a way to introduce our project as a resource, and for us to keep current politically and socially." While these efforts represent rather conventional ways to attempt to affect policy, activists like Greig, Ritz, and members of La Finca del Sur are actively using the farm and garden programs they run to help strengthen democratic participation by members of the communities in which they work—individuals who, due to a variety of social, economic, and political patterns, often have limited political clout.

Constraints on Policy Making

Despite activists' efforts to engage in policy making, they have often faced the fundamental constraints of insufficient staff resources and comparatively less political clout than larger organizations and individuals working in more privileged communities. Their efforts include community organizing; some urban agriculture advocates use the tried-and-true method of "knocking on peoples' doors" to ask for support for policy change, as Karen Washington described her strategy for organizing in her neighborhood. Yonnette Fleming characterized successful policy advocacy as "years of work." These efforts take a toll on organizations with limited resources. Although activists try to work in solidarity with others to influence policy, they also know that their highest priority is to focus on core farming and gardening issues, lest their work as urban farmers and gardeners fall by the wayside. For example, Ortiz-Surun attributed the lack of staff for policy research and networking to the need to attend to the farm, explaining, "The time that I have has to be prioritized for such things as ordering seeds, making sure we have recruitment outreach, and that workdays are arranged and provisioned. I also am part of the actual farmer group; I teach and lead student and volunteer groups, which is balanced with all the rest of my life. It's sometimes hard to understand why we don't get to all the social functions connected to this movement; it's because a small, growing core group is actually hands-on doing this, and it's hard work."

And while networks can be effective at building a critical mass of groups in support of a particular policy, individual organizations can sometimes be pulled in different directions by policy campaigns that are not core to their interests. For example, Leticia Alanis noted the importance of developing activist campaigns within an organization, suggesting that a group cannot be simply plugged into others' existing campaigns. "I feel it cannot be imposed," she explained. "Sometimes the other groups . . . they already have the issue identified, or they already have identified in which campaigns they want to work, and they just want to kind of plug us in." She described the difficulty of participating in a rally to get grocery chain Trader Joe's to settle with the Coalition of Immokalee Workers, a national coalition that advocates for farm worker wages and rights: "I value that work because I know that farmers live in severe conditions," she explained, "but [it's] not all the time [that] you can just pull people and say, 'Oh, let's go to this!' you know. If it's not something that is holistic and is growing within the group, it's harder [to prioritize]." Bee Ayer at BK Farmyards noted:

> We have tried occasionally to talk with some of the local politicians about our work, or be involved in some of the citywide food policy task forces, that kind of stuff. But we had to scale back because we haven't found that it's actually that effective in reaching our goals. We find it very divided from the actual stuff that we do on the ground, and it can just make our staff tired. I think our staff is tired.

Inclusiveness is also critically important to policy networks made up of activists committed to achieving social justice. Access to political leaders and resources often depends on the strength and reach of a network of organizations. Urban agriculture activists recognize that the constituents in a network are critical to its success. For example, Ortiz-Surun noted that access to politicians requires cultivating connections and "is about whose attention you can align with your work and mission." Nevertheless, networks can be exclusionary as well as inclusive. To be effective, networks of urban agriculture activists must be committed to including diverse farmers and gardeners and other activists. Sometimes disparities within the network of urban agriculture groups can be quite visible: larger nonprofits often get access to resources more easily than smaller ones, making it more difficult for smaller groups to compete for those resources and to build capacity (Cohen and Reynolds 2015, 2014). The consequences for policy are significant, as the organizations getting public resources develop close relationships with agency officials responsible for funding or supporting them. These relationships may help them to gain access to additional resources. Moreover, well-supported organizations may continue to attract attention, enabling them to secure a disproportionate amount of philanthropic and government funds (Reynolds 2014).

In terms of working with government agencies, some of the activists we spoke with felt that their efforts had not always resulted in the policy changes that all involved had hoped to achieve. Bee Ayer described her frustrations in working with officials at the Department of Education (DOE) and other government agencies, academic institutions, and nonprofits in the city to develop soil quality standards for farms and gardens located on DOE property. At the request of the department, she organized a group of experts to advise DOE about safely growing edible crops on urban soils:

> We felt like it was a really big deal to actually create best practices that the DOE could use to help other groups to grow food on school land both for educational purposes and for producing food.... However, even after all the work, writing down standards and advice for best practices from a consensus of experts, the DOE hasn't made any moves to use them, or to support more projects. [So] maybe it's a good example of trying to work on policy and [work] with politicians and it not really getting anywhere.

A final factor limiting activists' ability to most effectively engage in policy development is simply the lack of technical capacity and time to sort through policies that are complex, conflicting, or simply a hindrance to gardening and farming. For example, La Finca del Sur had to unravel which among several different city and state transportation agencies controlled the site on which the farm is situated in order to continue to work there, and to do so in compliance with city regulations. Annie Moss described the difficulty of this process: "It was like a crazy mystery to find out; it took us a really long time to figure out who owned what and how the land was divided." For organizations with paid staff to spend time on this type of research, identifying landownership may have been less of an issue, but for an organization like La Finca, and indeed most of the groups discussed in this book, the majority of labor is volunteer, and so time is often allocated first to the in-the-moment tasks.

DISENGAGEMENT FROM POLICY MAKING

Many but not all urban agriculture activists are vocal participants in the new political spaces of policy making in New York City. Some choose to focus on the day-to-day practice of gardening and farming, seeing this work as neither political nor focused on policy controversies. Some activists, like Petula Gay, a Farm School NYC student and staff member at Snug Harbor Heritage Farm in Staten Island, are interested in and quite knowledgeable about how specific government programs and policies affect their farms or gardens but see policy advocacy as separate from their work with urban agriculture.

Meanwhile, some individuals or organizations may feel disconnected from policy-making processes and may therefore choose to disengage from policy advocacy in its more conventional form—especially since it is typically understood within the conventional framework of government agencies driving all decisions. The power of the new political spaces that give birth to contemporary urban agriculture policy lies not in projecting "policy activist" identities on individuals and groups that are uninterested in policy making but rather in seeing ways in which urban farmers and gardeners actually do affect policy process, whether through strategic networking, through framing of discourse, or through the act of cultivating urban spaces.

Policy Polyculture

As this chapter has illustrated, the urban agriculture policy landscape in New York City is quite varied. In part as a reaction to the proposed sale of community gardens in the 1990s (described in chapter 2), activists have focused their attention on developing relationships with a broader range of organizations. They have learned to work on numerous fronts to move policy forward, using a variety of strategies, in new political spaces. Through discursive processes they have attempted to change the nature of the policy discussion about urban agriculture from one that is narrowly focused on gardens and farms as food production sites to one that incorporates issues such as food and environmental justice, community control of land, and multigenerational, racialized poverty. Activists also work on policy at multiple levels and through formal and informal means. They engage in activities ranging from selling produce to cleaning vacant lots— activities that change agency practices and in turn have the potential to shape broader policies.

The notion of new political spaces includes conventional means as well as policy making beyond City Hall. Thus, in addition to developing relationships with other organizations and public officials that can translate into influence and power, activists recognize that they need to engage in more conventional policy development, sometimes supporting legislation to advance urban agriculture through traditional means. Fields, for example, suggested that urban food activists need to develop the capacity to push for change at all levels of government by working together more cohesively: "We've really got to build power legislatively on a city level, on a state level, and a federal level." To Fields, building power requires that groups like the New York City Community Garden Coalition figure out "how to legislate for land trusts and . . . how we [can] build a groundswell around that to make it happen." The farmers and gardeners we spoke with are lobbying lawmakers for local legislation or agency rule changes. Figueroa, as president of the Garden Coalition, continues to advocate for permanent preservation status for the city's community gardens. Activists like Karen Washington meet with government officials to offer input and recommendations on policy and to provide officials a sense of what different communities feel about certain issues. Moreover, urban agriculture activists work to empower their members and their communities so that they are able to engage in policy making as individuals.

Throughout the United States, policy making that deals with food and agriculture is relatively new for municipal governments. In New York City, although numerous agencies have some purview over aspects of farming and gardening, as of this writing there is no formal urban agriculture policy plan (though there are a few specific policies such as those pertaining to community garden tenure and beekeeping). As urban agriculture policy continues to evolve in the city alongside a renewed interest in economic equity and racial justice, urban agriculture activists, working in networks of like-minded groups, will increasingly help create policies that simultaneously advance farming, gardening, and a city that is more socially just at its core. However, such efforts also need to address uneven power dynamics that disadvantage urban agriculture programs situated in low-income communities, and particularly those led by people of color. These challenges, which are deeper than the common problem of lack of permanent land tenure or gardening resources, are examined in the next chapter.

CHAPTER 6

Addressing Uneven Power and Privilege

When we asked Karen Washington, a veteran urban farmer and community activist in the Bronx, about the challenges she encounters in her urban agriculture work, she immediately brought up the notion of power:

> There are so many people talking about food issues . . . and politicians having these food campaigns, but when you see exactly who's at the table, you don't see us. . . . I feel that I have a right to be at the table when some of these decisions are being made that directly affect my neighborhood and the people around me. And I think the challenge [is that] we don't, as people of color, have the power in New York City to have an impact on decision making. It's top down. It's people talking about us, talking for us. But when it comes to the power—the political power or people who have the money—we're not there.

Washington has delivered this message many times, from one-on-one conversations to the many public addresses she has given at sustainable agriculture and food systems conferences around the United States. This perspective on power is grounded in a firm belief that everyday people should have substantive control over what happens in their communities. Like many of the activists with whom we spoke, Washington is interested in building more socially just food systems in which people of color and working-class people have a meaningful voice in policy making and community advocacy, and in which they are able to take advantage of and create economic opportunities equal to those available to more privileged members of society. Like some of the other activists discussed in this book, she is also invested in strengthening the presence and clout of black farmers in the agricultural economy and alternative food movements and in expanding recognition of the long-standing food production and culinary practices of people of color in New York and nationwide. To Washington, a fundamental challenge in working to advance social justice through urban agriculture is the very fact that farming and gardening are embedded in racial and economic oppression, even in a diverse and cosmopolitan city like New York.

Washington's analysis of food and power were developed through her experiences as a Bronx resident and longtime community gardener and activist, and through her more recent engagement with national food justice movements. Her urban agriculture work began in the Bronx in the late 1980s, when she played an instrumental role in establishing a community garden called the Garden of Happiness on an abandoned lot near her home. In 1998, around the time of the Giuliani community garden battle described in chapter 2, she worked with residents and members of community gardens in nearby neighborhoods to found La Familia Verde Community Garden Coalition. The coalition, composed of five gardens in the Crotona, East Tremont, and West Farms neighborhoods of the Bronx, operates a farmers' market selling food grown by its gardens and by other regional farms. Washington has served as president of the New York City Community Garden Coalition, and she helped found La Finca del Sur, Farm School NYC, and Black Urban Growers. She has also been a member of urban agriculture policy task forces in the city and has developed working relationships with a number of government officials. Through collaboration with grassroots activists and other leaders in sustainable agriculture and food justice movements, Washington has helped bring questions about power inequities to the attention of a broader public. Still, as her comments suggest, imbalances of power and privilege remain and are among the key challenges facing many urban agriculture activists in New York City.

All of the activists highlighted in this book work in low-income communities. Most are people of color, and some have immigrated from the southern United States or from regions of the Global South. Many of these individuals have experienced the effects of structural racism, homophobia, patriarchy, or class discrimination in their own lives, and thus they understand structural forms of oppression from a deeply personal perspective. Urban agriculture is a strategy they use to confront these oppressive structures.

As described in previous chapters, some activists like Karen Washington, Yonnette Fleming, and Ray Figueroa frame their work in what more politically conservative people might consider "radical" analyses of injustice and ideas about how it should be addressed, distinguishing their work from more conventional urban agriculture projects. Yet the combination of working in communities with limited economic and political resources, the decidedly anti-oppression politics of their work, and at times the activists' own identities gives rise to another layer of challenges seated in the uneven power dynamics to which Washington refers.

Power and privilege are seldom recognized as fundamental challenges to urban agriculture. More commonly, advocates and policy makers focus on the basic needs: access to land, soil and compost, horticultural advice, and operating funds. These are often in short supply, hampering the success of any farm or garden. But a focus on the technical challenges to farming in the city, as significant as they may be, risks ignoring the social, economic, and political dynamics within an urban agriculture system that can privilege some farmers and gardeners over others. Again, gardening and farming exist within broader systems, and uneven power dynamics within these systems present additional challenges to less-powerful urban agriculture groups. As Washington and many of the other activists featured in this book have argued, racial, socioeconomic, gender, and political inequities are more formidable obstacles to their urban agriculture initiatives than lack of materials like soil and compost or horticultural know-how. This chapter begins with a brief overview of challenges common to urban agriculture in New York City. It then focuses on how the distribution of power affects who in the urban agriculture community gets resources, and thus why uneven power and privilege are the root challenges facing the groups examined in this book.

Common Challenges to Urban Agriculture in New York City

Urban farmers and gardeners in cities throughout the United States face a number of common challenges: lack of sufficient, long-term access to land; inadequate funding; the need for material supplies like soil and seeds; and the need for nonmaterial resources including technical assistance and supportive policies (Hodgson, Campbell, and Bailkey 2011; Kaufman and Bailkey 2000; Pothukuchi and Kaufman 1999; Cohen, Reynolds, and Sanghvi 2012; Cohen and Reynolds 2015; Reynolds 2011; Feenstra, McGrew, and Campbell 1999). Urban growers also run up against the perception that food production is not a legitimate or prudent use of urban space, or that urban food production is not really agriculture (ibid.), though supportive policies in increasing numbers of US and Canadian cities (e.g., Chicago, Seattle, Toronto) suggest that this perception has begun to change (Gilens 2012; Schlozman, Verba, and Brady 2012).

These common challenges to urban agriculture persist in New York. Lack of secure land tenure has long been one of the biggest challenges for community gardens in particular. Access to sufficient quantities of material supplies and other farming and gardening resources is also constrained, although GreenThumb provides some supplies (e.g., compost, lumber, seeds, tools) to its licensed gardens and the Department of Sanitation supplies compost to other city agencies and nonprofits. Some urban farmers and gardeners also need technical assistance, particularly with market gardening, small livestock, and commercial agricultural production. Cornell University Cooperative Extension's Master Gardener Program, along with city programs like GreenThumb, the Department of Sanitation's New York City Compost Project, the New York Botanical Garden's Bronx Green-Up program, and some of Just Food's programs provide assistance with horticulture, composting, pest management, and small-scale chicken keeping. Still, given the expansion of farming and gardening through-out the city, demand often outpaces supply.

As in many cities, a lack of municipal policies to support farming and gardening as a beneficial use of urban space presents an additional challenge. Elsewhere in the nation, some cities have established plans to support urban agriculture (e.g., Minneapolis; see City of Minneapolis 2011) or have included farms and gardens in their municipal plans (e.g., Seattle; see Mukherji and Morales 2010), but New York City has no formal urban agriculture plan (Cohen, Reynolds, and Sanghvi 2012). Despite support from individual agencies, the city's lack of an overarching commitment to grant permanent tenure to gardens and farms on city property keeps these agriculture projects in a risky position. (See Cohen, Reynolds, and Sanghvi 2012 and Cohen and Reynolds 2015 for a more detailed examination of policy and resource needs for urban agriculture in New York City.)

Challenges to Urban Agriculture in Underresourced Communities

All farms and gardens face common challenges regardless of their leaders' socioeconomic status. However, for activists in communities that have been marginalized by economic and political systems, status quo power arrangements present additional, and more formidable, roadblocks to achieving their social justice goals.

LACK OF PRIVILEGE

Access to private funding, government resources, and city services often results from being part of influential networks. Frequently, being part of those networks is connected to social and economic privilege that often comes from higher socioeconomic status. The staff members, volunteers, board members, and neighbors involved in urban agriculture programs in underresourced communities may be less well connected to sources of financial support than are those in more privileged communities. As a result, it can be more difficult for them to secure needed grants, donations, and contracts than it would be if members had strong social and professional connections with wealthy and politically powerful groups.

These patterns were discussed conceptually in preceding chapters, and the urban agriculture activists we spoke with gave examples of how connections or the lack thereof had created disparities among groups citywide. Deborah Greig at East New York Farms! noted that connections to city agencies or political officials had enabled some groups to get access to land and to procure material resources and city services more easily and reliably than others. Tanya Fields at the BLK ProjeK argued that "if [relatively affluent] Park Slope has a vacant lot, it's a lot easier for those folks to get hold of that lot and turn it into a community garden . . . than someplace like the Bronx." Annie Moss at La Finca del Sur recounted the difficulty the organization had in getting the city to provide fencing around its South Bronx site, which is controlled by two different city agencies. Meanwhile, we learned from the white director of an organization that had received much media attention that the city had approached him with an offer to convert some vacant land into a farm.

Disparate social connections also affect organizations' ability to secure funding for their programs. One South Bronx farmer described having hosted a fish fry with the goal of raising $500 to purchase a generator for the farm. The event raised only half that amount, and members of the surrounding low-income community paid for the difference out of their own pockets. Farmers in a low-income Brooklyn neighborhood reported that their operation was "bare bones," without enough funding for basic operating expenses like office heating bills. Greig explained that ENYF! gets a lot of its materials by "just being kind of scroungy"—in other words, using salvaged materials to build the farm's infrastructure. To be sure, many urban agriculture organizations choose to use reclaimed materials for environmental reasons, but finding those materials can be time consuming and somewhat unpredictable and thus of limited reliability as a supply strategy. Though ENYF! is concerned with the environment, its habit of being "scroungy" is as much a result of its financial limitations.

Though most of the activists we spoke with told similar stories of insufficient budgets, there are in fact numerous well-connected urban agriculture programs and businesses securing large grants for their projects in New York City. For example, a highly publicized program at a public school in Greenwich Village received, through a combination of government grants and private donations, more than $1 million to install a rooftop greenhouse (Decker 2012). In recent years, some rooftop farms in the city have received hundreds of thousands of dollars in public subsidies; by and large, the projects receiving this magnitude of funding have been white-led.

These examples suggest that funding is highly uneven and that projects led by better-connected groups (and often led by white people) have easier access to capital and operating funds than those in low-income neighborhoods and led by people of color. Even identifying opportunities to apply for relevant grants requires some degree of familiarity with the philanthropic world (e.g., how funder priorities are set; funding cycles and time lines; how to approach foundation representatives), and connections with foundation staff and previous grant recipients facilitate this type of familiarity. As discussed in preceding chapters, these privileges are more often experienced by whites. People who are struggling financially often lack the funds or the time to contribute to political campaigns or to take time off from work to attend public meetings held during working hours; they may therefore be less likely to develop working relationships within influential networks. The inability to build social and political capital limits a group's ability to strengthen its financial viability or to influence policy makers.

Further, inadequate farm and garden budgets can prevent activist groups from hiring fundraising staff (or any staff, in some cases) and from attracting board members who are well connected and therefore more easily able to solicit donations and grants. These obstacles can make it hard for organizations in low-income communities to become financially stable, limiting their ability to grow or deepen the scope of their work. By contrast, individuals and communities of higher socioeconomic status, or that have social and political connections with privileged groups, often are more readily able to rely on government officials and private funders for support. And funders often privilege those with a funding track record. These are tangible examples of the ways that racial, social, and economic power and privilege present opportunities for some and barriers for others within New York's urban agriculture system.

SCARCITY OF VOLUNTEER TIME

As noted above, lack of time among staff and volunteers is a general challenge for community-based organizations, but time is a doubly scarce resource among gardeners and farmers who grow food while also struggling to make ends meet. The difficulty of securing funds for activities that go beyond gardening and farming requires organizations running community and youth education programs, farmers' markets, and other activities to rely on volunteer or minimally compensated labor (including their own). In some communities, finding volunteers who are willing and able to work on farms and gardens is relatively easy, particularly in light of the current popularity of urban agriculture in cities like New York. Yet this is not always true in lower-income communities whose residents often have longer commutes to work and might have to work multiple jobs or during nights and weekends to make ends meet. For example, Greig explained that many members involved with ENYF! work full-time jobs and that "this farming thing is like a passion and it's not their full-time job. So . . . when we ask them to come to a million meetings, it feels terrible. And they come, and I think it's because they have a really strong commitment, but I also feel bad that I'm [asking them to spend their time with us]."

Assembling a core group of participants is a challenge that not only affects how many hands are available to plant, tend, and harvest food, or to rally for political change, but how resources from agencies and donors are distributed. Donors and public agencies typically fund groups that demonstrate active community involvement, which usually is measured by the number of volunteers and the amount of time people commit to a garden or farm project or related activities. Keeping track of the number of people involved in a group's activities requires at least some degree of record-keeping skills and can be a challenge in light of limited volunteer time. As a result, it can be difficult to convince supporters to invest money and other resources.

LIMITED FINANCIAL RESOURCES IN THE COMMUNITY

Several activists noted that the amount of fund-raising and in-kind donations groups can solicit from local residents and business owners is limited when the potential donors may themselves face significant financial constraints. Maggie Cheney at Ecostation:NY, which oversees Bushwick Campus Farm, contended that "if you [have] a community garden in an affluent place in Manhattan, you're going to have more resources pooled to you purely [because of] who's attending that garden. . . . [You're] going to have a lot less income going towards [a] project in Brownsville, Bushwick, or East New York [in Brooklyn]." Community-based fund-raisers are also apt to raise larger amounts of money in wealthier neighborhoods, where residents have more personal financial resources and may also be able to solicit funds from friends and business colleagues.

While the activists described in this book obtain donations from businesses and individuals outside the communities in which they work, the success of such efforts is tied to the professional and social networks of their organizations' leadership, which can again be challenging in low-income communities. Greig provided an example of this challenge for ENYF!: "The restaurants in this area don't have the option to donate supplies, or space, or time. . . . We don't have a lot of relationships outside the neighborhood, because that's not what we're good at, and that's not what we do." Speaking about school gardens, Cheney explained, "A lot of after-school projects may be funded by the PTA. . . . If you're [at] a school that's in a really affluent area, you're going to get more money towards that urban agriculture project . . . through the PTA."

Financial limitations also make it difficult for organizations in low-income communities to support entrepreneurial ventures and small business development, a goal of several of the activists with whom we spoke. Some believe that their farms and gardens can foster the development of microenterprises, which they view as a way to advance self-determination and increase wealth and economic equity. However, scaling up cottage food production and complying with business and food-safety regulations requires access to capital. Washington pointed out that while many people in low-income communities have extensive experience producing value-added food products like jams or salsas, far fewer have the resources to turn these activities into income-producing small businesses. By contrast, Washington observed that many entrepreneurs producing artisanal foods for sale are young, middle-class whites who possess personal financial resources. Referring to the growing specialty food and beverage industry in New York City, she insisted, "I need to see my people get a piece of [the] pie. I don't want to see my people on the outside looking in, as people come in and make all types of beers, and all types of pickles, and all types of salsas. . . . I want to see an economy in which grants are given to low-income people to start enterprises and businesses." While larger projects like Farm School NYC were designed in part to help bridge this gap (the school also has courses on culinary arts and starting businesses), smaller urban agriculture projects that have limited or no development staff to raise funds for their work often are not able to provide the capital needed to help entrepreneurial gardeners and farmers realize an income from their culinary expertise.

STEREOTYPES

Beyond the reality of challenging economic conditions, simplistic stereotypes about underresourced communities can also pose challenges for activists situated in low-income communities. Farmers' markets associated with farms and gardens offer a telling example.

As discussed in chapter 3, many of the activists we spoke with run markets to provide fresh, healthy food, along with job training and part-time employment opportunities for youth and adults. These markets typically stock food produced at their farms or gardens, in addition to products sourced from farms outside New York City. Several accept USDA Farmers' Market Nutrition Program coupons and Health Bucks from the city's Health Department. These government programs are designed to provide low-income consumers with more purchasing power at farmers' markets by supplementing their emergency food benefits. Projects like ENYF! have been able to sustain and even expand their on-farm markets by accepting these emergency food payments, thereby increasing sales and the revenue that farmers derive from the markets, in addition to increasing food access in the community.

Yet by and large, attracting and retaining regional farmers willing to sell at markets in low-income neighborhoods like East New York, Bed-Stuy, and parts of the Bronx remains a challenge. Robert Jackson offered an example of a farmer from Brooklyn Rescue Mission's market who decided it would be more lucrative to sell at a market in higher-income Fort Greene, where he believed he could charge more. "It wasn't, 'I don't like your community,'" Jackson explained; rather, the decision was based on the farmer's perception of where sales would be highest. And while this particular example can be understood as rational business management by a farmer needing to maintain financial solvency, several activists, including Greig and Washington, noted that it was difficult to get farmers to sell at their markets. They attributed this difficulty to a stereotype that residents of low-income neighborhoods cannot afford to shop at farmers' markets, despite the fact that their markets had attracted a stable customer base by offering fresh, healthy, and culturally appropriate products and by increasing consumer buying power through use of federal food programs like SNAP.

Other racial and class stereotypes have also presented challenges to some of the farmers' market programs. For example, as discussed in chapter 3, Washington observed that some regional farmers' fear that low-income Bronx neighborhoods are inherently crime-ridden had limited the success of some of the markets she helped found. The fact that many neighborhoods in the Bronx have predominantly black or Latino/a populations suggests that this fear is rooted not only in stereotypes that all low-income communities have high rates of violent crime but in an often subconscious, erroneous association of people of color with illegal activities and violence (see chapter 1). Perceptions—even erroneous ones—can negatively affect markets in some of New York's lowest-income communities and communities of color, adding to the challenges the markets in these communities face.

Challenges to Urban Agriculture as Social Justice Activism

Most not-for-profit organizations rely on grants, donations, and other sources of charitable or in-kind support. Securing funding is a competitive process, and increasingly so for urban agriculture organizations: farming and gardening are growing in popularity, and thus the numbers of potential grant seekers have increased. Urban agriculture activists working on social justice issues, however, face additional challenges in raising funds to support their programs because funding that is available for farming and gardening is often targeted toward projects that aim to produce commonly understood benefits (such as food production or children's education) rather than for anti-oppression work.

The limited funding designated for activist work has led to intense competition that in some cases has disadvantaged existing activist organizations. For example, in researching this book, we learned about groups duplicating activities and offering services that other organizations had been providing for a longer time—in many cases with more expertise and greater capacity—because those activities and services had proven to be fundable. Fleming described competition for funding as "each one for himself," adding "[this] is a crazy thing, because this is a [social] movement." In the quest for grant money, some organizations may even extend their efforts beyond their primary areas of competency or launch activities outside their core mission. These are risky strategies for groups not well equipped to deliver particular types of services. Deborah Greig observed a trend of other organizations raising funds to do work similar to initiatives at ENYF! She noted the danger of this kind of "mission creep" to raise money for a nonprofit: "I think sometimes it's fine . . . if it's a very different aspect of an effort. But . . . there's just organizations that are good at certain things, and they should be supported to do those things." Though in some instances there can be benefits from organizations modeling their new activities on what they have learned or observed from other groups, there are also downsides to continually adding programs just because funding is available. As Greig noted, "When an organization tries to do too much, I think they can also spread themselves thin and confuse the message that they're trying to communicate" and what they are trying to accomplish.

There are a number of private foundations interested in speaking about and funding social justice work. Yet their numbers are small and their resources limited compared to the larger universe of funders that support the broad idea of food systems change without a more specific focus on social justice or social equity. Bee Ayer at BK Farmyards noted her own belief that "the funders . . . willing to fund projects that directly deal with racism, or talk about racism even, often have a lot less money . . . but still have their own ideas about what the organization that is doing that work needs to look like [in terms of structure and programming]."

URBAN AGRICULTURE AS A DE FACTO STRATEGY TO ADVANCE SOCIAL JUSTICE

A related challenge for urban agriculture organizations focused explicitly on social justice is competition from groups that use the rhetoric of social justice primarily to compete for funding. In keeping with the dominant narrative discussed in chapter 1, many groups describe their programming as advancing social justice by helping improve food access or supporting economic development—and they may in fact accomplish some of these goals. Yet some activists who have been working explicitly on social justice as a core mission, addressing issues of race and class oppression directly, see this rhetoric as opportunistic and inappropriately competitive, especially when farm and garden initiatives that get funding for social justice work address these issues only superficially. Yonnette Fleming, for example, criticized urban agriculture organizations that describe themselves as working on social justice when it is not their main focus. She observed, "They all say they are [social justice groups]. They all say they're doing exactly what I'm doing."

Further, sometimes catch phrases that are empty signifiers are used to describe organizations' social justice work. Figueroa suggested that the term "food justice" is being "co-opted, or conveniently used to add some kind of moral resonance to the work that [many groups are] doing, when [their work] has nothing to do with justice." He added that often the individuals ostensibly doing work to advance food justice have no deep understanding of the social, political, and economic injustices that lead to inequitable food access, hunger, malnutrition. Figueroa gave an example of a meeting he attended about food justice that was scheduled for the daytime (rather than after working hours), illustrating that the event organizers were insensitive to how holding meetings during the day could exclude those low-income or working-class individuals who cannot take the day off to attend a community meeting. He noted, "This is not going to [include] folks from the impacted community. It's folks [from outside the community] that are getting paid to do [this] work."

There are also concerns about what might be considered a form of "carpet-bagging," when groups initiate projects in communities they have never worked in because they have access to resources that allow them to do so and see an opportunity to fund the work. When groups receive funds to start new community-focused food projects (rather than partnering with or passing funds through to existing groups), existing organizations that have been committed to helping particular communities for many years, often while struggling to raise money to support their own efforts, may suffer from competition for funds; this hinders the growth potential of existing groups. As an example, Deborah Greig described the efforts of Slow Food's New York City group to create an educational garden in East New York: "A couple of years ago, they thought it would be really sexy to take over a garden in East New York and run it as a children's garden, which is awesome—I'm glad that a garden is being used, but . . . [if] that's not your forte and you have all these resources, why aren't you giving them directly to the community to do [the project] in their neighborhood? Why do you want to start another farmers' market, when ours is two blocks away? Let's work together!"

DIFFICULTY GETTING SUPPORT FOR "RADICAL" WORK

A more subtle way in which competition for resources disadvantages social justice–focused urban agriculture groups is that activists feel pressure to downplay what some funders and more conservative stakeholders might consider radical activism: initiatives that address politically controversial social justice issues like racial oppression, wealth disparities, or immigrant rights. Activists we spoke with described the difficulty of finding funders willing to support work that is critical of mainstream economic structures or that explicitly seeks to dismantle racism. Some activists explained that it was at times difficult to discuss social justice issues and the nature of oppression with funders plainly and frankly. Some thought that representing their organizations as stridently activist was also a liability when trying to secure funds.

Moreover, when funding goes to organizations that run educational or youth development programs that are *less* overtly political, it sends a signal to those focused explicitly on addressing oppression (a politically controversial notion) that they may have a harder time raising funds.

Fleming pointed to larger urban agriculture projects like Red Hook Community Farm, run by the nonprofit Added Value. The farm was founded and led by white directors beginning in 2000. When such programs attract a lot of funding, she explained, the message to groups like Hattie Carthan Community Garden is, "If I do what [Added Value] is doing . . . I might get funders. But if I'm linked in the way I'm linked in to the youths [that I work with] . . . and just cracking them wide open this way, I'm going to have [more] difficulty financing my program." Regardless of specific funding decisions, the success of more politically moderate organizations gives the impression that the politics of a group influences how well it raises money. This impression may dissuade certain activist groups from seeking particular sources of funds or may cause them to temper their messages or their work.

Similarly, according to Ray Figueroa, funding often goes to projects that attempt to increase the availability of fruits and vegetables in a community by subsidizing their cost, but less money is available for urban agriculture programs that address underlying unemployment, poverty, and the resulting psychological stresses. Figueroa noted that "well-meaning efforts such as the farmers' markets, [city-funded] Green Carts, [and] Healthy Bodegas [programs]—they're good, they're stepping in the right direction, but they still have not cracked the nut about poverty in the community." Successful grant applications for groups focused on these deeper issues usually are based on models of change that are more conservative than those that actually underlie the organization's work, or are written in such a way that the organizational and program goals appear to be allied with those of the prospective funder. Yet even if this strategy secures more grants, it can be detrimental to an organization if it influences the group's politics, mission, or methods over time.

An unwillingness to support radical change may also motivate government agencies, including local offices of citywide agencies, to withhold administrative, material, and financial support from organizations with a more explicitly anti-oppression praxis. Government agencies are typically organized to address particular mandates, not broader issues such as social justice. They are also inherently conservative in their approach to addressing the issues they do deal with. As a result, they may not support social justice programming, and urban agriculture organizations may end up conforming to policies not designed with social justice in mind.

For example, Ayer recounted the Department of Education's focus on whether the students participating in the Youth Farm at the city's High School for Public Service were being exposed to agricultural chemicals, rather than giving credit for the program's emphasis on teaching "health and justice and a more holistic form of education." Stephen Ritz, who is white, explained that in his experience, city agencies preferred to maintain the status quo and weren't always supportive of innovations. This preference creates challenges for urban agriculture programs like his Green Bronx Machine, which at the time of our interview operated within public schools to improve academic performance, build responsibility and self-esteem, and teach students how to participate in civic life. Ritz noted, "A lot of people don't want to see things change too much because [the system] works for a certain group of people, and it's worked for a long time. So when you tell people that you can change academic performance by growing vegetables, they don't want to hear that!"

Tanya Fields at the BLK ProjeK described her experience with a local police precinct that objected to her work: "[Calling out] a system of oppression got me into a bit of trouble, and the police in my community started to harass me and were refusing to give me [street activity] permits or anything. They had the ability to prevent me from being visible and being out in the community doing the work. . . . We wanted to do a block party for two years, [but] we weren't given street activity permits for anything we [applied] for. We weren't getting park permits for anything we put in for." Eventually, Fields found a supportive City Council member to work around the obstacle, but the example illustrates a broader problem: activist groups may face resistance to their political positions and have to confront city officials unwilling to support work that critiques the social and political status quo. While some individuals may have personal contacts and networks that include sympathetic officials who can help overcome obstacles, the structural barriers to anti-oppression work remain.

CEDING TO CONSERVATISM

To avoid alienating funders, activists with whom we spoke discussed the need to describe their anti-oppression activities using less politically charged terms ("food justice," for example, which is becoming common in mainstream discourse). Ayer observed that "there is a type of language that you have to use to get funding for projects, and if you are not willing to use that language, I think it is very difficult . . . if you are very up front and blunt about values, as far as dismantling racism, or equity in general. . . . I've found, in individual interactions with funders, that you can see them physically recoil from those kinds of things. I don't think that we are at a point where most people . . . in positions of power . . . [with] access to a lot of money are actually really interested in the promotion of dismantling their own position of power."

As Fleming noted, "The more you understand to speak that language [of funders], the more you can [get funding]. Somebody can start to listen to you, because it's almost like a code."

Learning to "speak the language of funders" often involves learning how to navigate structural forms of oppression such as social codes that make talking about wealth disparity and racism taboo in many high-income and white-dominated settings. Individuals who have not learned these communications styles through their own life experiences and social groups may be compelled to develop these skills to find support for their programs. The race and class dynamics of this reality notwithstanding, describing anti-oppression programs in more moderate terms may affect the integrity of the programs themselves. While cautious phrasing may seem like an innocuous and strategic way to obtain resources from funders or government agencies, when activists must use code words or phrases that may mean something significantly less challenging to the status quo (like "food access" rather than "workplace democracy" or "wealth redistribution"), they create certain expectations among funders and program staff that their work will be decidedly less radical than they actually intend. This mismatch between expectations and intent risks alienating funders who may at some point down the line learn that grantees' values are different from their own. Describing an organization's mission and activities using politically unobjectionable terms as a way of securing money from funders may also eventually change the identity of a group and the nature of its work if in doing so, the group focuses its efforts on projects that are less politically challenging.

Some of the activists with whom we spoke have come to terms with the fact that many urban agriculture groups receiving public or philanthropic resources have different goals, including the goal of farming for profit, or that groups approach social justice in very different ways. As Greig explained, "Our model is really different from somebody else's model, and that's fine. And I think it took me a long time to actually be OK with that, the fact that we have a really strong social justice mission, and I perceive another organization as not having the same social justice mission, and that's OK. It took me a really long time to stop being angry about that, I guess." But the differences among groups may nevertheless influence the missions, programming, and success of activist organizations, even if those organizations come to accept that others are more focused on production or profit.

DOCUMENTING SOCIAL JUSTICE OUTCOMES

Yet another constraint on urban agriculture activists who are focused on advancing social justice is the complexity of demonstrating results that are difficult to quantify. Funders and policy makers who support urban agriculture often evaluate success in terms of easily quantifiable outcomes such as the number of youth participants or pounds of food produced. Yet the activists with whom we spoke explained that an emphasis on such quantifiable outcomes made it difficult to obtain funding for operational costs associated with activities like anti-racism training, which might not be related to easily measurable activities such as food production. To Fleming, the problem is that "when you talk about a food movement and food system, a funder really doesn't understand what you're saying, and how . . . you could think your work could even impact many of these things." Understaffed organizations may also lack capacity to conduct the types of evaluations that funders increasingly require, not only at the end of a funded project but during the application stage, as proof of an organization's track record.

Moreover, the focus by funders and policy makers on narrow and easily measurable results can make it difficult to secure support for activities like educational programming on social justice issues that do not match narrowly defined curriculum standards. The importance placed on quantitative evaluation of outcomes also hinders organizations that lack the staff time and expertise to evaluate their own work, and organizations whose work involves long-term social justice outcomes like community building, empowerment, and shifting attitudes about one's role in society, which are difficult to measure. In the view of Stephen Ritz, who uses urban agriculture to motivate his students to learn both core curriculum content and how to become productive citizens, education administrators have very narrow criteria for measuring his students' success. In Ritz's words, "It's really about test scores. . . . I could cure cancer, and cure AIDS, and that would be wonderful . . . but people would say, 'That's great! What about test scores?'"

Organizational Challenges for Activist Groups

In addition to the difficulty of raising funds on an uneven and increasingly competitive playing field, some urban agriculture activist organizations also confront organizational barriers. Philanthropies generally require their grantees to have specific organizational structures that many small farm and garden groups lack, such as 501(c)(3) nonprofit status and a board of directors, along with a track record of securing previous funding. Having such requirements may seem reasonable from the perspective of fiduciary responsibility, but these requirements may also (and inadvertently) disadvantage very new organizations, small groups, and farms and gardens lacking administrative support—precisely the types of organizations that often work in low-income communities and communities of color in New York City. Fiscal sponsors like Green Guerillas can pass through funds to some small groups, but their reach is limited.

Several of the activists we spoke with suggested that the application process for a grant is often so complex, requiring lengthy and detailed paperwork even for small requests, that applying is beyond their available time and administrative capacity. The process of securing funding—networking to develop relationships with funders, writing compelling proposals, and filling out documents—requires attention, accounting capacity, administrative expertise, and prior fund-raising success, all scarce resources for small and understaffed organizations that lack dedicated grant-writing and administrative staff.

The complexity of securing and then reporting on the use of philanthropic or city dollars has caused some groups to give up seeking grant funding to support their projects. What they considered a slim chance of being funded did not, in their opinion, justify the time and effort required to prepare applications. When underresourced groups give up on fund-raising, better-resourced groups may fill the void, obtaining available funding and further exacerbating disparities between large and small, established and new, white- and nonwhite-led organizations. Moreover, organizations that do not apply for grants because of capacity constraints may not have other sources of money, like major donors or membership dues. Rather, as exemplified by many of the groups discussed in this book, they generally make do with less and may forgo opportunities to strengthen and expand their programs. The use of fiscal sponsors to provide nonprofit status and assist with grant administration can also lead to complications, as fiscal sponsors (which can be nonprofits themselves) in some cases compete with the organizations they are assisting for philanthropic resources.

Several of the activists we spoke with described this as a form of racism in the philanthropic community, hindering their efforts to get funding for their projects. As Figueroa explained, "For some reason—and it's de facto institutionalized racism, and I don't mean in the narrow sense of discrimination—there is a structure that resources accrue to groups that are already resourced. . . . And we see that because of how dollars seem to be flowing. And so folks like Karen Washington, myself, and others that are in the community, we're beginning to lift this up. We're beginning to lift this up on the urban agriculture task force, we're going to lift this up with the funders, that there has been a real disparity in the so-called Food Justice Movement."

The Challenges of Not Being Trendy

Curiosity and the attention paid to unusual agriculture projects often drives support. Several activists pointed out that projects that are considered innovative because they occur on rooftops or use new and intriguing technologies (e.g., aquaponics or hydroponic greenhouses) cost more but also tend to attract larger grants than more traditional on-the-ground growing techniques. The interest in such projects can often disadvantage groups that do not have access to large grants for capital investments, or those that choose to focus on growing lower-cost produce on conventional sites, using techniques that are familiar to their community and don't require expensive investments. Moreover, the use of new technologies isn't always appropriate for organizations focused on growing produce, training community members in farming, and doing educational and social justice work. For example, Greig explained that while "people are . . . obsessive about rooftops, . . . in East New York it just doesn't make sense [because] there's a lot of vacant land, and [rooftop agriculture is] really expensive. . . . So if a funder's like, 'Oh, but we have this money, are you interested in doing a rooftop?,' [we say,] 'No, we're not.'"

There are several potential reasons for the bias toward the new and trendy. Government officials tend to support what they believe the public is interested in, and their beliefs are influenced by what the media portrays as fashionable. Philanthropic organizations often seek to support what they consider innovations that have the potential to change practices. Both government agencies and private funders are often interested in technologies that might have ancillary benefits, including job creation. Media also tend to showcase trendy or high-tech projects or well-known, well-funded projects and those run by individuals comfortable interacting with reporters (Reynolds 2014). Beyond shifting attention to food production techniques that may be unaffordable or inappropriate for the social justice groups we interviewed, media coverage of technologies like rooftop greenhouse production or aquaponics systems can contribute to maintaining the power of dominant groups (Entman 2007; Ryan, Carragee, and Meinhofer 2001). As Maggie Cheney at Bushwick Campus Farm argued,

> There are just certain groups of people who like rooftop farming—they're like these icons. And they're usually white. And they have a lot [of] . . . access to media coverage. Versus [a] just-as-or-even-more-talented community gardener in a different area [who is] maybe black, or Latino, or a recent Asian immigrant . . . just not doing what they're doing to get [in the] public eye. I think there's a disparity there.

As discussed in the beginning of this book, less media attention to low-tech or underresourced urban agriculture groups—and conversely a focus on newer, capital-intensive technologies—has the potential to distort the popular understanding of who is engaged in urban farming and gardening in New York City. This misunderstanding hinders the efforts of activists situated in low-income communities and communities of color seeking support for their work.

Challenges of Political Disenfranchisement

We heard from interviewees in different contexts about urban agriculture activists of color "not having a seat at the policy table" and about the unwillingness of those in power to share or relinquish their power and privilege. This concern was raised in reference to decisions about the development of license procedures for community gardens, the development of former City Council speaker Christine Quinn's FoodWorks policy plan (and subsequent City Council legislation), and efforts by city agencies to identify additional parcels of land for urban agriculture. Yonnette Fleming echoed Washington's observation at the beginning of this chapter: "When we look at the writers and the authors [of food policy documents], we find out that these are the same people that have been involved in every single food agenda in New York—meaning the oppressive ones too, that held us [back]. So, to me, it's 'How do we get everyone involved, and speaking, and addressing their concerns in an equitable way?'"

"Not having a seat at the policy table" is a phrase that describes a number of ways activists can experience political inequality. The most direct effect is to be left out of policy-development processes by, for example, being excluded from committees drafting policy documents or not being invited to testify before City Council committees. While open-government laws and public-participation requirements enable anyone to provide opinions and recommendations on pending laws and regulations, those invited to be advisors or scheduled to speak at the start of a hearing are given more visibility and thus a more prominent voice in the process. Moreover, despite the broader mix of stakeholders involved in policy in recent years, government documents like strategies and reports can be written without public input. Those documents can dramatically shape policy discourse when released.

"Having a seat at the table" also means that one's ideas are taken seriously and that policy is designed to meet one's needs. If a community is less involved politically by virtue of lower voting rates, smaller political contributions, or exclusion from established political networks, as communities of lower socioeconomic status tend to be, they will have less power within the political system than communities of higher socioeconomic status. Structural barriers to political participation (e.g., higher incarceration rates, foreign citizenship status) and higher rates of poverty in communities of color have tended to give more power to predominantly white communities. Gender-based disparities that mirror the larger world of agriculture exist as well. According to Fleming, "Like the bigger picture of farming, where the brunt of the work is shouldered by women, we find that same phenomenon here. However, we do not find a unified voice or a focused vision that places women at the core of this work . . . often the tasks that are relegated to us are more of the burden work, as with agriculture historically, as exists everywhere."

Unequal political influence can also result in less media attention, less interest in an organization by funders, and less attention by city officials, in a vicious circle leading to further political disempowerment. Because resources often flow to communities and organizations that are considered politically important, influential, and thus able to make change, activist groups that are considered politically marginal often have a harder time raising funds for their work, which in turn keeps them struggling and politically marginalized. The feeling of disempowerment, which can come from seeing relatively empowered communities getting desired policy changes while those with less clout struggle for that "seat at the table," can lead to policy disengagement. For example, Tanya Fields described how the ease with which white, upper-middle-class activists gain access to vacant city parcels for gardens or farms can perpetuate a myth of white superiority, contributing to a sense of disempowerment among low-income people of color, further alienating individuals from the political system. According to Fields, "It's insulting and painful, and it is a manifestation of the sort of racist paradigm that we live in, that continues to promote this myth of white superiority that sort of 'formally well-educated' white people can come into a community and make more headway than you can in the community you live in, and you have got to work twice as hard to accomplish half of what they can when they come in."

She went on to explain that when white-led organizations come into communities of color to work on urban agriculture and food issues,

> it continues to perpetuate this missionary ideology that young white people will come into communities to save "the natives" . . . and you have the people that have lived there for a very long time that have tried to do this work and [they] come

up against obstacle, obstacle, obstacle, and a lot of times they can't even find help from their own elected officials. It continues to perpetuate this sort of paradigm of white people as the arbiters of justice and goodness and rightness, and associating whiteness with rightness and the rest of us as sort of the recipients of altruism from white folks.

Fields added: "One of the biggest challenges for me is how to direct that in a way that creates productive conversation that doesn't alienate people and doesn't make white folks feel like . . . they are somehow not welcome to do good things."

As discussed in chapter 4, many of the activists we spoke with insisted that to create more socially just systems, people who have historically been least advantaged in various ways within US society (i.e., people of color, women, people with both low incomes and low intergenerational wealth) must be recognized for leading change in their communities. To these activists, leadership requires power. Some of that leadership can be generated internally, as organizations train and support farmers and gardeners, but effective leadership within broader systems also requires recognition by people and institutions beyond the organizations themselves. Urban agriculture programs embedded in communities that lack power face significant challenges that even leaders are unable to surmount.

Rooting Out Power Dynamics

As this chapter has illustrated, urban agriculture activists and organizations that are focused on social justice—particularly those in low-income communities and communities of color—often face numerous challenges that are rooted in, and made more formidable by, the very structural forms of oppression that their programs are intended to address.

In addition to typical challenges such as securing land tenure, funding, or supplies, the uneven power dynamics within a city's social system impede the success of activists working in communities that have limited economic or political power. Garnering sufficient funding is more difficult for such groups because of the relatively limited ability of neighborhood residents to provide financial donations and because larger sums are often obtained via connections with influential and well-resourced individuals—connections that are more common in economically privileged communities. The ability to secure land for new farms and gardens can also be tied to activists' working relationships with influential groups, including city agency staff, elected officials, or private landowners, in addition to activists' familiarity with policies that govern land use. Privileged members of society often develop these types of relationships and specific forms of knowledge through day-to-day experiences, while those in less privileged communities may not.

Moreover, to remain true to their goals to confront and dismantle oppressive structures in their work for social justice, activists often must speak out about racism, class disparities, and other forms of structural oppression. Yet within a society that privileges white culture and capitalist structures, their theories about what underlies inequality may make even the most progressive government agencies or philanthropies uncomfortable, unwilling, or unable to support their programs. This outcome can perpetuate resource disparities between groups. Without adequate resources and policy support, anti-oppression initiatives are less successful or far-reaching than they could be. As a result, these challenges reduce the potential of urban agriculture overall to advance social justice. The work of activists such as those described in this book may not be as trendy as rooftop, hydroponic, or other higher-tech projects (though activists focused on social justice can and do also engage in these forms of food production). But until equitable food and environmental systems have been achieved, work to advance social justice through urban agriculture will continue to be relevant and important.

While deeply entrenched in existing policies and dominant societal norms, the challenges discussed in this chapter can be solved. The urban agriculture activists highlighted in this book are creating strategic opportunities to overcome the dual barriers structural oppression creates—to their farm and garden programs and to their communities—and thus to create a more socially just city. Their work provides models for additional urban farmers and gardeners, particularly leaders invested in building power in their own communities.

These challenges also underscore the strong need for urban agriculture initiatives whose goal is the advancement of social justice to focus on uneven power dynamics. Activists described in this book do this through their activities (chapter 3), by putting into practice their visions of socially just society (chapter 4), and by working for policy change (chapter 5). Much of this work involves collaborations and networks with other individuals and groups.

Activists need not stand alone in their work. Government agencies, philanthropies, nongovernmental organizations, and other institutions and individual members of society can take active roles in creating these changes. This work "in the trenches" can also be complemented by initiatives that help shift society's understanding of urban agriculture as it relates to social justice. Such efforts are one of the strengths of scholarly work, the topic to which we turn next.

CHAPTER 7

Rethinking Scholarship to Advance Social Justice

One winter evening, we invited several urban agriculture activists, along with a few faculty members and staff from New York City colleges, to a public forum at The New School to discuss how researchers and community-based activists might work together more effectively to advance social justice.

During this forum, we asked questions about the roles that researchers (in educational institutions, government agencies, or the broader community) might play in advancing activists' work toward dismantling oppression. We were interested in identifying how the resources of non-land-grant institutions such as liberal arts universities, schools for design and public health, and community colleges could be used to help activist urban agriculture groups. We also wanted to publicly challenge the primacy of institutional expertise on urban agriculture in a realm of city life with which farmers and gardeners have generations of experience. The goals of the forum were therefore to initiate a public dialogue about the intersection between academic and community-based urban agriculture activism in New York City, and to highlight that while academic "experts" often have support from institutions and recognition of their knowledge in the public sphere, farmers and gardeners are experts in their own right.

Although we were aware of examples of innovative and mutually supportive working relationships between academics and community-based groups, many of the activists we spoke with have generally viewed academic research as irrelevant at best and exploitative at worst. The forum provided a venue to confront this perception head-on by highlighting activists' experiences working with academic researchers and, in the process, to discuss strategies to make campus-community collaborations more effective in advancing social justice through urban agriculture. Panelists including Leticia Alanis, Maggie Cheney, Ray Figueroa, and Yonnette Fleming pointed to the need for more collaborative research processes that break down power structures privileging professional expertise over lived experience. They emphasized community-organizing approaches and the importance of valuing diverse forms of knowledge. The discussion evolved to question the very idea of scholarship. Panelists underscored the fact that community-based activists can also be scholars; Fleming emphasized the point, urging her fellow scholars to "observe the power line" that is often drawn between university researchers and those working outside institutions of higher education.

The event amplified and extended themes that emerged in the individual interviews we conducted in researching this book, as well as ideas that have continually influenced our own action-oriented research. Scholarship can help legitimize the work of marginalized community-based initiatives, but it does not always do so, as the panelists at this event were clear to point out. Inequitable power structures can impoverish not only those at the bottom of a hierarchy, but also the very processes through which social and political structures are negotiated. These dynamics can surface in any system, including in the research process, despite the best intentions of those involved.

However, academic researchers are also community members, and can work with community-based activists to advance social justice. The forum made clear that seeing the world in dichotomies (e.g., researcher *or* activist; community member *or* academic; farmer *or* scholar) limits our vision of possibility and thus limits the potential to take action against oppression. Even though academics are not the sole creators or proprietors of knowledge, at times we have opportunities, fleeting though they might be, to broaden awareness about structural foundations of injustice.

Chapters 2–6 examined some of the structural and political dynamics of New York City's urban agriculture system, though not without consideration of individuals' identity and status. This chapter takes a more reflective approach, drawing from our interviews with urban agriculture activists, a subsequent focus group, and the public forum described above. It explores the roles that research and scholarship can play in advancing social justice through urban agriculture and food system activism more broadly, beginning with a discussion about how research can actually contribute to *in*justice and then suggesting strategies for research and scholarship that may be more liberatory. The chapter consciously questions the notion of scholarship and expertise and explores ways to overcome the uneven power dynamics among academics and community-based activists.

Acknowledging Research Injustice as a Step toward Change

Professional and ethical standards require researchers, regardless of their institutional affiliations, to avoid harm to individuals, and colleges and universities have institutional review boards to ensure that research conducted under their auspices follows protocols to protect research participants. But risks to communities and organizations rarely receive more than a brief mention in the professional and ethical literature, and as a result, few researchers consider, and review boards generally overlook, such risks.

However, just as farming and gardening projects can reinforce unjust structures underlying the specific conditions that members of a community and their supporters hope to change, even well-intentioned urban agriculture research can reproduce and perpetuate injustice at a community scale. As with other practices addressed in this book, urban agriculture research can do this by reinforcing dominant narratives about low-income communities of color as monolithic and unhealthy environments; by focusing primarily on deficiencies instead of community assets and innovations; by taking information from communities without returning valuable analysis; or by co-opting activists' ideas.

Often, these trends take root in the early phases of a study, when researchers select a site or group for a collaborative study. Researchers may decide to partner with larger or well-known organizations, providing time and expertise to already well resourced (and well connected) groups, overlooking those operating on shoestring budgets because they are presumably less influential or less representative of some fictitious "generalizable" reality. Conversely, researchers may choose to focus on underresourced organizations or low-income neighborhoods as research *subjects*, framing these subjects as deficient, rather than using the power of analytical writing to elucidate community assets and organizational successes in the face of challenging socioeconomic conditions. Individuals in small organizations may spend time contributing to studies that lead to accolades for the researchers (e.g., graduate degrees, promotions, and other forms of professional recognition) but little change for the community in question. The time invested can sap the human resources of a small organization for little direct return, even if the results advance theoretical knowledge or produce diffuse long-term benefits.

Tanya Fields at the BLK ProjeK explained how these risks had been manifested in her South Bronx community:

> Research has been the one [thing] that has been elusive and [that I] very much want. A lot of times researchers will align themselves with these very well funded [groups]. . . . So for smaller organizations, like [mine], getting a researcher to come in [is difficult]—unless it's like Columbia or NYU wanting to come in and talk about one of these dismal [public health] statistics that I am so sick of hearing about. We don't have access to researchers that can help us create reports that will be used to change the landscape on a legislative level, on a public health level, on a policy level, or [in terms of] what happens in our community. [I]t's one more way that we get disenfranchised and aren't able to make change.

EXTRACTIVE RESEARCH

The injustices that can result from research extend to the implementation and reporting phases as well. Many of the farmers and gardeners with whom we spoke had been asked on numerous occasions to participate in research projects, particularly studies documenting and describing urban agriculture activities in New York City. Several who agreed to participate felt that the researchers had gleaned information that was of interest to their own research programs or to their institutions but was not helpful to the activists' community-based organizations. Bee Ayer at BK Farmyards explained,

> Often it does not feel that research is driven by the groundwork. It is driven by whatever the researcher thinks they should research or are interested in. I think that [such] research doesn't have a place because it's not always useful. Even if it is the most amazing study it may not be applicable [to the community], or at that period of time, or [connect] with what people have the capacity to [do].

Deborah Greig at East New York Farms! expressed a similar concern, noting, "I think a lot of times people come in and do research and just talk to people and leave, and then there's this paper, and that actually doesn't really change anything on our level." Activists explained that these processes had often felt extractive, in that outside researchers had extracted information but had not returned the products of a study (e.g., insights, a report, or even some form of recognition) to the participating organizations or communities. As a result, some activists categorically declined the increasingly frequent requests to participate in outsider-led research.

Research can also be extractive by broadcasting "best practices," which often are presumed to benefit all stakeholders in a given system. On one hand, several activists spoke about the need for researchers to help urban agriculture organizations share best practices related to farming techniques, educational methods, and labor management. Ayer, for one, holds this view; she explained that while sharing information would be helpful, BK Farmyards doesn't "have the time or capacity to do that kind of work with other organizations." On the other hand, several activists raised the point that sharing their organizations' practices could also be exploitative because once a researcher identifies an innovation and disseminates it to other groups or funders, it is likely to be replicated or appropriated by others, diminishing its novelty and reducing the innovator's ability to secure future funding.

The Reverend DeVanie Jackson at Brooklyn Rescue Mission said that she had experienced this form of "extraction" when applying for grants. Although grant applications are not research per se, they typically require applicants to articulate theories of change, tell how their activities will lead to change, and document evidence of the effectiveness of their programs, which often requires baseline research. Though it is understandable that funders would need to understand the vision and impact of projects they support, this can be a double-edged sword; in detailing their innovative plans, strategies, and programs, activists make them available to other groups, which may end up hampering their future ability to obtain funds for the ideas they've developed. As Jackson explained, "Once you share a good idea with a funder, it's 'on blast!' And that's part of the agreement with the funding, too, [that] there are no secrets. So you might get one grant off, and [then] they're recommending all of your best practices to everybody else and you never get a chance to get that second grant [for that work]! So then you have to come up with something new again! And it's a vicious cycle! . . . I'm going to have to keep coming up with new projects every year and hope that some subjective funder finds my request for money attractive, [or] appealing!"

Similarly, Yonnette Fleming described the phenomenon of researchers writing about her innovations as akin to "stealing ideas . . . and the displacement of people with those ideas." She explained that

> once they get the idea, the person [behind the idea] is no longer relevant. The person's struggle is no longer relevant. The resources [needed] are no longer relevant . . . as long as they have the idea. When I am in a group meeting and someone says, "Oh, that's an excellent idea," I cringe. I cringe because I know the sound of that . . . [and] every time [I hear] that, the meeting is just over for me. Because then, next year, it's in [the academics'] space, and [the academics] have claimed it.

Academic researchers may thus replicate patterns of oppression in our research, collecting data without returning meaningful insights and knowledge to participants in research that we design. This can further reinforce the perception among community-based activists that academic research is an extractive process. Yet academic and nonacademic research and scholarship can be tools for dismantling oppression in the food system *if* we direct them toward these ends (hooks 1994).

Clearly, minimizing the risk that research will amount to intellectual exploitation is critical to the integrity of all scholarship, particularly work that engages with the ideas of social justice and anti-oppression. The unintended and potentially *un*just outcomes of research need to be acknowledged up front so that potential research projects can be designed to avoid well-worn power imbalances. This does not require resorting to the characterization of food justice initiatives in only "the most adulatory ways"—as Guthman has observed that sympathetic researchers often do to support the "food justice" movement (2008a, 432). Rather, it requires acknowledging research practices that create injustice as the first step to more productively engaging in research that contributes to advancing more socially just urban food and environmental systems.

Scholarly Work as Social Justice Praxis

In interviews and in public forums we conducted while researching this book, we explicitly asked activists whether there was a role for researchers to support their social justice work and, if so, what types of research would be most beneficial. Despite being disenchanted with past experiences with academic research, many of the activists with whom we spoke believe that collaboration with outside researchers, including those employed by colleges and universities, could benefit their programs, their communities, and New York City's urban agriculture system overall. Indeed, we believe this is one reason they were willing to participate in the interviews. Several reiterated the themes that led to this project: the role of scholarship in legitimizing activities that are often marginalized; describing how individual initiatives relate to broader socioeconomic and political systems; and identifying common frameworks that might help all of us understand and communicate about the use of urban agriculture to create more socially just urban systems.

HIGHLIGHTING AND LEGITIMIZING URBAN AGRICULTURE ACTIVISM

To geographers Gibson-Graham (2008), analytical thinking and writing, the products of scholarly activity, can advance social and economic justice. Gibson-Graham's perspective is important because it encourages academics to *actively* use scholarship as a tool for change. The notion that those in positions of relative power can use their status to legitimize one version of reality is not new; Foucault characterized this phenomenon as "power/knowledge" and used this analytical framing to discuss the emergence of "biopower"—states' control over human life beyond territorial control (Foucault 2008).[1] Through research and the communication of research findings, academics can help legitimize "marginalized" activities, lending strength to alternative social, economic, and political realities and providing openings for "freedom and possibility." This process is more actively engaged than "public scholarship," in which research and analysis are made available for public use (e.g., in policy advocacy) without researchers taking a particular stance or becoming invested in how their findings are used (see Piven 2010).

Activists outside academic settings are also well aware of the power of research, scholarship, and the authority granted to academics. Several of the urban agriculture activists we spoke with pointed out that working with academics could be advantageous to their anti-oppression initiatives. For instance, Maggie Cheney discussed the need to legitimize EcoStation:NY's social justice work with the Bushwick Campus Farm in the eyes of the New York City Department of Education (see chapter 3). Likewise, Tanya Fields explained that academics could "give legitimacy to the work we are doing" by documenting the social justice efforts of farm and garden projects.

It is also important not to reinforce uneven power dynamics in day-to-day interactions between academics and activists. One reason that academic work often lends legitimacy to grassroots groups is that there is a distinction drawn between academic "experts" and the "community" and a perception that academic researchers are neutral observers, unbiased and able to evaluate projects with more objectivity than practitioners.[2] But the perception that attention by academics confers importance to particular projects also accentuates the distinctions that many people make between formally recognized academic experts and those not affiliated with an academic institution who nonetheless have expertise and often equally complex analyses of a given issue. Tanya Fields summed this up, observing that

> [people from] these prestigious academic institutions . . . doing reports or papers or books are the same kind of people that were giving me grief before, [and now] are like, "Look at this wonderful report that talks about the intersections of class and race in food," and I'm kind of like, "I was talking about that!" But me as a single black mother, my lived experiences don't hold the same value in this society as, say, the experiences of a researcher or a food systems professor.

Academic research can be used as a tool to advance social justice through urban agriculture, but this requires individual researchers to disrupt inequitable relationships, including those that exist between academics and community-based activists. As Fields explained, "I think that where we work together is where [people within powerful academic] organizations understand the very system in which they exist and they are willing to challenge those systems and say, 'I am using this privilege—my privilege—to be an agent [of change].'" Fields saw this as one way that academic researchers could be engaged in "radical progress." As Gibson-Graham suggest, by stepping beyond merely documenting obvious injustices, a collaborative research process may help open spaces of freedom and possibility. Closer collaboration and ongoing communication between academics and community-based activists may also avoid the kinds of idea poaching that DeVanie Jackson and Yonnette Fleming identified, as long as academics are willing to share the role of "expert" and recognize the co-creation of knowledge that takes place through dialogue that is often part of social science research.

CONTEXTUALIZING URBAN FOOD CONCERNS

Activists we spoke with in researching this book articulate very clearly and passionately the ways in which structural oppression affects the food system in their communities. They are highly qualified and quite capable of contextualizing food system issues and revealing the oppression that underlies food disparities, as their comments throughout this book clearly demonstrate. Yet several offered ideas for how people with academic affiliations could also contribute to their efforts to contextualize their work. At the public forum described above, Leticia Alanis remarked that academics are well positioned to connect the work of La Unión to the political and economic structures that necessitate the community's activism. As an example, she pointed to the economic, geopolitical, labor, and related policies causing Mexican rural farmer displacement—which has caused many of La Unión's members to migrate from their farms in the Mixteca region of their homeland to the Sunset Park neighborhood of South Brooklyn. Academic research connecting those forces to La Unión's work, she said, would build support for the organization's initiatives by explaining how structural oppression shaping the global food system affects individual farmers, many of whom end up living in low-income immigrant communities in the United States. Fleming made a similar comment, suggesting that academics could help shift the narrative about food system problems from the focus on limited food availability and food "deserts" to the poverty grounded in structural oppression that limits the ability of people to keep their families well fed and healthy.

Social scientists like us are trained to analyze issues and events through specific theoretical frames, though we may also write and lecture about the structural foundations of social phenomena like inequity in broader contexts. While community-based activists may see the same structural origins of issues they work to change, analysis conducted by those with formal scientific training is often regarded as more valid than the same analysis offered by those without advanced academic degrees. This perception is part and parcel of the uneven power dynamics between "campus and community" that we and many other individuals strive to change. And yet, when looked to as experts—by the media, government agencies, foundations, and other influential stakeholders in a food or urban system—academics can use our positions as authoritative sources to try to bring structural injustices in the food system into public consciousness.

Further, faculty working in academic institutions often are paid or rewarded professionally to think, write, and engage the public on these issues, which can be a pragmatic advantage over staff at organizations who must focus on day-to-day management, fund-raising, farming, and other critical tasks and may thus have less time to devote to writing about the issues they work on, even though many have the creative and analytical capacity to do so.

Beyond the strategic value academics bring to the table because of our professional status, we have discipline-specific approaches and insights that can be useful in the broader project of liberation. For example, examining urban agriculture in terms of critical geography[3] and urban policy making (as we do throughout this book) can uncover how and when farming and gardening can be considered efforts to advance social justice and human rights. Thus, rather than understanding Alanis's and Fleming's comments above as arguments for rather conventional social scientific explanation, we understand them as recommendations that academics use their skills *and* professional positions to help rewrite the various narratives of food injustice—ranging from immigration policy to individual and public health—and to underscore those narratives' roots in structural oppression.

FRAMING URBAN AGRICULTURE ACTIVISM

Though we have offered a working definition of "social justice," this term means different things to different people. Likewise, "urban agriculture" conjures different ideas in people's minds. Because definitions can affect relationship building, access to funding and materials, policy formulation, and other important aspects of an urban agriculture system, activists must be able to communicate their work using language understood and respected by diverse people in contexts as different as a grassroots community garden and the formal chambers of the New York City Council.

As demonstrated throughout this book, many urban agriculture activists already present their work in multiple and strategic ways. Some are fluent in the terminology commonly used in food systems advocacy, grant-making, and government settings, regularly using concepts such as "food justice," "environmental justice," or "food sovereignty" to describe their work. Yet since these terms, too, can have a range of meanings, they are not always useful in describing precisely the goals or strategies of a particular organization or project. This can lead to one of the very issues that motivated our work on this book: urban agriculture is often understood as a strategy to advance social justice, but there is little consensus on what this process actually looks like on the ground and little recognition of how planting gardens might at times exacerbate *in*justice. Thus, it's important to understand the finer-grained organization of an urban agriculture system and the specific strategies activists use to dismantle oppression.

Conversely, the activists we spoke with also know that some of their community members consider the terms typically used to describe their social justice–oriented programs, such as "food justice" and "food sovereignty," overly abstract or irrelevant, even if the underlying concepts are quite relevant to the neighborhoods in which they are working. Some activists communicate about these issues using terms they feel people in the community can relate to more readily—like "accessing healthy food"—while others provide community-based education about the concepts, such as the "demystifying food justice" training that Fleming convenes in Bed-Stuy.

Several of the activists we spoke with have what some consider "radical" analyses of food system injustice and propose similarly radical solutions to make the system just. For example, the Reverend Robert Jackson described Brooklyn Rescue Mission's work in terms of African American economic self-determination, a standpoint also articulated by urban farmers in Detroit (White 2011a; see chapter 8). Ray Figueroa frequently referred to the work of the Black Panthers and the Young Lords, describing some of the *nonviolent* organizing techniques these groups used in their liberation struggles in the 1960s and 1970s. Cheney aligned her own work with the Gay-Straight Alliance with the work of gay rights groups in New York City and beyond. Fleming spoke of deep ecology, which emphasizes the inherent worth of both nonhuman and human life. Several other interviewees suggested that their work was also undergirded by some of these principles, even if they did not use these terms explicitly.

In many cases, these "radical" frameworks are core to the organizations' activities but much less prominent on their websites or in comments that activists make at public forums. Downplaying their "radical" perspective often is a pragmatic strategy for activists who recognize the need to appeal to a broad audience of program participants and partners without alienating potential funders or political allies. As a case in point, Ayer mentioned having replaced words that can provoke negative reactions, such as "antiracism," with more general and less controversial ones like "food justice" when speaking with potential funders. She adopted this practice after having been flatly told on at least one occasion that a specific foundation would not fund antiracism work. From the standpoint of activists attempting to garner financial and political support for their anti-oppression initiatives—initiatives that conservatives may view as radical—aptitude for framing their work in more politically acceptable terms can make a significant difference. On the other hand, using more moderate terms may move a group in a more moderate direction. Thus, many urban agriculture activists are judicious in how they describe their urban agriculture programs, tailoring their language to specific contexts.

Academics situated beyond the community setting may contribute in specific ways to reframing urban agriculture as social justice activism, to garner support for this work and to help create and strengthen alliances. For example, we might identify otherwise obscure common grounds among different activists and among grassroots urban farming/gardening groups and prospective supporters in government agencies, foundations, and larger nonprofit organizations. Academics may offer perspectives on shared objectives and identify shared narratives that enable seemingly diverse stakeholders to communicate more effectively, surmounting roadblocks that often needlessly stymie collaboration.

Academics may also have specific opportunities in settings such as policy forums or foundations' strategic planning efforts in which they can help reframe farm and garden programs as social justice activism. As discussed above, academics' messages might be given greater weight *because* we are looked to as experts who do not have a vested interest in advancing the concerns of one specific group over any other. That our allegiance is to the cause of dismantling oppression, not to an individual project, may be more easily understood and accepted in the dominant framework of "value-neutral" academic expertise.

"Explaining" systems is one part of public scholarship, but as Piven (2010) notes, the more difficult aspect of scholar-activism—and one part of what makes this stance unique—is using research to help *advocate* for those with the least amount of power. Although we insist that academics are not necessarily more knowledgeable about aspects of urban agriculture than are farmers and gardeners, and although we have divested from the dichotomy of expert/activist, we remain aware that academics are often granted the authority of knowledge. While questioning it, we recognize this granted authority as an opportunity to facilitate the use of urban agriculture to counter social and political oppression, though as Tanya Fields's comments above suggest, doing so requires challenging the systems in which we are embedded and using our academic privilege to be "agents of change."

Future Research Needs:
Not New Questions but Anti-Oppression Approaches

Most discussions about the research needs of urban agriculture focus on specific problems of food production, organizational development, and program design that some groups feel they lack the technical capacity or time to analyze and solve themselves. Indeed, urban agriculture activists with whom we spoke discussed the need for technical assistance in conducting evaluations (particularly because of how time-consuming program evaluation is), documenting complex program outcomes, and understanding specific policies and key policy-making leverage points.

Figueroa summed up the value of program evaluations, stating: "I would love to knock policy makers over the head with all the benefits of community gardens . . . air filtration, carbon sequestration, value-added [products], environmental education, community stabilization, alternatives to incarceration—I just would like to knock them over the head with this, you know, because, that's the language that they understand. That's the language that they speak." Tanya Fields suggested that "in terms of what metrics look like, I think it's up to us to redefine that," so that evaluation of farms and gardens helps these projects evolve to meet community needs, rather than simply aligning with funders' and policy makers' priorities. Through informal conversations with foundation representatives, we learned that funders were likewise interested in understanding the harder-to-quantify benefits of urban agriculture programs. A number of funders wanted to find a way to support urban agriculture programs focused on social justice but explained that they needed to document the social benefits in order to get their boards of directors to approve specific funding streams.

Several organizations have recently developed tools to document social and educational outcomes of urban agriculture projects (see, for example, Cohen, Reynolds, and Sanghvi 2012; Altman et al. 2014; Bauer and Fletcher 2014) and to assess the impact of food system policies and programs on racial justice more broadly (Giancatarino and Noor 2014). These are examples of how researchers can use their expertise help challenge the existing evaluation methods and devise alternative means of demonstrating value in specific contexts (e.g., policy making, philanthropy, or scale-spanning movements).

Yet urban agriculture research and evaluation can be organized either in ways that result in the reproduction of injustice or in ways that help advance social justice through strategic communication and specific forms of technical assistance. Rather than asking what questions need research, then, we think that it is more fruitful to identify research *approaches* that may support activists' anti-oppression work. Technical questions may change from group to group and over time, but figuring out how to create productive and mutually respectful relationships among academics, community-based researchers, and activists is more fundamental to meeting the needs of activists committed to social justice. And rethinking the research process will lead to new questions, new methods for inquiry, and benefits for urban agriculture activists and scholars.

COMMUNITY-CENTRIC AND COLLABORATIVE RESEARCH

By and large, the urban agriculture activists we spoke with felt that research should be driven by community needs rather than solely by the interests of researchers and the priorities of the institutions in which they work. Many activists were weary of participating in studies they found irrelevant to their communities' needs. Throughout the interviews and in follow-up meetings, there was a general disinterest in research for research's sake or in meetings that were "just a conversation" focused on information exchange with no identifiable next steps.

From the perspective of activists, hours spent on studies designed primarily to advance theories, or that are beneficial to community members only in the long run, are hours *not* spent on activities like grant writing, educational programming, or growing and distributing food—activities essential to their organizations' work. Many of the activists suggested that they would be more willing to be involved in research, including academic studies not directly related to their own research needs, if the process of designing research questions, methods, and goals was collaborative, with the overarching goal of producing tangible results for the community-based groups. As Fleming explained, "I like academics. Part of me respects [academia] a lot. Academic researchers are incredibly important. But what is more important is that the research that they do comes back to us. No researcher should come and sit with me to document my project for their PhD while I stay in my same condition. After all, it's my sweat equity [that they're documenting]. That [research] has to translate to experience and credentials for the community people that are doing [the work]."

To avoid these organizational and community risks, at minimum, academics should include the eventual research participants in study design and should fashion their scholarship around a community's expressed needs. Research processes can also originate in, and be driven by, the communities in question. To this end, Figueroa suggested using a community-organizing approach to identify critical research questions: "Community organizing starts off with your hot button. What is pressing your hot button? What is in your face? What is pissing you the blip off? What is not right, and what is not just? And what I am suggesting by that is—we can talk about food, but there can be a very top down, paternalistic assumption [about what's helpful when researchers say,] 'Oh, let's discuss food; let's discuss your relationship to food.' That may not be the top thing that's in a person's face. Community organizing starts where folks are at, you know, and if folks are at a housing issue—housing court, being caught up in family court, being decertified from Food Stamps—we work with that."

The process itself needs to be collaborative, as Nancy Ortiz-Surun at La Finca explained:

> Researchers come, and you've got projects or certain goals or whatever, but we emphasize that [researchers] need to partner with, and give credit to, the farmers. No longer [should it be] this thing [where] you come in and study and [talk about] what's going to be done *for* this community, but [rather] what is going to be done in tandem *with* this community. Is there a role for researchers? Of course. But when it's not a community entity [leading the research], there needs to be a high level of respect and engagement and an honest, open way of communicating the agenda with the farmers. That's how I see that role. It's not just coming in and doing "your" work and reporting "your" findings, but being accountable about how our work and people—not someone's subjects—are represented. A statement of how [a given study] will benefit the understanding of La Finca, urban agriculture, and the South Bronx, as well as sharing of the final product, have also become requisite for us.

Another strategy is to use the research process to break down the barriers between academics and practitioners. One way to do that is for projects to be designed so that community-based activists could conduct research alongside credentialed researchers. As Ortiz-Surun noted: "We ourselves can be and are more commonly becoming the researchers."

Designing research in such a way that the results will be useful to activists is a key to improving the success of academic-community projects. Several activists we spoke with cited examples of community-focused, collaborative research that had been successful because the organizations had obtained useful information through the study. Cheney explained that EcoStation:NY and Bushwick Campus Farm had worked with students and professors at several colleges (including one of the authors of this book) to examine funding and curricular sources. She also described partnerships in which graduate students had led multiyear social-action projects with Bushwick High School students: "With their help we've been able to do a real expansion on the food justice component of our work, [including developing] a Youth Food Policy Council." Greig explained that "the most successful research that has happened at East New York [Farms!] was with [a graduate student who] came down from Cornell. She was doing work on soil management and cover crops in urban gardens and she [used] farmer field school methods, with small groups of gardeners who are involved directly in that research. I thought that was incredibly empowering, and it's actually made a really big huge change in what people have been doing."

PARTICIPATORY ACTION RESEARCH

In addition to research designed to help organizations meet their goals, activists also emphasized the need for processes that recognize the assets in their communities instead of merely describing and analyzing deficiencies. This point is particularly important in low-income communities, communities of color, and communities of recent immigrants, which are often erroneously seen as "deficient" in human and cultural capital because they lack economic resources or have experienced historical disenfranchisement. To this end, several activists felt that participatory action research (PAR) could be useful as a tool for community empowerment.

As a framework or approach, rather than a method, PAR envisions research as a tool to advance social change through having academic or professional researchers work with community members to design, implement, analyze, and, when relevant, report on findings from a study. PAR was developed and has been used in a range of academic and professional fields from business and worker improvement to education to liberation theology (Reason and Bradbury 2008). Critical participatory action research (cPAR), a branch of PAR more closely tied to anti-oppression activism, is rooted in a number of disciplines and traditions including educational theory (e.g., Freire 1993), postcolonial studies (e.g., Fals-Borda and Rahman 1991), social psychology (e.g., Lewin 1948), and the influential work of scholar and civil rights activist W. E. B. DuBois (see Torre et al. 2012). The cPAR approach disrupts the idea that research expertise is solely the purview of academically trained professionals, placing community members in control of data collection and knowledge generation.

Several of the activists we spoke with discussed their interest in and experience with these approaches. Ray Figueroa explained: "I'm a big one for collaborations, particularly the PAR model where community folk are out there, really observing." He noted that "we do this with our young people on an informal basis. One summer it was the best job out of [the city's] Summer Youth Employment Program—right here in Brook Park! They were involved in doing a community survey. I had gotten an in-kind grant from Columbia [University], from their mapping guys." Leticia Alanis explained how PAR could help (and had helped) advance La Unión's work. She explained:

> We don't like too much the role of an external person, a person who doesn't live in the community [as the] expert researcher, and we are going to be the object of study. I think that maybe youth could help investigate something, the adults too. But of course we need expertise, you know, the expertise of somebody who is going to do it in a way that will not render good resources invalid, you know. You [want] to come up with valid findings. But I think that the [community] people also have to contribute, because maybe the researcher doesn't have the way to reach the com-

munity, or doesn't [speak] the language of the community. So I think it will be more beneficial if it's kind of participatory.

Participatory action research and other community-centric and collaborative research methods could be more useful to urban agriculture/social justice activism than the conventional model of data collection that some interviewees described as exploitative or disconnected from community realities. Community-based research has long been used in the fields of community and agricultural development, education, and organizational management. Recent collaborations between academic and community-based food activists also serve as examples. For example, Block et al. (2012) have described collaborations between university researchers and urban agriculture groups in Chicago, drawing parallels between their own work and Saul Alinsky–inspired community-organizing approaches that begin with "what the community knows" (213). In Gainesville, Georgia, academics and community-based activists have worked to connect local and historical civil rights and environmental justice praxes to contemporary food justice activism and have written collectively about their collaborations (Newtown Florist Club Writing Collective 2013). A number of research centers and collaborations throughout the United States and Canada also serve as institutional homes for food system action research. Examples include the Food Action Research Centre (FoodARC) at Mount Saint Vincent University, Arcus Center for Social Justice Leadership at Kalamazoo College, and the Public Science Project at the City University of New York.

ACKNOWLEDGING ACADEMICS' INTERESTS AND CONSTRAINTS

Academics are often challenged by the need to conduct research that is viewed as theoretically robust in order to advance in our careers or even keep our jobs (Piven 2010), and this requirement can stymie the types of community-based and action research discussed above. Academic institutions may not value applied research, such as evaluation or community food assessments, in terms of their contribution to theory and may question place-based research in terms of its reproducibility and implications for other social or geographic locations. Skeptics may deem findings from collaborative and participatory research less reliable or less valid than "objective" research conducted and controlled by "neutral" academics; action research may be seen as biased because it is constructed around an explicit focus on social change.[4] On the flip side, during our conversations with urban agriculture activists, we detected a common but often mistaken assumption that academics situated in private liberal arts universities (as we both were at the time of our research) have access to an abundance of funding and policy maker attention.

Academics work in diverse institutions, departments, and disciplines, and we also have varied degrees of status within our institutions' (often hierarchical) organizational structures. Faculty without tenure, those hired for limited-term appointments, and adjunct faculty generally have far less power within an institution than those with tenure or senior status. Tenure-track faculty are expected to conduct research that conforms to the tenure requirements that will determine whether or not they keep their jobs. Adjunct faculty are employed mainly to teach, not to do research, write, or collaborate with community-based groups, making this work, though personally rewarding, either more challenging or not feasible. Those who obtain sizable research grants from external funders often enjoy higher status than those whose work attracts smaller amounts.

In addition to the status of individual academic researchers, the status of the institutions in which we are situated can determine whether and to what extent certain types of research can be conducted or funded, since some universities have more resources than others to support faculty research. Liberal arts colleges generally require their faculty to devote more time to teaching and may expect (and support) less research than major research universities. Community colleges have different goals and objectives than four-year institutions, being primarily focused on teaching, and generally have access to much less funding through student tuition and donors (Bellafante 2014). An institution's reputation can also affect access to resources needed to conduct time-consuming research, since institutional status and political influence help garner funding and other forms of support. These differences affect the type of research that may be possible within a given institution.

Another challenge to conducting the sort of research favored by some of the activists we spoke with is that timelines often differ. Academic research and writing tends to take longer than on-the-ground research and the kinds of writing that have more immediate effects. As a result, it is challenging to align academic research with community needs (and vice versa). As a case in point, we have at times struggled with the gap between the time needed to produce this book and the drive to have our work on this project advance community-based activists' anti-oppression work. While we cannot claim to have resolved this dilemma while researching and writing *Beyond the Kale,* we have heeded a suggestion by Robert Jackson at Brooklyn Rescue Mission to be open and transparent about our research and writing processes. Also, using a practice common in action research, we are actively seeking ways to build on what we have learned collectively by pursuing opportunities for participatory action research and collaborative work with the activists whose perspectives informed this book.

And yet it is true that academics' interests may extend beyond community-based research to include the type of theorizing that is often critiqued as being irrelevant to everyday life. Indeed, the ability to do theoretical work is one reason many of us choose careers in academia rather than in other, more inherently applied sectors. Having spent much time reflecting on these dilemmas, we believe that it is incumbent on academics to explain our work's relevance to those who may not understand the workings of academic settings, and at the same time it is important for people situated outside academia to consider the value of scholarship that deeply, and with integrity, engages with social and political complexities—just as it is important to value the work of farmers and gardeners who choose to grow food for reasons that have nothing to do with activism or political change. Considering our interests, capacities, and professional requirements—and acknowledging the existing constraints that many academics face—is a key part of exploring roles for *academics* in advancing social justice.

As our own work on *Beyond the Kale* has evolved, we have begun to develop collegial relationships with several of the activists we quote here, having sat together on panels that explored policy making and antiracism in the food system, invited them to share their expertise in a public forum, and participated as cofacilitators or speakers at activists' educational events. Of course, our efforts represent a work in progress, and we would be remiss to omit the fact that there have also been missteps along the way. For instance, we have been misquoted in media pieces in which we aimed to broaden public awareness of structural racism and support organizations' work, and we have at times sensed the same wariness about our efforts that activists have discussed with regard to past participation in outsiders' research. We have also (re)learned that there are times when research on urban agriculture or food systems is not needed or desired by community-based activists. As DeLind (2013) has suggested, supporting urban agriculture through scholarship also involves a willingness to step back.

Enacting Theories of Change

Digging beneath the surface to reveal inequities in the food system is a necessary part of advancing social justice through urban farming and gardening. So, too, must urban agriculture research and scholarship attend to structural roots of oppression, both within and beyond the pale of the ivory tower. What we have learned throughout our research for this book project suggests to us that there are openings for academics to support the work of urban agriculture activists, but if this work is about social justice, it must take seriously some of the ideas elaborated by activists described in this book and must actually (not merely theoretically) take power to task (e.g., see Piven 2010).

As discussed in chapter 1, Gibson-Graham's work on bringing "alternative realities" to the foreground has been critiqued for giving short shrift to power structures. We have tried to avoid this shortcoming in *Beyond the Kale*. In this chapter we have reflected on the uneven power dynamics between academics and community-based activists. Our hope is that this project might help reframe narratives and shift practices related not only to urban agriculture but to the nature of collaboration between activists within and beyond institutions. This potential role of action-oriented research and writing that *is* based in academic institutions falls in line with Gibson-Graham's ideas that scholarship can help social actors look beyond false dichotomies such as scholar/community member or academic/activist to see possibilities for mutually supportive work. As Ray Figueroa suggested, "The idea is to honor folks as the experts about what affects them, and what impacts them, and to work from that. And then, ultimately, we're going to be able to address [important] issues."

In all, we feel hopeful that collaborations between academics (who may also be activists) and community-based urban agriculture activists (who may also be scholars) can help advance social justice when—and if—such advancement is needed. This requires mutual respect for individuals' interests, priorities, and constraints. To repair trust between people in socially privileged positions (such as academics and upper- and middle-class whites) and people who do not have these advantages also requires developing authentic relationships in which uneven power dynamics are acknowledged and reconciled.

While our research for this book has primarily examined work being done in New York City, the focus on power, privilege, politics, and the leadership of urban agriculture activists of color and anti-oppression activists extends beyond New York City's borders. The final chapter begins with a few examples from other regions and suggests both a vision and practical steps for advancing social justice through critical urban agriculture praxis.

CHAPTER 8

Taking a Collective Step
Beyond the Kale

The 2012 HBO documentary *Weight of the Nation* featured the activist efforts of Kebreeya Lewis, a seventeen-year-old resident of Goldsboro, North Carolina, who led a campaign to get a salad bar installed in her high school as part of her own initiative to improve her family's and community's health. Lewis prevailed after conducting surveys of her high school peers, meeting with school lunch administrators, and appealing to the City Council for support. Her drive to work on food system issues grew out of her own experience, and she learned her organizing skills by participating in a youth program called Students Working for an Agricultural Revolutionary Movement (SWARM) based at the Center for Environmental Farming Systems (a partnership between North Carolina Agriculture and Technical State University and the North Carolina Department of Agriculture and Consumer Services). Since it was created in 2009, SWARM has engaged young people of color, low-income youth, and youth living on the nearby military base in food system initiatives that range from community gardening to bicycle-powered produce delivery. Shorlette Ammons, community food systems outreach coordinator at the university, explained that the group emerged as members of the local Wayne (County) Food Initiative recognized the need to get young people of color interested in agriculture and growing food. "SWARM was . . . an innovative way to get youth to not just work in the community gardens—to get interested in agriculture—but to also inject a fuel of activism as a means to explore where their food comes from [and] how they're directly impacted by the food system."

Nearly eight hundred miles away, the Detroit Black Community Food Security Network's (DBCFSN) Food Warriors Youth Development Program focuses on distinct but related themes. The program operates in partnership with two charter schools (one African-centered) and a church-based community center in Detroit, helping youth understand food, agriculture, and healthy eating. The Food Warriors program also focuses on helping African American and black youth grasp the rich agricultural legacy of their ancestors and understand food production as a path to community empowerment and self-reliance. As a part of the program, youth visit DBCFSN's seven-acre D-Town Farm, where community farmers grow organic vegetables, tend beehives, conduct educational tours, run summer urban agriculture internships, and host an annual harvest festival. Malik Yakini, executive director of DBCFSN, cofounder of D-Town Farm, and former principal at another school that was involved with the Food Warriors program, explained that much of this work centers on "rekindl[ing] the spirit of African people—in [the Detroit community] in particular—of doing for self." DBCFSN's programs emphasize appreciation of and education about the experiences of African Americans and people of African descent in the food system. Through the Food Warriors program, D-Town Farm, a food-buying cooperative, and policy advocacy efforts, DBCFSN seeks to increase access to healthy food, advance food sovereignty and social justice in the food system, and cultivate leadership in food justice and food security initiatives among members of Detroit's black community.

In Texas, at El Paso's Downtown Art and Farmers Market, La Semilla Food Center sells Malabar spinach, a variety that does well in the hot desert region, along with various chiles and other vegetables grown at its community farm. The farm stand is just one of many projects of La Semilla, a nonprofit organization in the Paso del Norte borderland (the region of Las Cruces, New Mexico, and El Paso, Texas) that has been working since 2010 to create a healthy, fair, self-reliant, and sustainable local food system. La Semilla runs school gardens, farm-to-school programs, and nutrition and culinary education programs and provides outreach and assistance to enable families on federal food subsidies to shop at farmers' markets. The organization is also involved in policy advocacy and runs a fourteen-acre demonstration farm dedicated to helping the region's farmers solve the agricultural challenges of the border region, such as high-salinity irrigation water. According to Food Planning and Policy Coordinator Krysten Aguilar, La Semilla focuses on ways to "address the underlying issues that come from who holds power in the food system, and why that power is being held there." The organization is particularly committed to teaching youth about race and equity in the food system, community-based solutions to food system injustice, and how to influence public policy on food and agriculture (including urban agriculture). It sends participants to the national Rooted in Community youth leadership conference to learn about food justice and has organized community listening sessions that focus on food sovereignty. According to Aguilar, "A lot of our work is focused [on the] reasons inequities exist, because of institutionalized [and] structural racism, or institutionalized socioeconomic bias." La Semilla also operates with a shared leadership organizational structure—influenced by the Zapatistas in southern Mexico[1]—that embodies and reinforces its social justice values.

These three vignettes, drawn from cities that are very different from New

York, illustrate that the movement to advance social justice through urban agriculture reaches far beyond the five boroughs. Urban agriculture activists, many of whom are people of color, are working to advance social justice in diverse locales with differing populations, geographies, histories, and politics. While these groups conduct activities common to all urban farms and gardens—growing and selling food, supporting economic development projects, teaching children, providing spaces for community building, improving the environment, and advocating for policies that support gardening and farming—they also incorporate analyses of structural oppression and actions intended to build into their work the framework for a more equitable society.

These stories also exemplify an important component of a number of urban agriculture programs throughout the United States that focus explicitly on social justice concerns: their work to foster critical consciousness and leadership among youth of color. This fundamental part of their work helps create a cadre of new leaders within communities that experience the brunt of many food system and environmental inequities—in addition to providing individual youth with educational and skill-building opportunities. In addition to their urban agriculture initiatives and their focus on dismantling oppression, what activists at SWARM, DBCFSN, and La Semilla have in common with many of the New York City–based activists highlighted in this book is their vision for a food system in which youth of color and low-income youth are leaders both in their own communities of today and in creating more liberatory social systems in the long term. We revisit this important, forward-looking aspect of their work at the end of this chapter.

Dismantling Oppression to Advance Social Justice

The programs described throughout this book are models of urban agriculture groups that are actively working to dismantle oppression—by conducting activities grounded in specific theories and traditions, by embodying leadership structures that reflect activists' social justice values and that are representative of those with whom they work, and by engaging with other activists and organizations to advance policies that support not only urban food production but a more equitable urban environment. These are lessons that other activists may incorporate into their farm and garden initiatives, and they are also instructive to those in policy making, philanthropy, academia, and other sectors who support urban agriculture and social justice activism.

Dismantling oppression requires participation among people and institutions in all social positions. To this end, we emphasize two related perspectives on the intersection of urban agriculture and anti-oppression initiatives. First, additional urban agriculture activists, funders, policy makers, academics, and other supporters need to take seriously the fact that food system injustice is rooted in broader systems of inequity and structural oppression. The need for such awareness reaches far beyond academic exercise. Initiatives that seek to use urban food production as a way to solve food system and public health disparities without addressing the root causes of those disparities risk becoming stopgap measures that allow racialized, gendered, and classed inequities to remain. Understanding that the problems urban agriculture can address are rooted in structural oppression compels thinking about how to undo the complexities of social injustice. As such, urban agriculture can figure in the design of policies and governmental programs to support healthy communities; funding initiatives focused on the social, educational, and public health benefits of farming and gardening; action-oriented research aimed at contributing to the work of community-based activists; and new farm and garden programs.

In addition to understanding the problem, urban agriculture activists and supporters also need to recognize anti-oppression initiatives as potential strategies to bolster food system, environmental, and health justice. Various social justice concepts related to food (e.g., food justice, food sovereignty), environment, and health can take on different meanings depending on who is using them and how they are used. As discussed in previous chapters, these concepts and terms can be overused or co-opted, making it difficult to discern which urban agriculture activities have the deepest social justice effects. As we have illustrated throughout this book, activists' anti-oppression frameworks are often informed by specific experiences and theories of change that, if well elucidated, can show the powerful connections between urban farming or gardening and social justice.

Activist Scholarship

Through conversations with the individuals described in this book, we have explored the very concept of "scholarship" and have agreed that scholar-activist work that grants the authority of knowledge creation and the identity of "scholar" only to those employed by institutions of higher education serves to perpetuate uneven balances of power. Some concerns about this imbalance came from urban agriculture activists' past experiences with outsider research that had yielded little community benefit and had even resulted in their own ideas being appropriated. Still, the individuals we spoke with remained open-minded about research processes that are truly collaborative. Several had been involved with research that had been designed with respect for the knowledge of community members and the need for community benefit, and the communities involved had had the opportunity to take ownership in research design and findings. Activists viewed this type of research as successful and recommended similar standards for research focused on supporting food system and social justice work.

Yet research and scholarship are not synonymous. "Research" can be as simple as reading about the best variety of tomato for the local environment, without necessarily requiring in-depth knowledge about agronomy, climate, or tomatoes. "Scholarship" connotes a certain level of expertise that can be held by people both inside and beyond academia. Thus, although designing research projects that support the work of community-based activists is a critical part of action-oriented social justice research, it is also important to reframe ideas about scholarly expertise as a part of anti-oppression work.

Agriculture, like so many pursuits, is a process of problem solving, and urban farms and gardens are engaged in multidimensional community problem solving as part of a long tradition in agriculture of co-creating knowledge and solutions. Farmers manage food production with a combination of informal and formal knowledge, know-how, intuition, and collective judgment. Indeed, the farmers and gardeners we spoke with both generate their own knowledge and incorporate the research of others into their work. Moreover, they may incorporate lessons from both formal educational programs and informal study into their programs. Many are seasoned public speakers and use music and visual and material arts to communicate about the principles of their work. Many have published articles, chapters, and books based on their knowledge and experience. "Scholars" thus include not only people situated in academic institutions but people like the activists described in this book who have engaged in developing and sharing in-depth understanding of specific aspects of the world. Breaking down distinctions between types of scholars is a fundamental part of certain strands of critical or participatory action research and liberatory education.

Conversely, just as scholarship is not the domain of academics alone, neither are thinking and analysis the only activities in which academics may engage. Academics may support alternative realities through documentation and "theorizing," but we may also work alongside community-based activists in strategic moments, or on sustained projects that are *not* removed from everyday life. "Activists" thus include not only grassroots community organizers but other individuals who have invested themselves in creating change.

Additionally, it is important to recall that academics often face challenges in conducting community-oriented research. Academic researchers and scholars do not all have the same types of professional positions, levels of institutional power, or financial privilege. These disparities can present challenges to some academics who hope to engage in collaborative social justice–oriented scholarship.

Dissolving the "power line" between academic and community-based scholar-activists thus involves acknowledging the differences between social location and commitment, and divesting from uneven power dynamics that often pervade research involving individuals from both within and outside specific communities. And yet, although it is easy enough to theorize about socially just re-search processes or to reconceptualize urban agriculture scholarship, we must not forget that writing or talking about these issues should not be the end goal. Research and scholarship that seek to improve conditions in specific communi-ties require commitment—on the part of individuals and institutions—to out-comes beyond the "products of scholarly work" (Gibson-Graham 2008).[2]

The activists we spoke with discussed a number of ways that research pro-cesses could be designed to better address social justice issues in their com-munities. Research could disrupt power dynamics; be relevant in and needed by communities involved in research; recognize and make use of community knowledge and community assets; engage activists and other community mem-bers in all stages of research; and ensure that findings and benefits come back to the community.

Our conversations with urban agriculture activists suggested that similar re-search processes might be more useful in advancing food system and environ-mental justice than studies that involve outsiders documenting farm and garden activities. Specific research may include program evaluation that helps farmers, gardeners, policy makers, and funders understand the quantitative *and quali-tative* impacts of social justice–focused urban agriculture programs. As Karen Washington explained, measuring urban food production and its economic im-pact are important in demonstrating the economic potential of growing food in the city. She suggested that such measurement could potentially lead to gov-ernment funding to support urban agriculture, one step toward achieving eco-nomic justice in low-income communities. Bee Ayer explained that it would be helpful to have "evaluation that specifically looked at how our activities [align with] our values, and the actual effects that [our programs] have in terms of so-cial justice." She added that support from other organizations, particularly those groups that use urban agriculture as a tool for education, would be helpful at the Youth Farm that BK Farmyards manages.

As noted in chapter 7, several activists felt that it was important for organi-zational leaders to be involved in designing qualitative and quantitative metrics themselves—defining what success looks like, and communicating this infor-mation to potential supporters in philanthropy and government so that their programs were evaluated based on how well they met community needs. Tanya Fields added that there could be opportunities to partner with researchers who could "help us create reports that will be used . . . to change the landscape on a legislative, . . . public health, [or] . . . policy level to what happens in our com-munity." She feels that it is often difficult for smaller organizations like the BLK ProjeK to get access to academic researchers. Academics interested in support-ing social justice–oriented urban agriculture work could engage in this type of partnership. Such processes would require academics to remain cognizant of our privilege and the power often granted to our words, particularly when we are asked to stand as "experts." As Fields suggested, this academic privilege should be used for community benefit.

As Piven (2010) has noted, activist research and scholarship requires a commitment to the issues at hand, despite challenges related to power and privilege. In this way, academic activism is not *entirely* dissimilar from community-based activism. Scholarship and activism that include authentic, collaborative relationships can more effectively challenge the status quo power dynamics that underlie food and environmental injustice, in the interest of liberation. And this requires building trust and taking risks.

Recognizing Existing Leadership

There is a long-recognized need to increase racial and ethnic diversity within mainstream environmental and food organizations. This concern remains salient because many organizations (and the movements of which they are part) continue to be dominated by whites. Increasing overall racial and ethnic diversity in such organizations is critical to achieving equity and representation. It is also important in terms of incorporating the unique perspectives that people of color may have about key food and environmental issues.

Yet creating more socially just food systems, movements, and related institutions cannot stop at inclusion in white-led groups. It must also involve advancing *leadership* among people of color and addressing the uneven balance of power—not simply an organization's or movement's overall phenotypic diversity. Ignoring power imbalances within white-dominated organizations can give rise to diversity initiatives that do little to disrupt implicitly racist practices, and may even contribute to disparities between organizations led by whites and those led by people of color.

Moreover, white dominance in the leadership of urban agriculture organizations not only risks limiting the effectiveness of programs but also detracts from the success of the movement for social justice in food and environmental systems overall. Addressing leadership demographics and power dynamics within organizations and movements is therefore key to the integrity of social justice–oriented urban agriculture work.

It is also critical to recognize that people of color are already leading initiatives to manage environmental and food system problems, as they have for generations (e.g., see Taylor 2000, 2011; Mares and Peña 2011). As demonstrated throughout this book, activists of color are addressing issues like food insecurity, lack of economic and educational opportunity, environmental racism, and poverty in their own communities. Understanding this truth is significant because it illuminates community assets and can help shift problem-solving approaches from reliance on people and resources *outside* the community (e.g., well-intentioned white activists beginning gardens in communities of color in an attempt to address food insecurity) to self-reliance *within* communities that experience the most negative effects of food and environmental inequities. Those of us hoping to help communities of which we are not inherently a part need to listen and to remain open to the idea that sometimes outside help is neither needed nor desired.

We do not mean to suggest that all initiatives to address food and environmental problems must be led solely by neighborhood residents, or that innovations from outside the neighborhood are not valuable. Initiatives to improve conditions at the neighborhood scale often are, and must be, linked to policies and programs at a city, state, regional, or national scale. The key point is that communities that experience the brunt of food and environmental injustice, even if they have historically been sidelined from mainstream economic systems and political decision making, have within them talented people who can and do lead such initiatives. Advancing social justice through urban agriculture thus includes recognizing leadership where it already exists and supporting ongoing work.

Cultivating New Leaders

Urban agriculture programs can provide opportunities to cultivate new leaders within communities most directly affected by social, environmental, economic, and political injustice. Leadership development components of urban agriculture initiatives can help build power among community members, including youth. And yet, to avoid the trap of suggesting that all urban-agriculture-based youth development programs necessarily build participants' capacity to create less-oppressive systems, it is important to look more deeply into how these programs are structured and the analyses of injustice (and justice) they espouse. Urban-agriculture-based youth development programs, too, should be led by members of communities that experience the most negative effects of food and environmental inequity, like many of the activists and community leaders described herein. And like SWARM, DBCFSN, and La Semilla, these programs should help youth participants understand both the structural forms of oppression and the ways in which people who have experienced its negative effects can *and do* liberate people.

As illustrated throughout this book, most of the New York City activists we spoke with also engage youth as leaders through intergenerational programs that enable community elders to share the agricultural and cultural knowledge they possess. Moreover, some of the activists see youth development programs as one part of their efforts to solidify long-term leadership within their own cultural or geographic communities. For example, Ray Figueroa spoke about some of Friends of Brook Park's programs as not only growing new leaders but also promoting and developing "institutional permanence that will support community capacity"; Karen Washington emphasized the importance of youth in her community learning from family elders about their own food and agricultural heritages in order to understand the strength in their own histories and to see themselves as the next generation of community leaders. This emphasis on youth is a critical element of sustained movement toward social justice.

Conclusion as Beginning

To some, urban gardening and farming is merely a way to grow vegetables. To others, the mere act of growing food is a means to transform the food system and change society. We have shown that both perspectives are misguided. Urban agriculture can be a powerful force to dismantle multiple forms of oppression and advance social justice—but only if we make it so. Washington went so far as to suggest that urban agriculture is "the new civil rights movement—the food civil rights movement [that involves] growing food."

Without naively suggesting that members of a given system of activists, farmers, gardeners, academics, policy makers, and funders can simply begin to work together in solidarity if they desire to do so, we suggest that a key part of advancing social justice is recognizing that all of these actors can be—in fact, need to be—involved.

Moving beyond the kale is about re-envisioning urban agriculture—an activity many view as a curiosity or benign anachronism—as a social justice project that can produce tremendous social benefits if we commit the required multilayered and collaborative activist work. Recognizing the *potential for* urban agriculture to be used in advancing social justice—and recognizing such efforts as an existing reality—can help us see openings for "freedom and possibility" in the farms and gardens situated in what some people see as unlikely places. This vision we share for an urban agriculture–social justice praxis is one in which anyone can engage.

APPENDIX 1

Research Methods

Data presented in this book were collected in two distinct phases. First, through the Five Borough Farm project, between 2010 and 2012 we conducted in-depth interviews with thirty-one individuals who had unique knowledge about aspects of urban agriculture in New York City. Those interviewed included urban farmers and gardeners; representatives of nongovernmental organizations that provided support or advocacy for urban agriculture; representatives of organizations that had recently funded urban agriculture programs; and local government officials directly involved with urban agriculture activities. The Five Borough Farm project, coordinated by a New York City nonprofit, involved a team of seven researchers and design professionals and one urban farmer who worked collaboratively over the two-year span to conduct research, develop policy and evaluation strategies, and depict New York City's urban agriculture system through photography and information graphics.

Following that study, we conducted follow-up interviews with practitioners and organization representatives to gather more specific information about the ways in which race-, class-, and gender-based disparities have surfaced within New York's urban agriculture system, and the strategies being used to address food system and environmental injustice through urban agriculture. In addition to data derived from these two distinct sets of interviews, we also drew from reviews of New York City policy documents and reports prepared by local food system organizations, as well as from our own participation in food-policy-making processes and food system activism in New York City. This approach allowed us to ground our research-based analysis in everyday experiences.

Elements of New York City's Urban Agriculture System

A Networked System

The persistence of urban agriculture in New York City depends not only on the availability and forms of spaces to grow food and flowers but on relationships among the individuals and organizations in many related sectors. Urban farmers and gardeners often collaborate with each other, both informally and formally, on specific projects and campaigns. Their programs are also connected through a network of technical assistance providers, advocacy organizations, philanthropies, researchers, government agencies, and private businesses. The networked nature of this system is not unique to New York but is distinct in that it reflects the city's social, demographic, political, and physical characteristics. Here we provide a brief overview of the people and types of entities engaged in New York City's urban agriculture system.

Farmers and Gardeners

Community gardeners and urban farmers reflect the city's diversity, though the geographic distribution of sites and the racial and ethnic diversity of farmers and gardeners result from urban agriculture's roots in the city's many low-income communities, communities of color, and immigrant communities. Black and Latino/a gardeners (the latter having heritage in Central or South America) represent the majority of community gardeners in the city (Eizenberg 2013, 2012b, 2008), and some gardens, such as Evergreen Community Garden in Flushing, Queens, are managed primarily by Asian residents. Urban agriculture sites, particularly community gardens, are concentrated in low-income neighborhoods and neighborhoods with primarily black and Latino/a residents (Ackerman 2011; Eizenberg 2013, 2012a, 2012b, 2008). Meanwhile, although there has been no empirical documentation of the changing demographics of urban agriculture in New York City, observers have noted a recent increase in the proportion of young, white urban agriculture practitioners, mirroring a national trend in urban agriculture (e.g., see Crouch 2012; Tortorello 2012). This change has coincided with gentrification taking place in historically low-income neighborhoods (see Curran and Hamilton 2012; Pearsall 2012), including parts of Brooklyn, where many new urban agriculture projects have been developed.

Government Agencies and Public Officials

A number of key municipal and state agencies provide support for urban agriculture in New York City, whether through specific programs or legislation or as a part of their mandates to provide services (such as water, which gardeners use for irrigation): the Department of Parks and Recreation, the Department of Sanitation, the Department of Environmental Protection, the New York State Department of Agriculture and Markets, and Cornell University Cooperative Extension.

Supporting Organizations

A number of not-for-profit and nonprofit organizations and informal groups also provide technical assistance, training, and organizational support for New York City farmers and gardeners. These include the long-standing Green Guerillas, the New York Botanical Garden's Bronx Green-Up program (which began in 1988), United Community Centers in East New York (which was established in the 1950s and has operated its East New York Farms! project since 1998), and Just Food, a food justice organization operating citywide since 1995. The nonprofit International Rescue Committee coordinates opportunities for refugees in New York to practice urban agriculture, and Farming Concrete, a citizen science project, helps urban gardeners track how much produce they have grown as a means to support the gardeners as well as to document the value of the gardens to policy makers (Farming Concrete 2014). The organization 596 Acres identifies, maps, and helps New York City residents organize to gain access to farm vacant parcels (596 Acres 2014).

Organizations also provide opportunities for networking and advocate for urban agriculture throughout the city. For example, Black Urban Growers (BUGS), a citywide (and increasingly nationwide) organization, has convened annual conferences since 2010 to address issues of concern to black urban and rural farmers and gardeners. Members also network with black farmers and advocates in other cities and remain connected through social media and by speaking at national conferences.

At times, some of these groups also engage in policy activism to strengthen the urban agriculture system. For example, the New York City Community Garden Coalition has taken the lead in advocating favorable terms for occupying city-owned garden sites, testifying at public hearings and legal proceedings, and networking with other urban agriculture organizations in support of long-term or permanent tenure for gardens (Hernandez 2010; Figueroa-Reyes and Dekhan 2014).

Funders

Private philanthropies and municipal, state, and federal government agencies have provided some financial support for urban agriculture projects in New York City. Members of a Northeast regional funder affinity group called the Community Food Funders have made grants to nonprofit organizations and educational institutions to conduct on-the-ground farming and gardening projects as well as urban agriculture research (including major support for the Five Borough Farm project and micro-grants for aspects of our work on this book). City and federal agencies have also provided grant funds for urban agriculture projects focused on the agencies' goals. For instance, in 2011 the New York City Department of Environmental Protection granted nearly $600,000 to the Brooklyn Navy Yard to construct a 40,000-square-foot commercial rooftop farm in partnership with Brooklyn Grange, which runs its own nearly one-acre rooftop farm in Queens. The New York State Department of Environmental Conservation has supported community-based urban agriculture initiatives in the city. Through various granting programs, the US Department of Agriculture has provided funds to nonprofit organizations including Just Food, which supported the development of Farm School NYC, and United Community Centers, which houses East New York Farms!

Academics and "Scholars"

Academics and scholars, both those affiliated with educational institutions and those in other sectors, engage in urban agriculture in New York City through research, education, and technical assistance. The City University of New York has a food policy research center that explores wide-ranging issues related to the food system, many of which intersect with many urban agriculture groups' initiatives on topics such as food production and distribution. Two community colleges that are part of the City University system have food and agriculture programs: Kingsborough Community College in Brooklyn runs an educational farm that connects with its culinary program, and Hostos Community College in the South Bronx is launching a food studies associate's degree program that addresses social justice, environment, policy, and public health and includes a course on urban botany. The New School and New York University have four-year degree programs in food studies, with occasional urban agriculture course offerings. Several high schools in the city have urban farms that are used as cocurricular learning spaces. Cornell University Cooperative Extension provides horticultural advice to farmers and gardeners in New York City and statewide.

Farms and Gardens in New York City

In New York City, gardens and farms are regularly created, abandoned, and occasionally cleared for development, so any estimate of the number in operation is quickly outdated. In 2011 there were nearly 500 GreenThumb gardens, approximately 600 gardens at NYCHA sites, and at least 150 community gardens owned and overseen by land trusts and the New York Restoration Project. There were also an estimated 300 public school gardens, two dozen community-operated farms, and a handful of commercial farms (Ackerman 2011; Cohen, Reynolds, and Sanghvi 2012; Gittleman, Librizzi, and Stone 2010; authors' calculations). These numbers continue to rise as new gardens and farms are created on the nearly 5,000 acres of vacant land in the city (though not all of this is suitable for production) and as innovative forms of urban agriculture such as rooftop farming and aquaponics expand (Ackerman 2011). An update to a 2012 study of New York City's urban agriculture system published in 2014 identified approximately 900 food-producing gardens and farms operating within the five boroughs (Altman et al. 2014).

Numerous studies have proposed typologies of urban agriculture based on legal definitions (e.g., the USDA definition of a farm or whether the group is a formally constituted nonprofit organization), scale, technology, output, or purpose (for recent examples, see Ackerman 2011; Hodgson, Campbell, and Bailkey 2011; Cohen, Reynolds and Sanghvi 2012; Reynolds 2011; McClintock 2013; Rogus and Dimitri 2015). While we feel that farms and gardens often do not fit neatly into categories, we provide an overview here to help conceptualize the forms of urban agriculture in New York City.

COMMUNITY GARDENS. Community gardens, which were at the heart of urban agriculture activism beginning in the 1960s and 1970s, still represent the majority of urban agriculture sites in New York City today. Community gardens typically consist of parcels divided into individual plots that are maintained by member gardeners. They range in size from less than one city lot to the five-acre Evergreen Community Garden in Flushing, Queens. Community gardens are typically not-for-profit, as they are overseen by city agencies or nonprofit organizations. Nearly 90 percent of the existing gardens are under the jurisdiction of either the NYCHA or the Department of Parks and Recreation's GreenThumb program. The remaining sites are owned and protected by land trusts, including the national Trust for Public Land and borough-based land trusts in Brooklyn and Queens, the Bronx, and Manhattan. Nonprofits (such as the New York Restoration Project) and private individuals own and/or manage the rest.

COMMUNITY FARMS. Broadly speaking, community farms feature contiguous growing spaces, rather than individual plots, that are managed by staff, apprentices, and volunteers. Like community gardens, they grow produce and may also have chickens or beehives. Producing food for distribution and sale (often at low or sliding-scale prices) is an integral part of these operations, though community farms typically prioritize community and educational goals. They achieve these goals through programs such as formal curricula, youth leadership training, and informal community workshops. Though community farms may be for-profit or nonprofit, they usually emphasize a social mission rather than focusing primarily on maximizing production or profit.

INSTITUTIONAL FARMS AND GARDENS. A number of farms and gardens operate as programs of government agencies or nonprofit institutions, such as schools, churches, prisons, and supportive housing developments, and many are established to fulfill the mandate or mission of the sponsoring organization. Some provide food to their affiliated institution or agency, either as a supplement to other food sources or as part of related health or nutrition education programs; for others the practice of horticulture for education or therapy is the main objective rather than maximizing food production. Schools are a particularly important institution connected to urban agriculture. As noted above, an estimated 300 New York City schools have active gardens. Other extensive institutional garden programs include the NYCHA Garden and Greening program, through which residents of the city's 334 public housing developments maintain approximately 600 gardens, 245 of which grow food.

ROOFTOP FARMS AND GREENHOUSES. In addition to having a large number of conventional (i.e., in-ground) gardens and farms, New York City has a growing number of rooftop farms and greenhouses. Larger-scale, commercial rooftop farms include a nearly one-acre farm (Brooklyn Grange) located on top of a commercial building in Long Island City, Queens, and a rooftop greenhouse operated by the for-profit company Gotham

Greens at a Whole Foods Market in Brooklyn. City housing agencies have integrated rooftop agriculture into affordable housing projects.

INNOVATIVE CULTIVATION METHODS. In addition to rooftop innovations, some farms and gardens use soilless technologies like hydroponics and aeroponics (which feed nutrients to plant roots through water and air, respectively) or integrate fish and vegetable production in aquaponic growing systems.

Urban Agriculture and Community Groups Highlighted in This Book

The descriptions below summarize the organizations and groups featured in this book as it goes to press. We recommend that readers interested in learning more about the specific work of or the most up-to-date information about any of these groups consult the websites listed here. Additional photos of the farms and gardens are found at www. beyondthekale.org.

BK Farmyards

BK Farmyards is a decentralized farming network that helps start and support urban farms in Brooklyn. It manages The Youth Farm (a project of the nonprofit organization Green Guerillas) at the High School for Public Service in Crown Heights, Brooklyn, and its members run farm-based education and consulting projects. Its mission is to build a local food network to enhance the health of "our culture, our people, and our environment."

WEBSITE: http://bkfarmyards.com/

Black Urban Growers

Black Urban Growers (BUGS) is a volunteer organization that builds networks and community support for black farmers and gardeners in both urban and rural settings through education and advocacy. BUGS hosts community events, including an annual conference, to bring together grassroots organizations and activists.

WEBSITE: http://blackurbangrowers.org/

The BLK ProjeK

The BLK ProjeK is an organization dedicated to addressing food justice and health issues for women of color. It offers health classes and runs a community meal series. It is developing an abandoned lot as an urban farm and has refitted a school bus as a mobile food market. Its mission is to address issues of food justice, public health, and mental health as they relate to underserved women of color through culturally relevant education, beautification of public spaces, urban gardening, and community programming.

WEBSITE: http://theblkprojek.org/

Brooklyn Rescue Mission Urban Harvest Center

Brooklyn Rescue Mission Urban Harvest Center is a community-based organization in Central Brooklyn that develops creative solutions to change what its leaders see as an unhealthy food environment, to eliminate health disparities, and to address the economic challenges the community endures on a daily basis. The organization serves over twenty thousand Brooklyn residents annually through its community food center, its urban agriculture educational program, and two community farmers' markets. It envisions communities that are healthy, sustainable, empowered, safe, and economically secure. Its mission is to establish an entire food chain at the grassroots level to transform the community.

WEBSITE: http://www.brooklynrescuemission.org/

Bushwick Campus Farm

Bushwick Campus Farm was founded as a partnership between the four high schools at Bushwick Campus, a public school in Bushwick, Brooklyn, and the nonprofit EcoStation:NY, an organization dedicated to addressing social and environmental justice through community food and urban agriculture. It operates as a living classroom, a job-training site, and a garden-to-cafeteria program for the Bushwick Campus schools. Its mission centers on sustainable urban agriculture and social justice.

WEBSITE: www.ecostationny.org/BCF/

East New York Farms!

East New York Farms! is a project of the community-based organization United Community Centers, in partnership with residents of the Brooklyn neighborhood of East New York. It consists of two urban farms, two community farmers' markets, and a youth internship program focused on social and environmental justice. It also supports a network of over fifty backyard and community gardens throughout the area. The mission of ENYF! is to organize youth and adults to address community food justice through local sustainable agriculture and community-led economic development.

WEBSITE: http://www.eastnewyorkfarms.org/

Evergreen Community Garden

Evergreen Community Garden is a five-acre GreenThumb garden in Kissena Corridor Park in Queens that serves as a growing space for members of the community.

Farm School NYC

Farm School NYC, originally a project of the food justice organization Just Food, offers a two-year certificate in urban agriculture as well as individual courses on a wide range of topics including social justice issues, urban planting techniques, and grassroots community organizing. Its mission is to train New York City residents in urban agriculture to build self-reliant communities and inspire positive local action for food access and social, economic, and racial justice issues.

WEBSITE: http://www.farmschoolnyc.org/

Friends of Brook Park

Friends of Brook Park is a community-based environmental organization in the South Bronx that provides recreational, environmental, and educational activities for children and adults in the community. It leads gardening and agriculture activities in Brook Park, including a community garden, rainwater harvesting, beekeeping, and chicken keeping. Friends of Brook Park also engages formerly incarcerated, as well as currently court-adjudicated youth, from the South Bronx in an alternatives-to-incarceration program through its Brook Park Youth Farm project.

WEBSITE: http://www.friendsofbrookpark.org/

Green Bronx Machine

Green Bronx Machine is a nonprofit organization focused on sustainable agriculture education, leadership development, and healthy eating for K–12 school communities. It provides educational and consulting services on greenscaping, urban agriculture, and workforce and community development. It is creating a National Health, Wellness, and Learning Center, a community wellness space that will include a vertical farm and a training kitchen.

WEBSITE: http://greenbronxmachine.org/

Green Guerillas

Green Guerillas is a nonprofit organization that helps New York City's community gardeners sustain vital grassroots networks and cultivate vibrant community gardens. It does this through plant giveaways, community organizing activities, fundraising assistance, and youth engagement programs.

WEBSITE: http://www.greenguerillas.org/

Hattie Carthan Community Garden

Hattie Carthan Community Garden is a multigenerational, multicultural garden space operating since 1991 in Bedford-Stuyvesant, Brooklyn. The garden hosts several culinary festivals annually, provides gardening and cooking demonstrations, and organizes public discussions addressing neighborhood issues. Its mission is to preserve the agricultural heritage of Brooklyn while serving as an intergenerational space for reflection, inspiration, education, and training for those who visit.

WEBSITE: http://www.hattiecarthangarden.com/

Hattie Carthan Community Market

Hattie Carthan Community Market, also located in Bedford-Stuyvesant, is a community-based revitalization project led by people of color to increase access to fresh food and the resources needed to grow and distribute it. It operates a "Learn and Earn" program that recruits, trains, and employs local teenagers in its two weekly markets, which operate from July through November. In addition to its farmers' markets, it runs an artisanal solstice market for local women producers and homesteaders and hosts food justice training and events.

WEBSITE: http://www.hattiecarthancommunitymarket.com/

Hattie Carthan Herban Farm

Hattie Carthan Herban Farm is an educational and health justice farm promoting the use and inclusion of herbs for individual, communal, and environmental health. It hosts women's leadership teach-ins, seasonal communal rituals, herbalism workshops, sound healing councils, and plant medicine councils.

WEBSITE: http://yonnette.wix.com/hcherbanfarm

La Familia Verde

La Familia Verde is a coalition of five community gardens in the Bronx whose activities include social justice programs such as voter registration and a farmers' market. Its mission is to sustain the neighborhood, culture, and the environment through education, community service, and horticulture.

WEBSITE: http://www.lafamiliaverde.org/

La Finca del Sur

La Finca del Sur is a nonprofit organization in the South Bronx that runs a community farm, hosts a farmers' market, and organizes community activities centered on food justice and food education. It receives support from New York City's GreenThumb program. Its goal is to address issues of food access, environmental justice, and community empowerment for women of color and their allies in the South Bronx.

WEBSITE: http://bronxfarmers.blogspot.com/

La Unión

La Unión is a nonprofit organization that works for educational justice and immigration reform, as well as food justice and youth justice. It runs the urban farm Granja Los Colibries in Sunset Park, Brooklyn. Its mission is to improve the health of the community through growing healthy food; to build intergenerational relationships; to connect to the traditions and cultures of members' home countries; and to value the process of raising animals and growing food.

WEBSITE: http://la-union.org/

Loisaida United Neighborhood Gardens

Loisaida United Neighborhood Gardens (LUNGS) is a coalition of forty-eight community gardens in New York City's Lower East Side. LUNGS sponsors a community-supported agriculture program, a summer youth employment program, and community events and celebrations, and it advocates for the preservation and protection of member gardens. Its garden sites include GreenThumb gardens, Manhattan Land Trust Gardens, and New York Restoration Project Gardens.

WEBSITE: http://www.lungsnyc.org/

The Point Community Development Corporation

The Point Community Development Corporation is a nonprofit organization that seeks to engage the people of Hunts Point in the Bronx in creating livable spaces and generating economic opportunity. It focuses on cultural and economic revitalization and youth development, including after-school and summer programming, arts and culture events, and community development activities. It also engages in advocacy and community education about open space and waterfront access in the Bronx.

WEBSITE: http://thepoint.org/

Snug Harbor Heritage Farm

Managed by the Snug Harbor Cultural Center and Botanical Garden on Staten Island, Snug Harbor Heritage Farm produces fruits and vegetables with the aim of feeding, inspiring, and educating the local community. It works to increase awareness of the importance of eating locally and to improve the quality of life for those who live in, work in, or visit the New York City area.

WEBSITE: http://snug-harbor.org/heritage-farm/

Taqwa Community Farm

Taqwa Community Farm is a farm and garden space operating in the Bronx. It includes a hydroponics growing system as well as poultry and beekeeping, and it hosts a community market.

Select Population Characteristics
of New York City
and Community Districts

New York City and Community Districts (*Neighborhoods*)	Economic Characteristics (2012) [a]			Racial and Ethnic Composition (2010) [b]				
	Median Household Income (2012)	Poverty Rate (2012)	Unemployment Rate (2012)	% White Non-Hispanic (2010)	% Black Non-Hispanic (2010)	% Hispanic Origin (2010)	% Asian and Pacific Islander Non-Hispanic (2010)	% Other Non-Hispanic (2010)
New York City	$51,750	21.2%	10.6%	33.3%	22.8%	28.6%	12.6%	2.7%
Bronx								
BX01 (*Mott Haven/Melrose*)	$19,443	46.1%	16.0%	1.6%	25.9%	70.9%	0.6%	1.0%
BX02 (*Hunts Point/Longwood*)	$19,443	46.1%	16.0%	1.3%	22.1%	74.8%	0.7%	1.1%
BX03 (*Morrisania/Crotona*)	$20,933	46.4%	20.9%	1.2%	39.4%	57.7%	0.5%	1.3%
BX04 (*Highbridge/Concourse*)	$27,408	37.0%	18.2%	1.5%	32.3%	63.1%	1.5%	1.6%
BX05 (*Fordham/University Heights*)	$21,959	42.3%	17.9%	1.4%	28.7%	66.8%	1.5%	1.6%
BX06 (*Belmont/East Tremont*)	$20,933	46.4%	20.9%	7.5%	25.9%	64.2%	1.1%	1.3%
BX07 (*Kingsbridge Heights/Bedford*)	$31,039	30.1%	14.5%	7.2%	18.8%	65.3%	6.6%	2.1%
BX08 (*Riverdale/Fieldston*)	$55,882	17.1%	9.9%	38.5%	11.2%	43.4%	5.0%	1.9%
BX09 (*Parkchester/Soundview*)	$34,349	28.9%	13.9%	2.8%	30.8%	57.7%	5.8%	3.0%
BX10 (*Throgs Neck/Co-Op City*)	$52,196	13.5%	11.6%	34.5%	22.2%	36.6%	4.6%	2.1%
BX11 (*Morris Park/Bronxdale*)	$43,360	18.4%	15.8%	27.4%	20.3%	42.2%	7.7%	2.4%
BX12 (*Williamsbridge/Baychester*)	$42,077	21.3%	15.7%	7.1%	65.0%	22.9%	1.9%	3.0%
Brooklyn								
BK01 (*Greenpoint/Williamsburg*)	$51,143	31.5%	6.1%	60.8%	5.2%	27.2%	5.1%	1.7%
BK02 (*Fort Greene/Brooklyn Heights*)	$77,014	23.3%	8.5%	46.1%	28.0%	14.2%	7.8%	3.8%
BK03 (*Bedford Stuyvesant*)	$38,742	31.6%	15.6%	10.9%	64.6%	19.9%	2.3%	2.3%
BK04 (*Bushwick*)	$35,616	33.4%	17.5%	8.5%	20.1%	65.4%	4.3%	1.7%
BK05 (*East New York/Starrett City*)	$34,249	30.8%	15.3%	3.4%	51.6%	36.7%	5.0%	3.4%
BK06 (*Park Slope/Carroll Gardens*)	$88,610	10.5%	7.4%	62.7%	10.5%	18.2%	5.3%	3.3%
BK07 (*Sunset Park*)	$42,116	31.6%	10.5%	23.3%	2.9%	45.5%	26.4%	1.9%
BK08 (*Crown Heights/Prospect Heights*)	$42,401	26.9%	12.7%	16.7%	65.5%	11.9%	2.8%	3.0%
BK09 (*S Crown Heights/Lefferts Gardens*)	$39,250	22.9%	13.2%	19.1%	68.0%	9.3%	1.3%	2.3%
BK10 (*Bay Ridge/Dyker Heights*)	$53,285	16.5%	8.2%	61.5%	1.4%	14.4%	20.7%	2.1%
BK11 (*Bensonhurst*)	$50,860	19.8%	11.2%	49.9%	0.7%	13.3%	34.6%	1.5%
BK12 (*Borough Park*)	$38,451	32.4%	6.9%	65.4%	2.3%	13.0%	17.7%	1.7%
BK13 (*Coney Island*)	$30,458	27.5%	11.8%	57.0%	12.9%	16.7%	11.8%	1.7%
BK14 (*Flatbush/Midwood*)	$41,759	18.7%	9.9%	37.1%	35.4%	15.7%	9.5%	2.4%
BK15 (*Sheepshead Bay*)	$48,138	18.3%	10.8%	71.9%	3.3%	8.2%	15.1%	1.6%
BK16 (*Brownsville*)	$28,838	36.4%	12.7%	1.0%	76.2%	20.1%	0.7%	2.0%

Neighborhood								
BK17 (East Flatbush)	2.2%	1.2%	6.8%	88.4%	1.4%	12.2%	17.1%	$49,437
BK18 (Flatlands/Canarsie)	2.2%	3.8%	8.4%	59.6%	26.0%	11.4%	12.1%	$62,546
Manhattan								
MN01 (Financial District)	3.4%	17.4%	7.9%	4.3%	66.9%	4.6%	7.4%	$104,603
MN02 (Greenwich Village/Soho)	2.8%	13.9%	6.2%	1.8%	75.3%	4.6%	7.4%	$104,603
MN03 (*Lower East Side/Chinatown*)	2.3%	33.8%	24.6%	6.9%	32.4%	9.1%	25.1%	*$41,512*
MN04 (Clinton/Chelsea)	2.8%	13.2%	17.7%	6.2%	60.1%	7.2%	11.5%	$87,726
MN05 (Midtown)	2.5%	18.1%	7.7%	4.1%	67.7%	7.2%	11.5%	$87,726
MN06 (Stuyvesant Town/Turtle Bay)	2.4%	14.0%	7.6%	3.5%	72.6%	5.5%	9.1%	$93,983
MN07 (Upper West Side)	2.4%	7.6%	15.0%	7.6%	67.4%	6.8%	11.1%	$93,361
MN08 (Upper East Side)	2.1%	8.6%	7.1%	3.2%	79.0%	6.0%	7.6%	$100,994
MN09 (Morningside Heights/Hamilton)	2.7%	6.9%	42.7%	24.6%	23.0%	11.7%	29.0%	$41,090
MN10 (*Central Harlem*)	2.8%	2.4%	22.2%	63.0%	9.5%	13.5%	27.5%	*$37,460*
MN11 (*East Harlem*)	2.1%	5.6%	49.2%	31.2%	12.0%	8.6%	31.2%	*$31,537*
MN12 (Washington Heights/Inwood)	1.5%	2.5%	71.0%	7.3%	17.6%	17.1%	25.3%	$36,872
Queens								
QN01 (Astoria)	3.3%	14.1%	27.6%	9.8%	45.3%	7.8%	16.3%	$52,727
QN02 (Woodside/Sunnyside)	2.8%	32.0%	34.6%	1.9%	28.7%	7.4%	16.0%	$50,684
QN03 (Jackson Heights)	2.0%	15.8%	64.2%	6.2%	11.9%	8.9%	24.2%	$43,842
QN04 (Elmhurst/Corona)	2.1%	33.2%	52.3%	5.3%	7.2%	8.1%	24.8%	$42,366
QN05 (Ridgewood/Maspeth)	1.4%	7.7%	34.7%	1.4%	54.9%	7.8%	14.5%	$51,723
QN06 (Rego Park/Forest Hills)	2.7%	25.9%	13.6%	2.5%	55.3%	6.2%	13.3%	$64,236
QN07 (*Flushing/Whitestone*)	2.0%	49.4%	16.6%	2.2%	29.8%	9.5%	14.6%	$53,200
QN08 (Hillcrest/Fresh Meadows)	4.2%	31.2%	17.0%	12.6%	35.0%	10.0%	16.1%	$65,192
QN09 (Kew Gardens/Woodhaven)	9.3%	21.9%	40.9%	8.4%	19.6%	10.2%	16.1%	$56,581
QN10 (S. Ozone Park/Howard Beach)	15.6%	18.3%	23.1%	17.1%	25.9%	11.5%	14.5%	$60,877
QN11 (Bayside/Little Neck)	1.6%	39.3%	10.0%	2.1%	47.0%	7.9%	7.4%	$73,315
QN12 (Jamaica/Hollis)	6.7%	9.0%	17.3%	65.3%	1.7%	14.0%	18.1%	$51,574
QN13 (Queens Village)	5.2%	14.7%	11.8%	55.2%	13.1%	10.6%	10.9%	$74,226
QN14 (Rockaway/Broad Channel)	2.7%	2.3%	21.0%	38.8%	35.2%	12.5%	18.5%	$49,757
Staten Island								
SI01 (St. George/Stapleton)	2.5%	7.5%	28.5%	22.0%	39.6%	7.9%	19.7%	$57,325
SI02 (South Beach/Willowbrook)	1.7%	11.4%	13.2%	3.0%	70.7%	6.5%	7.3%	$72,495
SI03 (Tottenville/Great Kills)	1.0%	4.2%	8.4%	1.0%	85.4%	7.0%	6.5%	$83,441

SOURCES:
[a] NYU Furman Center 2014
[b] US Census Bureau 2010 Census
Italics denote neighborhoods detailed in this book.

Urban Agriculture Activities of Select New York City Organizations and Agencies

Organization	Farm or Garden	Food Distribution	Education	Research	Tech. Assistance	Advocacy	Government	Land Trusts	For further information
596 Acres	•			•	•				596acres.org
BK Farmyards	•		•						bkfarmyards.com
Black Urban Growers (BUGS)		•	•			•			blackurbangrowers.org
The BLK ProjeK	•	•	•			•			theblkprojek.org
Bronx-Manhattan Land Trust	•			•	•			•	manhattanlandtrust.org
Brooklyn Botanic Garden			•	•					bbg.org
Brooklyn-Queens Land Trust	•							•	bqlt.org
Brooklyn Rescue Mission Urban Harvest Center	•	•	•						brooklynrescuemission.org
Bushwick Campus Farm	•		•						ecostationny.org/BCF
Cornell Cooperative Extension				•	•		•		nyc.cce.cornell.edu/Pages/home.aspx
Design Trust for Public Space					•				designtrust.org
East New York Farms!	•	•	•			•			eastnewyorkfarms.org
Evergreen Community Garden	•								no website
La Familia Verde	•				•	•			lafamiliaverde.org
Farming Concrete				•	•				farmingconcrete.org
Farm School NYC			•			•			farmschoolnyc.org
La Finca del Sur	•		•	•	•	•			bronxfarmers.blogspot.com
Friends of Brook Park	•		•						friendsofbrookpark.org
Green Bronx Machine	•		•	•		•			greenbronxmachine.org
Green Guerillas			•		•	•			greenguerillas.org
GreenThumb (Department of Parks and Recreation)					•	•	•		greenthumbnyc.org
GrowNYC		•	•			•			grownyc.org
Hattie Carthan Community Garden	•		•			•			hattiecarthangarden.com
Hattie Carthan Community Market									hattiecarthancommunitymarket.com
Hattie Carthan Herban Farm	•		•	•	•				yonnette.wix.com/hcherbanfarm
Horticultural Society of New York			•	•					thehort.org
Hostos Community College				•			•		hostos.cuny.edu

Organization	Website
John Bowne High School	johnbowne.org
Just Food	justfood.org
Kingsborough Community College Urban Farm	kbcc.cuny.edu/cewd/urban_farm
Laurie M. Tisch Center for Food, Education, and Policy	tc.columbia.edu/tisch/
Lower East Side Ecology Center	lesecologycenter.org
LUNGS – Loisaida United Neighborhood Gardens	lungsnyc.org
More Gardens!	moregardens.org
The New School	newschool.edu
New York Botanical Garden	nybg.org/green_up/
New York City Beekeepers Association	bees.nyc
New York City Community Garden Coalition	nyccgc.org
New York City Food Policy Center at Hunter College	nycfoodpolicy.org
New York City Housing Authority Garden & Greening Program	nyc.gov/html/nycha/html/community/garden.shtml
New York Restoration Project	nyrp.org
The Point! Community Development Corporation	thepoint.org
Snug Harbor Heritage Farm	snug-harbor.org/heritage-farm
Taqwa Community Farm	facebook.com/pages/Taqwa-Community-Farm/111780142194555
Trust for Public Land	tpl.org
La Unión	la-union.org

Based on authors' research

NOTES

Chapter 1: Seeing Beyond the Kale

1. The environmental justice movement emerged in contrast to perceived shortcomings of the mainstream environmental movement, particularly the exclusion of people of color from leadership in the movement and the neglect of environmental issues relevant to low-income communities of color. The environmental justice movement grew in the 1980s as grassroots activists began to reveal the disparate risks that low-income communities and communities of color faced as a result of the regulatory, legal, and procedural mechanisms by which chemical manufacturing and disposal facilities were disproportionately located in and near those communities (Gottlieb 2005; Pellow 2000; Taylor 2000, 2011; Sze 2007; Bullard 1993; Mohai, Pellow, and Roberts 2009; Alkon and Agyeman 2011; Peña 2002).

The environmental justice movement broadened its scope in 1991 at the first People of Color Environmental Leadership Summit, when participants coalesced around a shared interest in re-envisioning the environment within "an overall framework of social, racial, and economic justice" (Dana Alston, cited in Gottlieb 2005, 32). Today, environmental justice activists work on a range of issues, including long-standing air pollution and anti-toxics campaigns but also food system justice and climate justice.

2. Food justice is a concept and related movement that considers the social and political roots of inequities in the food system and holds that these fundamental issues must be addressed to solve problems such as disparate access to healthy food, race- and gender-based inequities in restaurant wages, or exploitation of farm workers' labor. Drawing inspiration from the environmental justice movement, many food justice activists insist that people who have been marginalized from food system decision making—often people of color and working-class people—should lead initiatives to realize food justice in their own communities (Alkon and Agyeman 2011; Bradley and Herrera 2015; Gottlieb and Joshi 2010; Redmond 2013).

3. As defined at the Nyéléni Forum for Food Sovereignty in Sélingué, Mali, in 2007, food sovereignty is "the right of peoples to healthy and culturally appropriate food produced through ecologically sound and sustainable methods, and their right to define their own food and agriculture systems. It puts the aspirations and needs of those who produce, distribute and consume food at the heart of food systems and policies rather than the demands of markets and corporations" ("Declaration of Nyéléni" 2007).

Chapter 2: New York City's Urban Agriculture System

1. Just as farms and gardens in New York City do not fit neatly into categories, the farmers and gardeners we spoke with described themselves differently depending on the context, or spoke about their sites as "gardens" but referred to themselves as "farmers." Throughout the book, we have used the words the activists used to describe their sites and themselves.

Chapter 3: Growing More than Just Food

1. The Bronx High School of Science is a prestigious magnet school specializing in math and science and is consistently one of the top-ranked schools in the United States.

2. Though we use the term Latino/a throughout the book, we retain "Hispanic" for accuracy when citing government statistics using this term.

3. The "school-to-prison pipeline" refers to policies and practices that push a disproportionate number of youth of color out of the school system and eventually into the criminal justice system (Wald and Losen 2003).

Chapter 4: Embodying Socially Just Systems

1. We use the word "mainstream" to refer to movements and organizations that have dominated popular understandings of these activist efforts. The mainstream environmental movement traces its roots in the United States to milestones including the Progressive Era conservation movement, the publication of Rachel Carson's *Silent Spring* in 1962, the first national Earth Day in 1970, and passage of the federal Clean Air Act (1963) and Clean Water Act (1972). Accordingly, mainstream environmental *organizations* include the "Big Ten" environmental groups (including the Sierra Club, the National Wildlife Federation, and the National Parks and Conservation Association) and other large nongovernmental organizations and government agencies that have driven the movement. The mainstream environmental movement and its organizations have long been critiqued for being dominated by upper- and middle-class whites and espousing a vision of the environment as "pristine" wilderness areas mostly uninhabited by humans. With regard to food movements and organizations, we follow Mares and Peña's (2011, 200) characterization of the "mainstream alternative food movement" as that which includes such diverse movements as veganism, organic and local food, and community food security. According to these authors, these movements do not encompass a structural analysis of social justice in their visions for a "better" food system. Mainstream alternative food movements and organizations have been critiqued as being dominated by white people and their cultural values. They have also been criticized for creating alternative food systems that are economically inaccessible to low-income consumers, thereby reinforcing existing oppressive structures (see also Guthman 2008b; Slocum 2007, 2006; Yakini 2013; Herrera 2015; US Census Bureau 2012).

2. See, for example, Slocum's (2006) and Morales's (2011) recounting of the now-defunct Community Food Security Coalition's less-than-successful attempt to address the concerns of its Outreach and Diversity Committee, and the subsequent formation of the Growing Food and Justice for All network.

3. Taylor (2014, 73) found that increasing racial and ethnic diversity was seen as beyond the scope of some mainstream environmental organizations. In our experience with

food systems activism, we have heard similar statements from leaders of mainstream alternative food organizations. In light of persistent institutionalized and structural racism, and considering intersectionality theories, one could reasonably expect that if racial and ethnic diversity is not considered part of an organization's mission, supporting leadership among people of color and recent immigrants—arguably more radical ideas—would also be seen as beyond the scope of groups not explicitly focused on these issues.

4. The Institute of Cultural Affairs is a global consortium of nonprofit organizations that provides facilitation training.

Chapter 5: Cultivating Policy

1. Westchester and Putnam Counties are more affluent areas surrounding New York City.

2. This point is particularly salient in light of the high proportion of farmers of color in New York City and the fact that USDA programs have historically underserved, and in some cases discriminated against, minority racial and ethnic groups, including black and Native American farmers.

3. The term *food desert* refers to an urban or rural community that has limited access to nonemergency sources of healthy and affordable food. Government agencies have increasingly embraced this term as a catch-all for food access issues, particularly in low-income urban communities (see Wrigley 2002 for one account of how the term came into use in policy making in the 1990s). The USDA expanded the use of this term when it developed a searchable map of food deserts across the United States. However, many activists dismiss the term because it suggests that low-income communities are devoid of human culture; because it overlooks long-term structural oppression and political decisions that lead to food inaccessibility; and because people living in neighborhoods often referred to as food deserts were not involved with "naming" their communities as such. Moreover, the USDA definition of a food desert is narrowly construed as the lack of a large grocer, which ignores other retail channels and suggests that the solution is a particular type of retail outlet. It also ignores the phenomenon of a "food mirage," where poor people living in affluent areas cannot afford the food in the grocers that exist to serve higher-income residents (e.g., see Short, Guthman, and Raskin 2007).

4. New York City is divided into fifty-nine community districts, represented by community boards that address neighborhood land use, budget, and service delivery issues; some activists attend board meetings to make political connections as well as to comment on the topics being discussed.

Chapter 7: Rethinking Scholarship to Advance Social Justice

1. See also Kurtz, Retburg, and Preston (2015, 5) for an application of this analysis to food sovereignty initiatives in rural Maine.

2. The explicit change-oriented perspective of activist-oriented research does not connote permission to engage in biased research. Research methodologies must still be sound, and the researchers do not alter the findings. It is the analysis and application that contribute to the action-oriented agenda.

3. Critical geography is an approach to geographic scholarship that analyzes the roots of social developments and simultaneously recognizes that scholars are part of the social

world. Critical geographers seek to connect theory to practice by questioning not only social and political systems but their roles in them.

4. Critiques of the validity and generalizability of action-oriented research, along with a long-standing debate about objectivity in social scientific research, have been well rehearsed (e.g., see Anderson and Herr 1999; Habermas 1987 [1971]; Herr 1995). We do not dwell on these critiques or responses to them here. We do, however, note that an important aspect of understanding an approach like participatory action research as a framework or epistemology, rather than as a research *method*, is that it underscores the fact that the action-oriented stance does not inherently affect the rigor or reliability of data collection, analysis, or writing.

Chapter 8: Taking a Collective Step Beyond the Kale

1. The Zapatistas are a rebellion group composed mainly of rural indigenous people in the southern Mexican state of Chiapas. The Zapatista movement aligns with antiglobalization, antineoliberalization, and indigenous rights movements.

2. Models of this type of work include the Public Science Project at the City University of New York, whose staff members conduct participatory action research with New York City community members; nonprofit organizations such as the DataCenter, which supports grassroots organizing for social justice and sustainability through research and training in data collection; and the Bronx Community Research Review Board (a project akin to institutional review boards at universities) in which participating community members review research to be conducted through the Albert Einstein College of Medicine in the Bronx (*Community IRBs* 2012).

BIBLIOGRAPHY

596 Acres. 2014. "596 Acres." http://596acres.org/ (accessed July 30, 2014).

Aarsaether, Nils, Torill Nyseth, and Hilde Bjørnå. 2011. "Two Networks, One City: Democracy and Governance Networks in Urban Transformation." *European Urban and Regional Studies* 18, no. 3 (July): 306–20. doi:10.1177/0969776411403988.

Ackerman, Kubi. 2011. *The Potential for Urban Agriculture in New York City: Growing Capacity, Food Security, and Green Infrastructure.* New York: Urban Design Lab at the Earth Institute, Columbia University.

Agrawal, Arun, and Maria Carmen Lemos. 2007. "A Greener Revolution in the Making? Environmental Governance in the 21st Century." *Environment: Science and Policy for Sustainable Development* 49, no. 5: 36–45.

Agyeman, Julian, and Jesse McEntee. 2014. "Moving the Field of Food Justice Forward through the Lens of Urban Political Ecology." *Geography Compass* 8, no. 3: 211–20. doi:10.1111/gec3.12122.

Alkon, Alison Hope, Daniel Block, Kelly Moore, Catherine Gillis Nicole DiNuccio, and Noel Chavez. 2013. "Foodways of the Urban Poor." *Geoforum* 48: 126–35.

Alkon, Alison Hope. 2012. *Black, White, and Green: Farmers Markets, Race, and the Green Economy.* Geographies of Justice and Social Transformation 13. Athens: University of Georgia Press.

Alkon, Alison Hope, and Teresa Marie Mares. 2012. "Food Sovereignty in US Food Movements: Radical Visions and Neoliberal Constraints." *Agriculture and Human Values* 29: 347–59.

Alkon, Alison Hope, and Julian Agyeman. 2011. "Introduction: The Food Movement as Polyculture." In *Cultivating Food Justice: Race, Class, and Sustainability*, edited by Alison Hope Alkon and Julian Agyeman, 1–20. Cambridge, Mass: MIT Press.

Allen, Patricia. 2008. "Mining for Justice in the Food System: Perceptions, Practices, and Possibilities." *Agriculture and Human Values* 25: 157–61.

Allen, Patricia, and Julie Guthman. 2006. "From 'Old School' to 'Farm-to-School': Neoliberalization from the Ground Up." *Agriculture and Human Values* 23: 401–15.

Altman, Lee, Liz Barry, Martin Barry, Kaja Kuhl, Philip Silva, and Barbara Wilks. 2014. *Five Borough Farm II: Growing the Benefits of Urban Agriculture in New York City.* New York: Design Trust for Public Space.

Anderson, Gary L., and Kathryn Herr. 1999. "The New Paradigm Wars: Is There Room for Rigorous Practitioner Knowledge in Schools and Universities?" *Educational Researcher* 28, no. 5: 12–21, 40.

Ansell, Chris, and Alison Gash. 2007. "Collaborative Governance in Theory and Practice." *Journal of Public Administration Research and Theory* 18, no. 4: 543–71.

Apollon, Dominique, Terry Keheler, Jillian Medeiros, Natalie Ortega, Julia Sebastian, and Rinku Sen. 2014. *Moving the Race Conversation Forward: How the Media Covers Racism, and Other Barriers to Productive Racial Discourse.* New York: Race Forward: The Center for Racial Justice Innovation.

Aspen Institute Roundtable on Community Change. 2014. *Glossary for Understanding the Dismantling Structural Racism/Promoting Racial Equity Analysis* 1–2. http://www.aspeninstitute.org/sites/default/files/content/docs/rcc/RCC-Structural-Racism-Glossary.pdf (accessed August 8, 2014).

Bang, Henrik P. 2010. "Everyday Makers and Expert Citizens: Active Participants in the Search for a Knew Governance." In *Public Management in the Postmodern Era: Challenges and Prospects,* edited by John Fenwick and Janice McMillan. 163–91. Northampton, Mass.: New Horizon in Public Policy.

Bang, Henrik P., and Eva Sørensen. 1999. "The Everyday Maker: A New Challenge to Democratic Governance." *Administrative Theory and Praxis* 2, no. 3: 325–41.

Bauer, Caroline, and Rosamond Fletcher, eds. 2014. *Five Borough Farm Data Collection Toolkit: Protocols for Measuring the Outcomes and Impacts of Community Gardens and Urban Farms.* New York: Design Trust for Public Space and Farming Concrete.

Bellafante, Ginia. 2014. "How Can Community Colleges Get a Piece of the Billions that Donors Give to Higher Education?" *New York Times,* November 16.

Bellows, Anne C., Katherine Brown, and Jac Smit. 2003. "Health Benefits of Urban Agriculture." Working paper from members of the Community Food Security Coalition's North American Initiative on Urban Agriculture.

Bellows, Anne C., Verdie Robinson, Jennifer Guthrie, Troels Meyer, Natalie Peric, and Michael W. Hamm. 2000. "Urban Livestock Agriculture in the State of New Jersey, USA." *Urban Agriculture Magazine* 1, no. 2: 8–9.

Binz-Scharf, Maria Christina, David Lazer, and Ines Mergel. 2011. "Searching for Answers: Networks of Practice Among Public Administrators." *American Review of Public Administration* 42, no. 2: 202–25.

Blair, Dorothy. 2009. "The Child in the Garden: An Evaluative Review of the Benefits of School Gardening." *Journal of Environmental Education* 40, no. 2: 15–38.

Blecha, Jennifer L. 2007. "Urban Life with Livestock: Performing Alternative Imaginaries through Small-Scale Urban Livestock Agriculture in the United States." PhD diss., University of Minnesota.

Blecha, Jennifer, and Helga Leitner. 2014. "Reimagining the Food System, the Economy, and Urban Life: New Urban Chicken-Keepers in US Cities." *Urban Geography* 35, no. 1: 86–108.

Block, Daniel R., Noel Chávez, Erika Allen, and Dinah Ramirez. 2012. "Food Sovereignty, Urban Food Access, and Food Activism: Contemplating the Connections through Examples from Chicago." *Agriculture and Human Values* 29, no. 2: 203–15.

Bonacich, Edna, and Jake Alimahomed-Wilson. 2011. "Confronting Racism, Capitalism, and Ecological Degradation: Urban Farming and the Struggle for Social Justice in Black Los Angeles." *Souls* 13, no. 2: 213–26.

Bonilla-Silva, Eduardo. 1997. "Rethinking Racism: Toward a Structural Interpretation." *American Sociological Review* 62, no. 3 (June): 465–80.

Bowens, Natasha. 2015. *The Color of Food*. Gabriola Island, B.C., Canada: New Society Press.

Bradley, Katherine, and Hank Herrera. 2015. "Decolonizing Food Justice: Naming, Resisting, and Researching Colonizing Forces in the Movement." *Antipode: A Radical Journal of Geography* (June 17): Online first content, 1–18, doi:10.1111/anti.12165.

Bradley, Katharine, and Ryan E. Galt. 2013. "Practicing Food Justice at Dig Deep Farms and Produce, East Bay Area, California: Self-Determination as a Guiding Value and Intersections with Foodie Logics." *Local Environment* 19, no. 2: 172–86.

Broad, Garrett M. 2013. "Ritual Communication and Use Value: The South Central Farm and the Political Economy of Place." *Communication, Culture, and Critique* 6: 20–40.

Brown, Gavin. 2007. "Mutinous Eruptions: Autonomous Spaces of Radical Queer Activism." *Environment and Planning A* 39, no. 11: 2685.

Brown, Katherine H., Martin Bailkey, Alison Meares-Cohen, Joe Nasr, Jac Smit, and Terri Buchanan. 2002. *Urban Agriculture and Community Food Security in the United States: Farming from the City Center to the Urban Fringe*. Portland, Ore.: Urban Agriculture Committee of the Community Food Security Coalition.

Brown, Katherine H., and Anne Carter. 2002. *Urban Agriculture and Community Food Security in the United States: Farming from the City Center to the Urban Fringe*. Portland, Ore.: Urban Agriculture Committee of the Community Food Security Coalition.

"Brownfields to Greenfields: A Field Guide to Phytoremediation." 2011. New York: youarethecity. http://www.youarethecity.com.

Brustein, Joshua. 2009. "Beekeepers Keep the Lid On." *New York Times*, June 19. http://www.nytimes.com/2009/06/21/nyregion/21ritual.html?_r=0.

Bullard, Robert D., ed. 1993. *Confronting Environmental Racism: Voices from the Grassroots*. Boston: South End Press.

Cadji, Max. 2013. "Tools for Dealing with Gentrification." COMFOOD listserv. comfood@elist.tufts.edu.

Certomà, Chiara. 2011. "Critical Urban Gardening as a Post-Environmentalist Practice." *Local Environment* 16, no. 10: 977–87.

City of Minneapolis Community Planning and Economic Development Department. 2011. "Urban Agriculture Policy Plan: A Land Use and Development Plan for a Healthy, Sustainable Local Food System." February 22.

City of New York. 2007. *PlaNYC: A Greener, Greater New York*. City plan.

City of New York. 2014. *PlaNYC: A Greener, Greater New York, a Stronger, More Resilient New York: Progress Report 2014*. City plan. http://www.nyc.gov/html/planyc2030/downloads/pdf/140422_PlaNYCP-Report_FINAL_Web.pdf.

City of New York. 2015. *One New York: The Plan for a Strong and Just City*. City plan, July 2. http://www.nyc.gov/html/onenyc/downloads/pdf/publications/OneNYC.pdf (accessed July 13, 2015).

City Record, The, 2010. Addition of New Chapter 6 to Title 56 of the Official Compilation of Rules of the City of New York. 137 (176): 2549. September 13.

Cohen, Nevin, and Kubi Ackerman. 2011. "Breaking New Ground." *New York Times*, November 21. http://bittman.blogs.nytimes.com/2011/11/21/breaking-new-ground/.

Cohen, Nevin, and Kristin Reynolds. 2015. "Resource Needs for a Socially Just and Sustainable Urban Agriculture System: Lessons from New York City." *Renewable Agriculture and Food Systems* 30, no. 1: 103–14.

Cohen, Nevin, and Kristin Reynolds. 2014. "Urban Agriculture Policy Making in New York's 'New Political Spaces': Strategizing for a Participatory and Representative System." *Journal of Planning and Education Research* 34, no. 2: 221–34.

Cohen, Nevin, Kristin Reynolds, and Rupal Sanghvi. 2012. *Five Borough Farm: Seeding the Future of Urban Agriculture in New York City*. New York: Design Trust for Public Space.

Cohen, Nevin, and Katinka Wijsman. 2014. "Urban Agriculture as Green Infrastructure: The Case of New York City." *Urban Agriculture Magazine*, no. 27 (March): 16–19.

Colasanti, Kathryn J. A., Michael W. Hamm, and Charlotte M. Litjens. 2012. "The City as an 'Agricultural Powerhouse': Perspectives on Expanding Urban Agriculture from Detroit, Michigan." *Urban Geography* 33, no. 3: 348–69.

Cole, Luke, and Sheila R. Foster. 2001. *From the Ground Up: Environmental Racism and the Rise of the Environmental*. New York: New York University Press.

Coleman, Stephen. 2007. "Mediated Politics and Everyday Life." *International Journal of Communication* 1: 49–60.

Collins, Patricia Hill. 2000. *Black Feminist Thought: Knowledge, Consciousness, and the Politics of Empowerment*. 2nd edition. New York: Routledge.

Community IRBs and Research Review Boards: Shaping the Future of Community-Engaged Research. 2012. Bronx, N.Y.: Albert Einstein College of Medicine, The Bronx Health Link and Community-Campus Partnerships for Health. http://ccph.info.

Conley, Dalton. 1999. *Being Black, Living in the Red: Race, Wealth, and Social Policy in America*. 209. Berkeley and Los Angeles: University of California Press.

Cooper, Dara, Dennis Derryck, Ray Figueroa, Karen Washington, Anthony Giancatarino, Simran Noor, Mark Winston Griffith, Brenda Duchene, Qiana Mickie, Onika Abraham, Tanya Fields, Sheryll Durant, DeVanie Jackson, and Robert Jackson. 2015. "Community Recommendations for New York State Food Hub Task Force." Open letter. http://www.centerforsocialinclusion.org/community-recommendations-for-new-york-state-food-hub-task-force/ (accessed July 2, 2015).

Crenshaw, Kimberlée. 1991. "Mapping the Margins: Intersectionality, Identity Politics, and Violence against Women of Color." *Stanford Law Review* 43, no. 6: 1241–99.

Crouch, Patrick. 2012. "Evolution or Gentrification: Do Urban Farms Lead to Higher Rents?" *Grist.org* (online magazine), October 23. http://grist.org/food/evolution-or-gentrification-do-urban-farms-lead-to-higher-rents/.

Curran, Winifred, and Trina Hamilton. 2012. "Just Green Enough: Contesting Environmental Gentrification in Greenpoint, Brooklyn." *Local Environment* 17, no. 9: 1027–42.

Daftary-Steel, Sarita, and Suzanne Gervais. 2014. *East New York Farms! Retrospective Case Study*. N.p.

Decker, Geoff. 2012. "At Rooftop Garden Party, Candidates Tout Budding Principal." Gotham Schools (now Chalkbeat New York). http://gothamschools.org/2012/09/21/at-rooftop-garden-party-2013-candidates-tout-budding-principal/ (accessed April 10, 2013).

"Declaration of Nyéléni." 2007. Nyéléni Forum for Food Sovereignty. Nyéléni Village, Sélingué, Mali. February 27. http://www.nyeleni.org/.

Dekhan, Aziz. 2014. "Boardwalk Community Garden Lawsuit Update." New York City Community Garden Coalition (website), June 23. www.nyccgc.org/2014/06/board-walk-community-garden-lawsuit-update/.

Delgado, Richard, and Jean Stefancic. 2012. *Critical Race Theory: An Introduction.* 2nd ed. New York: New York University Press.

DeLind, Laura. 2013. "Raising Food or Razing Neighborhood: Coming to Terms with Urban Agriculture—A Self-Critique." Agriculture and Human Values conference, East Lansing, Mich.

DeLind, Laura. 2015. "Where Have All the Houses (Among Other Things) Gone?" *Renewable Agriculture and Food Systems* 30, no. 1: 3–7.

"Detroit Foodies Promote Urban Farming as Way to Fight Blight, Grow Economy." 2013. *Crain's Detroit Business.* Last modified August 12, 2013. http://www.crainsdetroit.com/article/20130812/NEWS01/130819989/detroit-foodies-promote-urban-farming-as-way-to-fight-blight-grow.

Dewey, John. 1917. "Enlistment for the Farm." *Columbia War Papers* 1, no. 1. New York: Division of Intelligence and Publicity of Columbia University.

Dooling, Sarah. 2009. "Ecological Gentrification: A Research Agenda Exploring Justice in the City." *International Journal of Urban and Regional Research* 33, no. 3: 621–39.

Draper, Carrie, and Darcy Freedman. 2010. "Review and Analysis of the Benefits, Purposes, and Motivations Associated with Community Gardening in the United States." *Journal of Community Practice* 18, no. 4: 458–92.

Dryzek, John S. 2010. *Foundations and Frontiers of Deliberative Governance.* Oxford: Oxford University Press.

Duchemin, Eric, Fabien Wegmuller, and Anne-Marie Legault. 2008. "Urban Agriculture: Multi-Dimensional Tools for Social Development in Poor Neighbourhoods." *Field Actions Science Reports: The Journal of Field Actions.* Vol. 1. http://factsreports.revues.org/113 (online since January 16, 2009; accessed October 10, 2012).

Egan, Michael. 2005. "Organizing Protest in the Changing City: Swill Milk and Social Activism in New York City, 1842–1864." *New York History* 86, no. 3: 205–25.

Eizenberg, Efrat. 2008. "From the Ground Up: Community Gardens in New York City and the Politics of Spatial Transformation." PhD diss., City University of New York.

Eizenberg, Efrat. 2012a. "The Changing Meaning of Community Space: Two Models of NGO Management of Community Gardens in New York City." *International Journal of Urban and Regional Research* 36, no. 1: 106–20.

Eizenberg, Efrat. 2012b. "Actually Existing Commons: Three Moments of Space of Community Gardens in New York City." *Antipode: A Radical Journal of Geography* 44, no. 3: 764–82.

Eizenberg, Efrat. 2013. *From the Ground Up: Community Gardens in New York City and the Politics of Spatial Transformation.* Farnham, Surrey, Eng.: Ashgate.

Elder, Robert Fox. 2005. "Protecting New York City's Community Gardens." *NYU Environmental Law Journal* 13: 769.

Englander, Diane. 2001. *New York City's Community Gardens: A Resource at Risk*. New York: The Trust for Public Land.

Entman, Robert M. 2007. "Framing Bias: Media in the Distribution of Power." *Journal of Communication* 57, no. 1: 163–73.

Fainstein, Susan S., and Norman Fainstein. 1989. "The Ambivalent State: Economic Development Policy in the US Federal System under the Reagan Administration." *Urban Affairs Review* 25, no. 1: 41–62.

Fals-Borda, Orlando, and Mohammad Anisur Rahman, eds. 1991. *Action and Knowledge: Breaking the Monopoly with Participatory Action Research*. New York: Apex.

Farming Concrete. 2014. "Farming Concrete." http://farmingconcrete.org/about/ (accessed July 30, 2014).

Farms to Grow. No date. www.farmstogrow.com (website).

Feenstra, Gail Whiting, Sharyl McGrew, and David Campbell. 1999. *Entrepreneurial Community Gardens: Growing Food, Skills, Jobs, and Communities*. ANR Publication 21587. Davis: University of California Agriculture and Natural Resources Publications.

Figueroa-Reyes, Raymond, and Aziz Dekhan. 2014. "Pack the Courtroom in Solidarity with Boardwalk Community Garden." New York City Community Garden Coalition (website), June 3. http://nyccgc.org/2014/06/pack-the-courtroom-in-solidarity-with-boardwalk-community-garden/ (accessed June 10, 2014).

Florida, Richard. 2002. *The Rise of the Creative Class: And How It's Transforming Work, Leisure, Community and Everyday Life*. New York: Basic Books.

Foucault, Michel. 2008. *The Birth of Biopolitics: Lectures at the Collège de France, 1978–79*. Edited by Michel Senellart. Translated by Graham Burchell. New York: Palgrave Macmillan.

Freire, Paolo. 1993. *Pedagogy of the Oppressed*, rev. ed. New York: Continuum.

Fuchs, Ester R. 2010. *Mayors and Money: Fiscal Policy in New York and Chicago*. Chicago: University of Chicago Press. (Orig. pub. 1992.)

Giancatarino, Anthony, and Simran Noor. 2014. *Building the Case for Racial Equity in the Food System*. New York: Center for Social Inclusion.

Gibson-Graham, Julie-Katherine. 2006. *The End of Capitalism (As We Knew It): A Feminist Critique of Political Economy*. 2nd ed., with a new introduction. Minneapolis: University of Minnesota Press.

Gibson-Graham, Julie-Katherine. 2008. "Diverse Economies: Performative Practices for Other Worlds." *Progress in Human Geography* 32, no. 5: 613–32.

Gilens, Martin. 2012. *Affluence and Influence: Economic Inequality and Political Power in America*. Princeton, N.J.: Princeton University Press.

Gittleman, Mara, Lenny Librizzi, and Edie Stone. 2010. *Community Garden Survey New York City: Results 2009/2010*. GrowNYC.

Glassman, Jim. 2003. "Rethinking Overdetermination, Structural Power, and Social Change: A Critique of Gibson-Graham, Resnick, and Wolff." *Antipode: A Radical Journal of Geography* 35, no. 4: 678–98.

Golden, Sheila. 2013. *Urban Agriculture Impacts: Social, Health, and Economic: A Lit-

erature Review. Davis: University of California Agriculture and Natural Resources Publications.

Gómez-Baggethun, Erik, Åsa Gren, David N. Barton, Johannes Langemeyer, Timon McPhearson, Patrick O'Farrell, Erik Andersson, Zoé Hamstead, and Peleg Kremer. 2013. "Urban Ecosystem Services." In *Urbanization, Biodiversity and Ecosystem Services: Challenges and Opportunities*, 175--251. Dordrecht: Springer Netherlands.

Gorgolewski, Mark, June Komisar, and Joe Nasr. 2011. *Carrot City: Creating Places for Urban Agriculture*. New York: Monacelli.

Gottlieb, Robert. 2005. *Forcing the Spring: The Transformation of the American Environmental Movement*. 2nd ed. Washington, D.C.: Island Press.

Gottlieb, Robert, and Anupama Joshi. 2010. *Food Justice*. Cambridge, Mass.: MIT Press.

Green Guerillas. 2014. "Green Guerillas." http://www.greenguerillas.org (accessed February 1, 2015).

Grow to Learn NYC. 2014. "Grow to Learn NYC." http://growtolearn.org/ (accessed June 26, 2014).

Guthman, Julie. 2008a. "Bringing Good Food to Others: Investigating the Subjects of Alternative Food Practice." *Cultural Geographies* 15, no. 4: 431–47.

Guthman, Julie. 2008b. "'If They Only Knew': Color Blindness and Universalism in California Alternative Food Institutions." *Professional Geographer* 60, no. 3: 387–97.

Habermas, Jürgen. 1987. *Knowledge and Human Interests*. Translated by Jeremy J. Shapiro. 3rd trans. edition. Oxford: Polity Press. (Orig. pub. 1971.)

Hajer, Maarten. 2003. "Policy without Polity? Policy Analysis and the Institutional Void." *Policy Sciences* 36, no. 2: 175–95.

Hattie Carthan Community Market. 2013. "Hattie Carthan Community Market." http://www.hattiecarthancommunitymarket.com/ (accessed December 27, 2013).

Hayden-Smith, Rose. 2006. *Soldiers of the Soil: A Historical Review of the United States School Garden Army*. 4-H Center for Youth Development Monograph Series. Davis: University of California, Davis.

Hayden-Smith, Rose. 2014. *Sowing the Seeds of Victory: American Gardening Programs of World War I*. Jefferson, N.C.: McFarland.

Hernandez, Javier C. 2010. "Community Garden Rules Receive Mixed Reaction." *New York Times*, September 3.

Herr, Kathryn. 1995. "Action Research as Empowering Practice." *Journal of Progressive Human Services* 6, no. 2: 45–58.

Herrera, Hank. 2015. Personal communication dated January 30.

Heynen, Nik, Hilda E. Kurtz, and Amy Trauger. 2012. "Food Justice, Hunger and the City." *Geography Compass* 6, no. 5: 304–11.

Heynen, Nik, and Jason Rhodes. 2012. "Organizing for Survival: From the Civil Rights Movement to Black Anarchism through the Life of Lorenzo Kom'boa Ervin." *ACME: An International E-Journal for Critical Geographies* 11, no. 3.

Hodgson, Kimberley, Marcia Caton Campbell, and Martin Bailkey. 2011. *Urban Agriculture: Growing Healthy, Sustainable Places*. Planning Advisory Service Report No. 563. Chicago: American Planning Association.

hooks, bell. 1994. *Teaching to Transgress: Education as the Practice of Freedom*. New York: Routledge.

hooks, bell. 2000. *Feminist Theory: From Margin to Center.* 2nd ed. Brooklyn, N.Y.: South End Press.

Howe, Marvine. 1994. "Neighborhood Report: Lower East Side; Trouble in the Gardens?" *New York Times,* May 15, www.nytimes.com/1994/05/15/nyregion/neighborhood-report-lower-east-side-trouble-in-the-gardens.html.

Hynes, H. Patricia. 1996. *A Patch of Eden: America's Inner-City Gardens.* White River Junction, Vt.: Chelsea Green.

Hynes, H. Patricia, and Genevieve Howe. 2004. "Urban Horticulture in the Contemporary United States: Personal and Community Benefits." In *ISHS Acta Horticulturae 643: International Conference on Urban Horticulture,* edited by R. Junge-Berberovic, J. B. Bächtiger, and W. J. Simpson, 171–81. International Society for Horticultural Science. doi:10.17660/ActaHortic.2004.643.21.

Innes, Judith E., and David E. Booher. 2010. *Planning with Complexity: An Introduction to Collaborative Rationality for Public Policy.* Abbington, Oxon: Routledge.

Jenkins, Dorothy H. 1943. "First Year Is Hardest: Despite Mistakes Victory Gardens Have Done Wonders and Can Do Even Better." *New York Times,* September 19.

Jenkins, Dorothy H. 1944. "Around the Garden." *New York Times,* July 23.

Just Food. No date. "Farm School NYC" (website). http://justfood.org/farmschoolnyc (accessed February 19, 2014).

Kandel, William. 2008. *Profile of Hired Farmworkers: A 2008 Update.* Economic Research Report No. 60. Washington, D.C.: Economic Research Service, US Department of Agriculture, June.

Kato, Yuki, Catarina Passidomo, and Daina Harvey. 2013. "Political Gardening in a Post-Disaster City: Lessons from New Orleans." *Urban Studies* 51, no. 9: 1–17.

Kaufman, Jerome L., and Martin Bailkey. 2000. *Farming Inside Cities: Entrepreneurial Urban Agriculture in the United States.* Cambridge, Mass.: Lincoln Institute of Land Policy.

Keleher, Terry, and Nayantara Sen. 2012. "Challenging Racism Systematically" (webinar). N.p.: Applied Research Center.

Kelly, Philip. 2005. "Scale, Power and the Limits to Possibilities. A Commentary on J. K. Gibson-Graham's 'Surplus Possibilities: Postdevelopment and Community Economies.'" *Singapore Journal of Tropical Geography* 26, no. 1: 39–43.

Kurtz, Hilda E. 2015. "Scaling Food Sovereignty: Biopolitics and the Struggle for Local Control of Farm Food in Rural Maine." *Annals of the Association of American Geographers* 105, no. 4, 859–73.

La Unión. 2014. "La Unión." http://la-union.org/ (accessed February 3, 2014).

Lai, Diane. 2009. "The Barnard Farmerettes of World War I." *Barnard Archives and Special Collections* (blog), December 1. https://barnardarchives.wordpress.com/2009/12/01/the-barnard-%E2%80%9Cfarmerettes%E2%80%9D-of-world-war-i/.

Laurie, Nina D. 2005. "Putting the Messiness Back In: Towards a Geography of Development as Creativity; A Commentary on J.K. Gibson-Graham's 'Surplus Possibilities: Postdevelopment and Community Economies.'" *Singapore Journal of Tropical Geography* 26, no. 1: 32–35.

Lawhead, Camille. 2014. "There's nothing hip or cool happening in Brooklyn. It's a war." *Brokelyn* (online magazine), October 28. http://brokelyn.com/fight-gentrification-brooklyn-battleground/ (accessed November 14).

Lawson, Laura. 2004. "The Planner in the Garden: A Historical View into the Relationship Between Planning and Community Gardens." *Journal of Planning History* 3, no. 2: 151–76.

Lawson, Laura J. 2005. *City Bountiful: A Century of Community Gardening in America.* Berkeley: University of California Press.

Lawson, Victoria. 2005. "Hopeful Geographies: Imagining Ethical Alternatives: A Commentary on J.K. Gibson-Graham's 'Surplus Possibilities: Postdevelopment and Community Economies.'" *Singapore Journal of Tropical Geography* 26(1): 36–38.

Let's Move. 2014. "Learn the Facts." http://www.letsmove.gov/learn-facts/epidemic-childhood-obesity (accessed July 30, 2014).

Lewin, Kurt. 1948. "Action Research and Minority Problems." In *Resolving Social Conflicts: Selected Papers on Group Dynamics,* edited by G. W. Lewin, 201–16. New York: Harper and Brothers.

Mares, Teresa M., and Devon G. Peña. 2011. "Environmental and Food Justice: Toward Local, Slow, and Deep Food Systems." In *Cultivating Food Justice: Race, Class, and Sustainability,* edited by Alison H. Alkon and Julian Agyeman. 197–220. Cambridge, Mass.: MIT Press.

Mares, Teresa M., and Devon G. Peña. 2010. "Urban Agriculture in the Making of Insurgent Spaces in Los Angeles and Seattle." In *Insurgent Public Space: Guerrilla Urbanism and the Remaking of Contemporary Cities,* edited by Jeffrey Hou. 241–54. New York: Routledge.

Markham, Lauren. 2014. "Gentrification and the Urban Garden." *New Yorker,* May 21. http://www.newyorker.com/business/currency/gentrification-and-the-urban-garden.

Markusen, Ann. 2006. "Urban Development and the Politics of a Creative Class: Evidence From a Study of Artists." *Environment and Planning A,* 38, no. 10: 1921–40.

Marsh, David. 2011. "Late Modernity and the Changing Nature of Politics: Two Cheers for Henrik Bang." *Critical Policy Studies* 5, no. 1: 73–89.

McCann, Eugene, and Kevin Ward. 2012. "Policy Assemblages, Mobilities and Mutations: Toward a Multidisciplinary Conversation." *Political Studies Review* 10, no. 3: 325–32.

McClintock, Nathan. 2010. "Why Farm the City? Theorizing Urban Agriculture through a Lens of Metabolic Rift." *Cambridge Journal of Regions, Economy and Society* 3, no. 2: 191–207.

McClintock, Nathan. 2012. "Assessing Soil Lead Contamination at Multiple Scales in Oakland, California: Implications for Urban Agriculture and Environmental Justice." *Applied Geography* 35, no. 1: 460–73.

McClintock, Nathan. 2013. "Radical, Reformist, and Garden-Variety Neoliberal: Coming to Terms with Urban Agriculture's Contradictions." *Local Environment* 19, no. 2: 147–71.

McIntosh, Peggy. 1990. "White Privilege and Male Privilege: A Personal Account of Coming to See Correspondences through Work in Women's Studies." Working Paper 189, New York State Council of Educational Associations.

McNeur, Catherine. 2011. "The 'Swinish Multitude' Controversies over Hogs in Antebellum New York City." *Journal of Urban History* 37, no. 5: 639–60.

Meenar, Mahbubur R., and Brandon M. Hoover. 2012. "Community Food Security via Urban Agriculture: Understanding People, Place, Economy, and Accessibility from a Food Justice Perspective." *Journal of Agriculture, Food Systems, and Community Development* 3, no. 1: 143–60.

Mendel, Richard A. 2011. *No Place for Kids: The Case for Reducing Juvenile Incarceration.* Baltimore: Annie E. Casey Foundation.

Metcalf, Sara S., and Michael J. Widener. 2011. "Growing Buffalo's Capacity for Local Food: A Systems Framework for Sustainable Agriculture." *Applied Geography* 31, no. 4: 1242–51.

Midgett, Jonathan. 2014. "Hope for the Motor City: Urban Farms Change Blighted Detroit Neighborhoods." *Powerhouse Growers.* Last modified on April 30, 2014. powerhousegrowers.com/hope-for-the-motor-city-urban-farms-change-blighted-detroitneighborhoods/.

Milbourne, Paul. 2011. "Everyday (In)Justices and Ordinary Environmentalisms: Community Gardening in Disadvantaged Urban Neighbourhoods." *Local Environment* 17, no. 9: 943–57.

Mitchell, Don. 2003. *The Right to the City: Social Justice and the Fight for Public Space.* New York: Guilford.

Mohai, Paul, David Pellow, and J. Timmons Roberts. 2009. *Environmental Justice: Annual Review of Environment and Resource* 34: 405–30.

Morales, Alfonso. 2011. "Growing Food and Justice." In *Cultivating Food Justice: Race, Class, and Sustainability*, edited by Alison H. Alkon and Julian Agyeman. 149–76. Cambridge, Mass.: MIT Press.

Moynihan, Colin. 2013. "Owner Takes a Chunk Out of an Unofficial Community Garden." *New York Times*, May 15.

Mukherji, Nina, and Alfonso Morales. 2010. "Zoning for Urban Agriculture." *Zoning Practice* 10, no. 3: 1–8.

Myers, Justin Sean, and Joshua Sbicca. 2015. "Bridging Good Food and Good Jobs: From Secession to Confrontation within Alternative Food Movement Politics." *Geoforum* 61: 17–26.

Nairn, Michael, and Dominec Vitiello. 2009. "Lush Lots: Everyday Urban Agriculture: From Community Gardening to Community Food Security." *Harvard Design Magazine* 31, no. 2.

New York City Community Garden Coalition. n.d. "New York City Community Garden Coalition" (website). http://nyccgc.org/ (accessed July 30, 2014).

New York City Council. 2010. *FoodWorks: A Vision of NYC's Food System* (report). http://www.council.nyc.gov/downloads/pdf/FoodWorks-%20A%20Vision%20of%20 NYC's%20Food%20System%20(speech).pdf.

New York City Housing Authority. 2014a. "Community Programs and Services: Garden Program." http://www.nyc.gov/html/nycha/html/community/garden.shtml (accessed July 30, 2014).

New York City Housing Authority. 2014b. "Green NYCHA" (website). http://greennycha.org/ (accessed February 1, 2015).

New York State College of Agriculture. 1943. "Victory Gardens in Greater New York: Instructions for Vegetable Growing in Urban Areas." New York: Greater New York Victory Garden Council. http://babel.hathitrust.org/cgi/pt?id=coo.31924000267280.

New York (State) Task Force on Transforming Juvenile Justice. 2009. *Charting a New Course: A Blueprint for Transforming Juvenile Justice in New York State.* 108. Governor David A. Paterson's Task Force on Transforming Juvenile Justice; Jeremy Travis, chair.

Newfield, Jack, and Paul Du Brul. 1981. *The Permanent Government: Who Really Rules New York?* New York: Pilgrim Press.

Newtown Florist Club Writing Collective. 2013. "Peas and Praxis: Organizing Food Justice Through the Direct Action of the Newtown Florist Club." In *Geographies of Race and Food: Fields, Bodies, Markets,* edited by Rachel Slocum and Arun Saldanha, 137–53. Burlington, Vt.: Ashgate.

NYU Furman Center. 2014. *The State of New York City's Housing and Neighborhoods in 2013.* New York: Furman Center. http://furmancenter.org/research/sonychan.

Office of Manhattan Borough President Gale A. Brewer. 2015. *How Our Gardens Grow: Strategies for Expanding Urban Agriculture* (report). April. http://manhattanbp.nyc.gov/downloads/pdf/GardenReport.pdf.

Office of Manhattan Borough President Scott Stringer. 2010. *FoodNYC: A Blueprint for a Sustainable Food System* (report). http://www.farmlandinfo.org/foodnyc-blueprint-sustainable-food-system.

Office of Manhattan Borough President Scott Stringer. 2009. *Food in the Public Interest: How New York City's Food Policy Holds the Key to Hunger, Health, Jobs and the Environment* (report). February. http://www.farmlandinfo.org/food-public-interest-how-new-york-citys-food-policy-holds-key-hunger-health-jobs-and-environment.

Omi, Michael, and Howard Winant. 1994. *Racial Formation in the United States: From the 1960s to the 1990s.* New York: Routledge Press.

Parr, Damian M., and Cary J. Trexler. 2011. "Students' Experiential Learning and Use of Student Farms in Sustainable Agriculture Education." *Journal of Natural Resources and Life Sciences Education* 40, no. 1: 172–80.

Patel, Raj. 2009. "What Does Food Sovereignty Look Like?" *Journal of Peasant Studies* 36, no. 3: 663–706.

Pearsall, Hamil. 2012. "Moving Out or Moving In? Resilience to Environmental Gentrification in New York City." *Local Environment* 17, no. 9: 1013–26.

Pearsall, Hamil, and Joseph Pierce. 2010. "Urban Sustainability and Environmental Justice: Evaluating the Linkages in Public Planning/Policy Discourse." *Local Environment* 15, no. 6: 569–80.

Peck, Jamie. 2005. "Struggling with the Creative Class." *International Journal of Urban and Regional Research* 29, no. 4: 740–70.

Pellow, David N. 2000. "Environmental Inequality Formation toward a Theory of Environmental Injustice." *American Behavioral Scientist* 43, no. 4: 581–601.

Peña, Devon G. 2002. "Environmental Justice and Sustainable Agriculture: Linking Ecological and Social Sides of Sustainability." Resource paper series. Second National People of Color Environmental Leadership Summit: Summit II.

Penniman, Leah. 2015. "Radical Farmers Use Fresh Food to Fight Racial Injustice and the New Jim Crow." *YES! Magazine* (online magazine), January 28. http://www.yesmagazine.org/peace-justice/radical-farmers-use-fresh-food-fight-racial-injustice-black-lives-matter.

Pinderhughes, Raquel. 2003. "Democratizing Environmental Ownership." In *Natural Assets: Democratizing Environmental Ownership*, edited by James K. Boyce and Barry G. Shelley. 299–312. Washington, D.C.: Island Press.

Piven, Frances Fox. 2010. "Reflections on Scholarship and Activism." *Antipode: A Radical Journal of Geography* 42, no. 4: 806–10.

Pothukuchi, Kameshwari, and Jerome L. Kaufman. 1999. "Placing the Food System on the Urban Agenda: The Role of Municipal Institutions in Food Systems Planning." *Agriculture and Human Values* 16, no. 2: 213–24.

Pudup, Mary Beth. 2008. "It Takes a Garden: Cultivating Citizen-Subjects in Organized Garden Projects." *Geoforum* 39, no. 3: 1228–40.

Quastel, Noah. 2009. "Political Ecologies of Gentrification." *Urban Geography* 30, no. 7: 694–725.

Raver, Anne. 1997. "Houses Before Gardens, the City Decides." *New York Times*, January 9.

Reason, Peter, and Hillary Bradbury. 2008. *The SAGE Handbook of Action Research: Participative Inquiry and Practice*. 2nd ed. London: Sage.

Redmond, LaDonna. 2013. "Food + Justice = Democracy" (presentation at TEDxManhattan). http://www.cfjn.org/.

Reynolds, Kristin. 2011. "Expanding Technical Assistance for Urban Agriculture: Best Practices for Extension Services in California and Beyond." *Journal of Agriculture, Food Systems, and Community Development* 1: 197–216.

Reynolds, Kristin. 2014. "Disparity Despite Diversity: Social Injustice in New York City's Urban Agriculture System." *Antipode: A Radical Journal of Geography* 47, no. 1: 240–59.

Rogus, Stephanie, and Carolyn Dimitri. 2015. "Agriculture in Urban and Peri-Urban Areas in the United States: Highlights from the Census of Agriculture." *Renewable Agriculture and Food Systems* 30, no. 1: 64–78.

Ryan, Charlotte, Kevin M. Carragee, and William Meinhofer. 2001. "Theory into Practice: Framing, the News Media, and Collective Action." *Journal of Broadcasting and Electronic Media* 45, no. 1: 175–82.

Sbicca, Joshua. 2012a. "Eco-Queer Movement(s): Challenging Heteronormative Space through (Re)Imagining Nature and Food." *European Journal of Ecopsychology* 3, no. 1: 33–52.

Sbicca, Joshua. 2012b. "Growing Food Justice by Planting an Anti-Oppression Foundation: Opportunities and Obstacles for a Budding Social Movement." *Agriculture and Human Values* 29, no. 4: 455–66.

Schiavoni, Christina. 2009. "The Global Struggle for Food Sovereignty: From Nyéléni to New York." *Journal of Peasant Studies* 36, no. 3: 682–89.

Schlosberg, David. 2004. "Reconceiving Environmental Justice: Global Movements and Political Theories." *Environmental Politics* 13, no. 3: 517–40.

Schlozman, Kay Lehman, Sidney Verba, and Henry E. Brady. 2012. *The Unheavenly Chorus: Unequal Political Voice and the Broken Promise of American Democracy*. Princeton: Princeton University Press.

Short, Anne, Julie Guthman, and Samuel Raskin. 2007. "Food Deserts, Oases or Mirages? Small Markets and Community Food Security in the San Francisco Bay Area." *Journal of Planning Education and Research* 26, no. 3: 352–64.

Sites, William. 1997. "The Limits of Urban Regime Theory New York City under Koch, Dinkins, and Giuliani." *Urban Affairs Review* 32, no. 4: 536–57.

Slocum, Rachel. 2006. "Anti-Racist Practice and the Work of Community Food Organizations." *Antipode: A Radical Journal of Geography* 38, no. 2: 327–49.

Slocum, Rachel. 2007. "Whiteness, Space, and Alternative Food Practice." *Geoforum* 38, no. 3: 520–33.

Smit, Jac, Annu Ratta, and Joe Nasr. 1996. *Urban Agriculture: Food, Jobs, and Sustainable Cities.* New York: United Nations Development Programme.

Smith, Christopher M., and Hilda E. Kurtz. 2003. "Community Gardens and Politics of Scale in New York City." *Geographical Review* 93, no. 2: 193–212.

Smith, Neil. 1996. *The New Urban Frontier: Gentrification and the Revanchist City.* New York: Routledge.

Solomon, Serena. 2014. "Activists Sue Developers to Take Control of Community Garden." *DNAInfo New York* (online magazine), March 10. http://www.dnainfo.com/new-york/20140310/lower-east-side/residents-sue-developers-take-control-of-community-garden.

Sørensen, Eva, and Jacob Torfing. 2005. "The Democratic Anchorage of Governance Networks." *Scandinavian Political Studies* 28, no. 3: 195–218.

Staeheli, Lynn A., Don Mitchell, and Kristina Gibson. 2002. "Conflicting Rights to the City in New York's Community Gardens." *GeoJournal* 58, no. 2–3: 197–205.

Stein, Joshua. 2010. "What an Urban Farmer Looks Like." *New York Magazine.* Accessed at http://nymag.com/restaurants/features/68297/.

Stephens, James M., Terry DelValle, Barbara Daniels, and Marcia K. Oehler. 1996. "Jacksonville's Urban Gardening Program: 1977–1996." *Florida State Horticultural Society* 109: 294–96.

Surls, Rachel, Gail Feenstra, Sheila Golden, Ryan Galt, Shermain Hardesty, Claire Napawan, and Cheryl Wilen. 2015. "Gearing Up to Support Urban Farming in California: Preliminary Results of a Needs Assessment." *Renewable Agriculture and Food Systems* 30, no. 1: 33–42.

Sze, Julie. 2007. *Noxious New York: The Racial Politics of Urban Health and Environmental Justice.* Cambridge, Mass.: MIT Press.

Taylor, Dorceta E. 2000. "The Rise of the Environmental Justice Paradigm: Injustice Framing and the Social Construction of Environmental Discourses." *American Behavioral Scientist* 43(4): 508–80.

Taylor, Dorceta E. 2009. *The Environment and The People in American Cities, 1600s–1900s: Disorder, Inequality, and Social Change.* 626. Durham and London: Duke University Press.

Taylor, Dorceta E. 2011. "Introduction: The Evolution of Environmental Justice Activism, Research, and Scholarship." *Environmental Practice* 13, no. 4: 280–301.

Taylor, Dorceta E. 2014. *The State of Diversity in Environmental Organizations* (report). Prepared for Green 2.0. July.

Tornaghi, Chiara. 2014. "Critical Geography of Urban Agriculture." *Progress in Human Geography* 38, no. 4: 551–67.

Torre, María Elena, Michelle Fine, Brett G. Stoudt, and Madeline Fox. 2012. "Critical Participatory Action Research as Public Science." In *APA Handbook Of Research Methods In Psychology,* edited by H. Cooper. 171–84. Durham, N.C.: American Psychological Association.

Tortorello, Michael. 2012. "Growing Everything but Gardeners." *New York Times,* October 31.

Travaline, Katharine, and Christian Hunold. 2010. "Urban Agriculture and Ecological Citizenship in Philadelphia." *Local Environment* 15, no. 6: 581–90.

Tremante, Louis P. 2000. "Livestock in Nineteenth-Century New York City." *Urban Agriculture Magazine* 2: 5–7. Accessed at www.ruaf.org.

US Census Bureau. 2010. Demographic Profile—New York City Community Districts 2000 and 2010. Compiled by the New York City Department of City Planning, Population Division. http://www.nyc.gov/html/dcp/pdf/census/census2010/t_sf1_dp_cd.pdf.

US Census Bureau. 2012. "U.S. Census Bureau Projections Show a Slower Growing, Older, More Diverse Nation a Half Century from Now" (website). December 12. https://www.census.gov/newsroom/releases/archives/population/cb12-243.html (accessed October 13, 2014).

Victory Gardens of World War Two. 1999. USA: On Deck Home Entertainment.

Vigil, David. n.d. "An Open Letter to the NY Post and the East New York Community." East New York Farms! (website). http://eastnewyorkfarms.org/ (accessed on November 25, 2014).

Viljoen, André, Katrin Bohn, and Joe Howe, eds. 2005. *Continuous Productive Urban Landscapes: Designing Urban Agriculture for Sustainable Cities.* 1st ed. Burlington, Mass.: Architectural Press.

Voicu, Ioan, and Vicki Been. 2008. "The Effect of Community Gardens on Neighboring Property Values." *Real Estate Economics* 36, no. 2: 241–83.

von Hassell, Malve. 2002. *The Struggle for Eden: Community Gardens in New York City.* 183 Westport, Conn.: Bergin and Garvey.

Wagenaar, Hendrik, and Noam S. D. Cook. 2003. "Understanding Policy Practices: Action, Dialectic, and Deliberation in policy Analysis." In *Deliberative Policy Analysis: Understanding Governance in the Network Society,* edited by Maarten A. Hajer and Hendrik Wagenaar. 139–71. Cambridge: Cambridge University Press.

Wakefield, Sarah E. L. 2007. "Reflective Action in the Academy: Exploring Praxis in Critical Geography Using a 'Food Movement' Case Study." *Antipode: A Radical Journal of Geography* 39, no.2: 331–54.

Wald, Johanna, and Daniel J. Losen. 2003. "Defining and Redirecting a School to Prison Pipeline." *New Directions for Youth Development* 99: 9–15.

Wallace, Deborah, and Rodrick Wallace. 1998. *A Plague on Your Houses: How New York Was Burned Down and National Public Health Crumbled.* New York: Verso.

Weissman, Evan. 2015a. "Brooklyn's Agrarian Questions." *Renewable Agriculture and Food Systems* 30, no. 1: 92–102.

Weissman, Evan. 2015b. "Entrepreneurial Endeavors: (Re)producing Neoliberalization through Urban Agriculture Youth Programming in Brooklyn, New York." *Environmental Education Research* 21, no. 3: 351–64.

Wekerle, Gerda R. 2004. "Food Justice Movements Policy, Planning, and Networks." *Journal of Planning Education and Research* 23, no. 4: 378–86.

White, Monica. 2013. Keynote address. Black Farmers and Urban Gardeners Conference. Brooklyn, N.Y., Nov. 9.

White, Monica M. 2011a. "D-Town Farm: African American Resistance to Food Insecurity and the Transformation of Detroit." *Environmental Practice* 13, no. 4: 406–17.

White, Monica M. 2011b. "Sisters of the Soil: Urban Gardening as Resistance in Detroit." *Race/Ethnicity: Multidisciplinary Global Contexts* 5, no. 1: 13–28.

Wrigley, Neil. 2002. "'Food Deserts' in British Cities: Policy Context and Research Priorities." *Urban Studies* 39, no. 11: 2029–40.

Yakini, Malik. 2013. "Building a Racially Just Food Movement." *Be Black and Green* (blog). http://www.beblackandgreen.com.

Young, Iris Marion. 2009. "Five Faces of Oppression." In *Geographic Thought: A Praxis Perspective*, edited by George Henderson and Marvin Waterstone. 55–71. New York: Routledge. First published in I. M. Young. 1990. *Justice and the Politics of Difference*. 39–65. Princeton: Princeton University Press.

Zukin, Sharon. 2011. *Naked City: The Death and Life of Authentic Urban Places*. Oxford: Oxford University Press. (Orig. pub. 2009.)

INDEX

Abraham, Onika, 72

action research. *See* participatory action research (PAR); scholars

activism, 135–39. *See also* urban agriculture activists

Added Value, 104

Advocates for Children, 77

African American farmers. *See* black farmers

African diaspora, 1–2

Aguilar, Krysten, 133

Alanis, Leticia, 43–46, 77, 80, 90, 120–21; on participatory action research, 127–28

alterNative, 65

alternatives-to-incarceration program, 55–56. *See also* Friends of Brook Park (FBP)

Ameroso, John, 67

Ammons, Shorlette, 132

animal husbandry, 23–24, 25, 26, 35

aquaponics, 3, 38, 40, 109, 110

autotopography, 43–44

Ayer, Bee, 90, 91, 105, 106, 117, 137; on BK Farmyard's leadership structure, 68–69, 71; on funding for social justice programs, 103; on queer farmers, 54–55; on sharing best practices, 117

Bed-Stuy Farm, 40–41

beekeeping, 35, 87, 88, 89

BK Farmyards: discussions on justice, 50; leadership structure of, 68–69, 71; safe space for queer farmers, 54–55

black farmers: Black Urban Growers (BUGS), 66–67, 95; community gardens as safe spaces, 53; historical experiences with agriculture, 42, 44–46, 132–33; political clout, lack of, 94

Black Farmers and Urban Gardeners conference, 44. *See also* Black Urban Growers (BUGS)

Black Panther Party, 55, 122

Black Urban Growers (BUGS), 66–67, 95; Black Farmers and Urban Gardeners conference, 44

BLK ProjeK, 83

Bloomberg, Michael, 34, 35

Bronx Green-Up program (New York Botanical Garden program), 21, 96

Brooklyn Rescue Mission, 40–41, 46

Brook Park Community Garden, 74–76

Bushwick Campus Farm, 50, 126; and safe space for queer youth, 54–55

Center for Environmental Farming Systems (North Carolina State University and North Carolina Department of Agriculture joint program), 132

Cheney, Maggie, 100, 110; and Gay-Straight Alliance, 122; on partnering with scholars, 126; on queer farmers, 54–55; on scholars and legitimacy, 119; on urban agriculture education, 5

Christy, Liz, 30

classism: and funding, 71, 99–100, 108–9; gentrification, 8–9, 29–30, 32; and intersectionality, 11–12; and leadership, 63–65; media attention favors middle-class white-led farms, 3, 7–8, 18, 71–72, 98, 110; and urban agriculture education, 49–53, 71.

GEOGRAPHIES OF JUSTICE AND SOCIAL TRANSFORMATION